POST-WAR RESTORATION
OF PROPERTY RIGHTS
UNDER INTERNATIONAL LAW

Several international mass claims programmes have recently been established to process individual claims arising from armed conflicts. These entities possess specific institutional and structural features allowing for an effective and efficient resolution of claims. Moreover, violation of international law protecting property during war gives rise to inter-State and individual reparation, mostly partial, for which monetary compensation is more frequent than return of property. These programmes have also developed specific procedures to handle the administration of evidence and new techniques to decide all of the claims within a reasonable period of time.

This two-volume set reviews modern-day mass claims practice. Volume I shows how new mass claims programmes have built upon traditional dispute resolution mechanisms, and also examines the substantive law rules protecting property rights. Volume II focuses on the administration of evidence and the technique developed to decide mass claims, including the use of statistical sampling.

HANS DAS has been legal counsel at the Claims Commission for Real Property in Bosnia and the Housing and Property Directorate in Kosovo. He then became a research assistant at Leuven University. His doctoral thesis "Evidence and Procedure in International Mass Claims Processes", financed by a grant from the Flemish Fonds voor Wetenschappelijk Onderzoek, served largely as the basis of this Volume. At present he is Deputy Head of Unit at the Directorate-General for Environment (DG Environment), European Commission.

HANS VAN HOUTTE is Professor of Law at Katholieke Universiteit Leuven, Belgium and President of the Eritrea–Ethiopia Claims Commission in The Hague. In the past he has served as a member of the Commission for Real Property Claims in Bosnia Herzegovina, as a member of the United Nations Compensation Commission, and as an arbitrator and senior judge at the Claims Resolution Tribunal for Dormant Accounts.

POST-WAR RESTORATION OF PROPERTY RIGHTS UNDER INTERNATIONAL LAW

VOLUME II: PROCEDURAL ASPECTS

HANS DAS AND HANS VAN HOUTTE

CAMBRIDGE UNIVERSITY PRESS

CAMBRIDGE UNIVERSITY PRESS
Cambridge, New York, Melbourne, Madrid, Cape Town, Singapore, São Paulo, Delhi

Cambridge University Press
The Edinburgh Building, Cambridge CB2 8RU, UK

Published in the United States of America by Cambridge University Press, New York

www.cambridge.org
Information on this title: www.cambridge.org/9780521898317

First published 2008

Printed in the United Kingdom at the University Press, Cambridge

A catalogue record for this publication is available from the British Library

Library of Congress Cataloguing in Publication data

Houtte, H. van.
Post-war restoration of property rights under international law /
Hans Das, Hans van Houtte.
p. cm.
Includes bibliographical references and index.
ISBN 978-0-521-89831-7 (2 hardback books)
1. War reparations. 2. Postwar reconstruction. 3. Restitution.
I. Das, Hans. II. Houtte, H. van III. Title.
KZ6785.D37 2008
341.6′6–dc22
2008021978

This volume ISBN 978-0-521-89830-0 hardback (Volume 2)
Volume 1 ISBN 978-0-521-89828-7 hardback (Volume 1)

Only available as:
ISBN 978-0-521-89831-7 Volume Set hardback

CONTENTS

TABLE OF CASES

Arbitral awards

Iran–US Claims Tribunal Cases (alphabetical order)

Other arbitral awards (chronological order)

International courts

ICJ cases (chronological order)

1

General introduction

The end of the twentieth century witnessed the development of a new discipline in international claims resolution. Mass claims processing emerged hesitantly with the creation of the Iran–United States Claims Tribunal in 1981.[1] The development gained prominence in the 1990s, with the establishment of at least eight ad hoc mass claims facilities. In 1991, the UN Security Council set up the United Nations Compensation Commission to process 2.6 million compensation claims resulting from the Iraqi invasion and occupation of Kuwait. In 1996, the Dayton Peace Agreement created the Commission for Real Property Claims in Bosnia, which received and decided over 240,000 property claims. A year later, the Claims Resolution Tribunal for Dormant Accounts was instituted in Switzerland. In 1998, the Holocaust Victim Assets Litigation (also known as the 'Swiss Banks litigation') in the United States resulted in a settlement agreement, making US $1.25 billion available for distribution among Holocaust victims. This was followed in October 1998 by the establishment of the International Commission on Holocaust Era Insurance Claims, which is mandated to supervise the processing of several tens of thousands of insurance claims from the Holocaust period. At the end of 1999, the United Nations Interim Administration in Kosovo (UNMIK) set up a Housing and Property Claims Commission to resolve the property rights crisis in the province. In 2000, a German Foundation entitled 'Remembrance, Responsibility and Future' came into existence to provide financial compensation to hundreds of thousands of former slave and forced labourers and other victims of National Socialist injustice.

---

[1] While this Tribunal is in many respects atypical, it is generally considered to be a useful starting point for the study of present-day mass claims processes. Howard M. Holtzmann, 'Mass Claims Settlement Systems: Potentials and Pitfalls', in The International Bureau of the Permanent Court of Arbitration (ed.), *Institutional and Procedural Aspects of Mass Claims Settlement Systems* (Kluwer: The Hague, 2000), p. 1.

Despite their different backgrounds and institutional settings, these claims programmes share a common goal: they are aimed at providing effective remedies to numerous individuals who suffered losses, damage or injuries as a result of an armed conflict or a similar event causing widespread damage. Moreover, they are all expected to accomplish this task within a reasonable period of time.

The prospect of deciding several thousands of claims within a reasonable period of time would make any well-established justice system pause for thought. Inevitably, mass claims resolution presents a myriad of difficult issues that challenge our understanding of justice and fairness. The sheer number of claims creates problems of delay, repetition and excessive transaction costs. Balancing the tension between individualised justice, on the one hand, and efficiency and speed, on the other, is the central challenge in all efforts to design and implement mass claims procedures.[2] Traditional individualised proceedings, which replicate the same facts and legal issues case after case, are not necessarily appropriate in mass claims situations. Rather, a balance must be struck between the traditional requirements of fairness and the imperative to provide justice quickly to all claimants. The larger the caseload, the more difficult this balance is to achieve.[3] Complex social choices are at stake and compromise is inevitable.

While this tension is present in virtually all aspects of mass claims adjudication, it is most clearly felt in the design of the procedural and evidentiary framework. Arguably, the most difficult series of decisions in the development of a mass claims facility involves the selection of procedural and evidentiary techniques.[4] Should the procedures resemble the classic adjudicative and individualised model, placing a premium on individualised treatment, or should they favour the administrative and standardised approach, which emphasises consistency and efficiency? Similarly, the selection of evidentiary techniques will have a direct bearing upon the level of outcome accuracy and the efficiency of the process.

Mass claims processing is well known in some domestic law systems. Proceedings in the context of mass torts, primarily in the United States, have developed sophisticated methods for processing many thousands

---

[2] Norbert Wühler, 'The United Nations Compensation Commission: A New Contribution to the Process of International Claims Resolution', *Journal of International Economic Law* 2 (2) (1999), 249, 265–6.

[3] Wühler, 'A New Contribution', 266.

[4] See also Francis E. McGovern, 'Claims Resolution Facilities and the Mass Settlement of Mass Torts: Foreword', *Law and Contemporary Problems* 53 (1990), 1, 2.

of cases, such as computer-supported verification methodologies, common issue determination and precedent-setting, sampling and regression analysis.[5] These developments have begun to show that for mass claims there may be significant advantages in using statistical and computer-supported techniques, including judicial economy and the expediting of proceedings. Moreover, when applied properly, such techniques might increase the general level of outcome accuracy while reducing the bias associated with individualised decision making.

These innovative techniques have gradually found their way into international mass claims processing. Several international mass claims programmes have come to recognise that the traditional method of individualised adjudication, if applied to mass claims, would result in unacceptable delays and substantially increased costs for both claimants and respondents.[6] Learning from national mass claims practice, they adopted radically new techniques and procedures. Similar innovations have been introduced with respect to the administration of evidence. In the interest of economy and time, most mass claims processes have operated on a documents-only basis. Because of the number of claims and the need to act swiftly, traditional oral hearings are obviously difficult, if not impossible, to organise in a mass claims programme with several hundreds of thousands of claimants spread across the globe. Moreover, when mass claims arise from an armed conflict, many claimants face significant difficulties in gathering and presenting sufficient evidence of their losses, damage or injuries. For these reasons, mass claims processes have eased the claimants' burden of proof, introduced relaxed standards of evidence and made extensive use of presumptions and inferences. These trends, and in particular their impact on the values of efficiency and outcome accuracy, require further analysis.

This study examines how international mass claims practice has dealt with the tension between individualised justice and efficiency in the administration of evidence and in the design of claims resolution

---

[5] For an overview of mass claims processing techniques, see Francis E. McGovern, 'The Intellectual Heritage of Claims Processing at the UNCC', in Richard B. Lillich, *The United Nations Compensation Commission – Thirteenth Sokol Colloquium* (Irvington, NY: Transnational, 1995), 187, 191–5.

[6] See for instance with respect to the UNCC, the Report and Recommendations Made by the Panel of Commissioners concerning the Fourth Instalment of Claims for Departure from Iraq or Kuwait (Category "A" Claims), 12 October 1995, UN Doc. S/AC.26/1995/4, para. 9.

techniques. It provides information and analysis from which principles for the design of future mass claims resolution procedures can be distilled.

The analysis is organised in three parts. This first introductory part starts with a brief overview of the mass claims processes covered in the research. It clarifies the concept of mass claims, maps the procedural landscape and explains the analytical approach. Part II focuses on three evidentiary techniques that have been applied by present-day mass claims processes. These techniques relate to the burden of proof, the standards of evidence and the use of presumptions and inferences. Part III, finally, examines five claims processing techniques, i.e. precedent-setting and common issue determination, computerised data matching, sampling and regression analysis.

PART I

Conceptual and analytical framework

This Part defines the framework, which will serve as the basis of this study. It first gives an overview of the international programmes that were set up to deal with mass claims, i.e. the Iran–US Claims Tribunal, the United Nations Compensation Commission, the Commission for Real Property Claims of Displaced Persons and Refugees, the Claims Resolution Tribunals for Dormant Accounts, the Housing and Property Claims Commission, the IOM Claims Processes under the German Forced Labour Compensation Programme and under the Holocaust Victim Assets Programme, as well as the International Commission on Holocaust Era Insurance Claims.

Moreover, a conceptual and analytical framework is given to clarify the phenomenon of mass claims and the substantial and process-related objectives of resolution facilities such as speed, economy and consistency. Finally, in spite of the diversity in mass claims programmes, common features – like the procedural precedents for determining eligibility and assessing claims, and values such as efficiency, outcome accuracy and consistency – are analysed.

2

International mass claims programmes: Overview

This volume covers a selection of nine international mass claims processes which reflect the broad range of procedural models that are available to resolve mass claims. All of these programmes are either international or 'internationalised'.[1] Their international – or in many cases 'internationalised' – nature stems from various factors. Several mass claims processes arise from international agreements, a UN Security Council Resolution or other texts governed by public international law. The membership of the claims tribunals is predominantly international. They serve an international claimant population spread over several different countries. They either apply international law or operate at the crossroads of national and international law. The latter point deserves particular attention: there are important differences in the governing law of the nine mass claims programmes, which needs to be kept in mind when assessing the relevance of national experience for the analysis of international mass claims programmes. While national mass tort programmes are directly governed by the applicable domestic law, international programmes tend to be closed and self-contained systems. They have their own applicable procedural and substantive law and they are governed by international law in a much looser sense.

The following overview focuses on what is relevant for the mass claims settlement procedures themselves. A full description of the programmes can be found in the first volume of this publication.

The Iran–United States Claims Tribunal

The Iran–US Claims Tribunal was established in 1981 as one of the measures taken to resolve the crisis that arose out of the detention of

---

[1] On the concept of 'internationalised' courts, see Project on International Courts and Tribunals, 'Internationalised Criminal Courts and Tribunals: Practice and Prospects', PICT Conference, Amsterdam, 2002, p. 3.

52 Americans at the US Embassy in Tehran in 1979 and the subsequent freezing of Iranian assets by the US.[2] It has jurisdiction to decide claims of US nationals against Iran and of Iranian nationals against the US, which 'arise out of debts, contracts [...], expropriations or other measures affecting property rights'.[3] It was established as an international arbitral tribunal, consisting of nine members, three appointed by each Government and three 'third-country' members.[4]

Claims were presented to the Tribunal either by the claimants themselves or, in the case of claims of less than US $250,000, by their Governments.[5] They were decided by the full Tribunal or by one of the three Chambers. The procedures are governed by 'the arbitration rules of the United Nations Commission on International Trade Law (UNCITRAL) except to the extent modified by the Parties or by the Tribunal to ensure that this Agreement can be carried out'.[6] The Iran–US Claims Tribunal received approximately 1,000 claims for amounts of US $250,000 or more, and 2,800 claims for amounts of less than US $250,000. While the Tribunal has been extremely successful in resolving commercial disputes, only a handful of the smaller claims were effectively resolved by the Tribunal. In 1990, the two Governments concluded a lump-sum agreement covering various small individual

---

[2] For a more detailed account of the genesis of the Tribunal, see Charles N. Brower and Jason D. Brueschke, *The Iran–United States Claims Tribunal* (The Hague: Nijhoff, 1998), pp. 3–10.

[3] Declaration of the Government of the Democratic and Popular Republic of Algeria Concerning the Settlement of Claims by the Government of the United States of America and the Government of the Islamic Republic of Iran, 19 January 1981, Art. II(1) (*American Journal of International Law* 75 (1981), 422). In addition, the Tribunal has jurisdiction over two other claims categories. This study is concerned with the first category of claims only. For more detail on the scope of the Tribunal's jurisdiction, see George H. Aldrich, *The Jurisprudence of the Iran–United States Claims Tribunal* (Oxford: Clarendon Press, 1996), p. 44.

[4] Iran–US Claims Tribunal Settlement Declaration, Art. II(1) and III(1).

[5] Iran–US Claims Tribunal Settlement Declaration, Art. III(3). See also Lucy Reed, 'Institutional and Procedural Aspects of Mass Claims Settlement Systems: The Iran–United States Claims Tribunal', in The International Bureau of the Permanent Court of Arbitration (edn), *Institutional and Procedural Aspects of Mass Claims Settlement Systems* (Kluwer: The Hague, 2000), p. 10.

[6] Iran–US Claims Tribunal Settlement Declaration, Art. III(2).

The Iran–US Claims Tribunal Rules of Procedure (3 May 1983) are available at www.iusct. org/tribunal-rules.pdf (visited October 2007). For a detailed account of the procedural rules applied by the Tribunal, see Mattie Pellonpää and David D. Caron, *The UNCITRAL Arbitration Rules As Interpreted and Applied: Selected Problems in Light of the Practice of the Iran–US Claims Tribunal* (Helsinki: Finnish Lawyers' Publishing, 1994).

claims, which were subsequently processed by the US Foreign Claims Settlement Commission.[7]

The United Nations Compensation Commission (UNCC)

In the wake of the Iraqi invasion of Kuwait in 1990, successive Security Council Resolutions reaffirmed Iraq's liability under international law 'for any loss, damage or injury arising in regard to Kuwait and third States, and their nationals and corporations, as a result of the invasion and illegal occupation of Kuwait'.[8] To give effect to its findings on liability, the Security Council also established the mechanism that would be used to award compensation.[9] The United Nations Compensation Fund was created as a special account of the United Nations. The Compensation Commission (UNCC) was set up as a subsidiary organ functioning under the authority of the Security Council.[10]

The UNCC was established to process claims and pay compensation for losses, damage or injuries suffered by individuals, corporations, Governments and international organisations as a direct result of Iraq's unlawful invasion and occupation of Kuwait.[11] The institutional set-up of the UNCC is *sui generis*, a hybrid between an administrative mass claims programme and an international tribunal.[12] It had a unique structure with three organs:

---

[7] Some 2,388 claims of less than US $250,000 were terminated by Award on Agreed Terms No. 483-CLTDs/86/B38/B76/B77-FT, filed 22 June 1990.

[8] See in particular UN Security Council Resolution 670, S/RES/670 (1990), 25 September 1990, *International Legal Materials* 29 (1990), 1334, para. 13; UN Security Council Resolution 674, S/RES/674 (1990), 29 October 1990, *International Legal Materials* 29 (1990), 1561, para. 8; UN Security Council Resolution 686, S/RES/686 (1991), 2 March 1991, *International Legal Materials* 30 (1991), 567, para. 2(b); and UN Security Council Resolution 687, S/RES/687 (1991), 3 April 1991, *International Legal Materials* 30 (1991), 847, para. 16.

[9] See UN Security Council Resolution 687 (1991), para. 18; Report of the Secretary-General Pursuant to Paragraph 19 of Security Council Resolution 687, S/22559, 2 May 1991, *International Legal Materials* 30 (1991), 1706, para. 13; and UN Security Council Resolution 692, S/RES/692 (1991), 20 May 1991, 30 *International Legal Materials* 864, para. 3.

[10] Report of the Secretary-General of 2 May 1991, para. 3 and 4.

[11] See UN Security Council Resolution 687 (1991), para. 16 and 18; UN Security Council Resolution 692 (1991), para. 3; and Report of the Secretary-General of 2 May 1991, Part 1.

[12] Hans Wassgren, 'The UN Compensation Commission: Lessons of Legitimacy, State Responsibility, and War Reparations', *Leiden Journal of International Law* 11 (1998), 473, 490.

- The Governing Council, composed of the representatives of the members of the Security Council[13], was responsible for establishing guidelines on the administration and financing of the Fund, the organisation of the work of the Commission and the procedures for the processing of claims, the settlement of disputed claims and the payment of awards from the Fund.[14] In addition, the Governing Council approved the reports and recommendations made by the Panels of Commissioners.[15] The Council could adjust the sums recommended by the Panels, but it could not alter the Panels' legal and factual conclusions.[16] The Council's decisions were final and are not subject to appeal or review.[17]

- Fifty-nine Commissioners, representing over forty nationalities, served as the backbone for the claims resolution process. Acting impartially and in their personal capacity, the Commissioners verified claims, determined whether the claimed losses were directly attributable to Iraq's invasion and occupation of Kuwait, assessed the amount of loss or damage, and recommended compensation awards for the Governing Council to approve.[18] Panels of three Commissioners were established to review a category or subcategory of claims.[19] Any recommendation or other decision of the Panel had to be adopted by a majority of Commissioners.[20]

- The UNCC secretariat administered the Compensation Fund and supported the Governing Council and the Commissioners.[21] It developed and maintained a computerised claims database, provided assistance in the collection of evidence and ensured uniformity and consistency in the handling of similar claims. The secretariat submitted the claims to the Panels, together with the secretariat's preliminary assessment and any other information deemed useful for the work of the Commissioners.

The UNCC was the largest of all of the mass claims processes examined in this book. It collected over 2.6 million claims, the vast majority of

---

[13] See Report of the Secretary-General of 2 May 1991, para. 10. The veto right, which is held in the latter by the five permanent members, has been expressly excluded in the UNCC. While decisions concerning the financing of the Compensation Fund require a consensus, other decisions can be taken by a majority of at least nine members.

[14] See Report of the Secretary-General of 2 May 1991, para. 10.

[15] UNCC Governing Council, Decision No. 10: Provisional Rules for Claims Procedure, S/AC.26/1992/10, 26 June 1992, *International Legal Materials* 31 (1992), 1053, Art. 40(1).

[16] UNCC, Provisional Rules, Art. 40(2).   [17] UNCC, Provisional Rules, Art. 40(4).

[18] Report of the Secretary-General of 2 May 1991, paras 25–6.

[19] UNCC, Provisional Rules, Art. 28 and 32.   [20] UNCC, Provisional Rules, Art. 33.

[21] Report of the Secretary-General of 2 May 1991, para. 12.

which were individual claims. The UNCC divided its caseload into six categories, according to the nature of the injured party and the type of loss, and developed specific procedures for each category. In particular for the smaller claims, the UNCC developed sophisticated techniques, relying on computer support and statistical science. Within approximately ten years, nearly all claims were resolved.

The Commission for Real Property Claims of Displaced Persons and Refugees (CRPC)

Property rights violations were an inherent part of the war which raged in Bosnia and Herzegovina from 1992 to 1995. Some 2.3 million people – more than half of the country's pre-war population – fled their homes.[22] Wartime legislation allowed municipal authorities to declare abandoned – and allocate to others – any property that was vacated by departing refugees and displaced persons. These property laws were applied in a corrupt and discriminatory manner in order to prevent refugees and displaced persons from repossessing their homes of origin. In certain parts of the country, minority owners were forced to sell their houses. In an attempt to prevent the eventual return of minorities after the conflict, many of the cadastre records and property books were destroyed, removed or tampered with, resulting in the collapse of the entire property registration system. By the end of the war, less than 45 per cent of the Bosnians were living in their homes of origin.[23] Many had lost their property rights or lacked any legal proof to reclaim their possessions.

The General Framework Agreement for Peace (commonly known as the Dayton Peace Agreement)[24] recognised the right of all refugees and displaced persons to freely return to their homes of origin and to 'have restored to them property of which they were deprived in the course of hostilities since 1991 and to be compensated for any property that

---

[22] Marcus Cox, 'The Right to Return Home: International Intervention and Ethnic Cleansing in Bosnia and Herzegovina', *International & Comparative Law Quarterly* 47 (1998) 599, 620–2.

[23] Cox, 'The Right to Return Home', 622.

[24] General Framework Agreement for Peace in Bosnia and Herzegovina, initialled in Dayton on 21 November 1995 and signed in Paris on 14 December 1995 (commonly known as the 'Dayton Peace Agreement'), *International Legal Materials* 35 (1996), 75, 138.

cannot be restored to them'.[25] Annex 7 of the Dayton Peace Agreement established the CRPC as the principal legal mechanism for implementing the right to return. Its mandate was to 'receive and decide any claims for real property in Bosnia and Herzegovina, where the property has not voluntarily been sold or otherwise transferred since April 1, 1992 and where the claimant does not now enjoy possession of the property'.[26] The CRPC's mandate included both private property rights and so-called occupancy rights to socially-owned apartments.[27] Claims could be for return of the property or for just compensation in lieu of return. In practice, compensation has not been awarded.[28] Instead, CRPC decisions simply confirmed the pre-war property rights of the claimants and authorised them to exercise these rights in any lawful manner. Decision holders who did not wish to return, could trade their property on the private market.

The CRPC was entitled to free access to any and all property records for the purposes of determining property title.[29] Mandated to adopt its own rules and regulations, the Commission was required to consider – but was not strictly bound by – domestic property law.[30] CRPC decisions were final and binding, and could not be reviewed by any domestic court.[31] The CRPC nevertheless established an internal procedure for reconsideration of decisions, which was available to any party who

---

[25] Dayton Peace Agreement, Art. I.

The right to return has also been incorporated in Art. II(5) of the new Constitution of Bosnia and Herzegovina (Annex IV of the Dayton Peace Agreement). See Madeline Garlick, 'Protection for Property Rights: A Partial Solution? The Commission for Real Property Claims of Displaced Persons and Refugees (CRPC) in Bosnia and Herzegovina', *Refugee Survey Quarterly* 19 (2000), 68; M. Stavropoulou, 'Bosnia and Herzegovina and the Right to Return in International Law', in Michael O'Flaherty and Gregory Gisvold (Eds.), *Post-war Protection of Human Rights in Bosnia and Herzegovina* (The Hague: Nijhoff, 1998), p. 127.

[26] Dayton Peace Agreement, Annex 7, Art. XI.

[27] For further detail on the nature of these occupancy rights, see Hans Das, 'Restoring Property Rights in the Aftermath of War', *International & Comparative Law Quarterly* 53 (2004), 429, 432 footnote 18.

[28] The Dayton Peace Agreement envisaged the creation of a compensation fund. The fund never came into existence. See Das, 'Restoring Property Rights', 441.

[29] Dayton Peace Agreement, Annex 7, Art. XII(1).

[30] Dayton Peace Agreement, Annex 7, Art. XV.

[31] Dayton Peace Agreement, Annex 7, Art. XII(7). On enforcement of CRPC decisions, see Marcus Cox and Madeline Garlick, 'Musical Chairs: Property Repossession and Return Strategies in Bosnia and Herzegovina', in Scott Leckie (edn), *Returning Home: Housing and Property Restitution Rights of Refugees and Displaced Persons* (Ardsley, NY: Transnational, 2003), pp. 65–81; Garlick, 'Protection for Property Rights', 78.

submitted new evidence or facts that had not yet been considered by the Commission.

The CRPC was a temporary ad hoc body of a *sui generis* nature. Its composition included both international experts appointed by the President of the European Court of Human Rights, and national members designated by the three domestic parties to the Dayton Agreement. Though decisions could be taken by majority vote, the Commission worked by consensus to ensure support for its work by the three ethnic groups.[32]

The Commission set up an Executive Secretariat, with its headquarters in Sarajevo and regional claims registration offices at various locations in the Balkans and in Western countries hosting significant numbers of Bosnian refugees. Through its field offices, the CRPC collected 240,223 claims relating to 319,220 real properties, suggesting that the institution has successfully reached a high proportion of the refugees and internally displaced persons (IDP). The Commission developed straightforward single-party procedures and a sophisticated set of eligibility criteria, which were laid down in two Books of Regulations.[33] When its activities terminated, the CRPC had issued 312,332 final decisions confirming property title.[34]

The Claims Resolution Tribunal for Dormant Accounts (CRT-I)

In June 1997, the Swiss Federal Banking Commission and the Swiss Bankers Association (SBA) agreed to establish a claims resolution process

[32] Hans van Houtte, 'Mass Property Claim Resolution in a Post-War Society: The Commission for Real Property Claims in Bosnia and Herzegovina', *International & Comparative Law Quarterly* 48 (1999), 625, 627.

[33] CRPC, Book of Regulations on the Conditions and Decision Making Procedure for Claims for Return of Real Property of Refugees and Displaced Persons, 8 October 2002; and CRPC, Book of Regulations on Confirmation of Occupancy Rights of Displaced Persons and Refugees, 8 October 2002, available at www.law.kuleuven.ac.be/ipr/eng/CRPC_Bosnia/CRPC/new/en/html/laws/lawsbookofregulations.htm (visited October 2007).

[34] These figures are somewhat deceptive. A claim may be for more than one real property and may be submitted by more than one person. Moreover, each real property consists of a number of 'property units'. Each decision covers a maximum of one real property. Each claimant, even from the same claim, receives a separate decision. To compare the number of claims and the number of decisions, one must therefore look at the relevant numbers of individual property units. In total, the CRPC received claims for 1,236,292 property units. Decisions were made for 999,758 of these units. Some 235,259 claimed units were 'struck out' for various reasons and 1,275 claimed units were transferred to the local authorities for further research and decision making.

(CRP) for dormant accounts in Swiss banks dating from before the end of the Second World War. The agreement provided for the creation of an independent and objective international claims resolution tribunal (CRT-I) to 'definitively and equitably decide claims, operating under liberal rules of evidence, with its decisions, in the form of written opinions, taken after due consideration of the representations of the claimants'.[35] An Independent Claims Resolution Foundation, governed by a Board of Trustees, was created to set up and supervise CRT-I. The Board of Trustees was responsible for promulgating the rules of procedure for the Tribunal and for appointing a chairperson and arbitrators.

CRT-I was set up as an international arbitral tribunal composed of a Chairman, a Vice-Chairman and fifteen arbitrators.[36] Decisions were rendered by Sole Arbitrators or Claims Panels of three arbitrators.[37] Pursuant to Article 30 of the Rules of Procedure, the Board of Trustees appointed a law firm to act as the secretariat of the Tribunal.

CRT-I received more claims than initially expected. In 1997, the SBA had published a list with 5,570 dormant accounts. Only 2,308 accounts were actually claimed before CRT-I.[38] For the vast majority of these claimed accounts, however, more than one person submitted a claim and, with an average of four different claimants for each account, the docket of CRT-I quickly grew to a total of 9,918 claims. The claimant population was spread over 70 different countries and claimants communicated with the Tribunal in more than 15 languages.

The adjudication of these claims was considerably more complex than anticipated. The dormant accounts under review were opened more than 50 years ago; records and documentation were sparse and the establishment of the relevant facts was difficult. CRT-I needed three and a half years to resolve all of the claims, awarding an aggregate amount of 65,251,159.99 Swiss Francs.[39] Approximately 31 per cent of all claims were approved and 69 per cent dismissed. The Tribunal's direct costs,

---

[35] Joint press release issued by the SFBC and ICEP on 27 June 1997, cited in *In re: Holocaust Victim Assets Litigation*, Plan of Allocation and Distribution, proposed by Special Master Judah Gribetz and approved by Judge Korman on 22 November 2000, p. 54.

[36] Board of Trustees of the Independent Claims Resolution Foundation, Rules of Procedure for the Claims Resolution Process (commonly referred to as the 'CRT-I, Rules of Procedure'), adopted on 15 October 1997, Art. 25, available at www.crt-ii.org/_crt-i/frame.html (visited October 2007).

[37] CRT-I, Rules of Procedure, Art. 3.

[38] See CRT-I, Final Report on the Work of the Claims Resolution Tribunal for Dormant Accounts in Switzerland (CRT-I), 5 October 2001, p. 3.

[39] CRT-I, Final Report, 3–4.

which were born by the participating banks and the SBA, totalled 32 million Swiss Francs.[40]

The Second Claims Resolution Tribunal for Dormant Accounts (CRT-II)

By the time CRT-I was finalising its caseload, a class action lawsuit filed against the two largest Swiss banks in New York was settled by an agreement known as the 'Global Settlement Agreement'.[41] The Agreement provided for a payment of US $1.25 billion to settle claims by members of five represented classes: the Deposited Assets Class, the Looted Assets Class, the Refugee Class, and two Slave Labor Classes.[42] The Plan of Allocation and Distribution, approved by Judge Korman on 22 November 2000, entrusted a new mandate to the CRT, namely to distribute US $800 million out of the US $1.25 billion Settlement Fund to so-called 'Deposited Asset Class Members'.[43] This new project is referred to as 'CRT-II'.

The Deposited Assets Class, for which CRT-II is responsible, consists of 'Victims or Targets of Nazi Persecution and their heirs, successors, administrators, executors, affiliates, and assignees who have or at any time have asserted, assert, or may in the future seek to assert Claims against any Releasee for relief of any kind whatsoever relating to or arising in any way from Deposited Assets or any effort to recover Deposited Assets'.[44] Concretely, CRT-II's task is (1) to determine whether the original owners of the published accounts are or were targets or victims of Nazi persecution, (2) to ascertain their heirs, if necessary, (3) to determine the amounts attributable to each account, (4) to explore the circumstances surrounding the closing of certain

---

[40] CRT-I, Final Report, 4.

[41] Settlement Agreement in the US Dictrict Court for the Eastern District of New York, Chief Judge Edward R. Korman presiding, *In re Holocaust Victim Assets Litigation (Swiss Banks)*, 4 November 2002, CV-96–4849, available at www.swissbankclaims.com/PDFs_Eng/exhibit1toPlanofAllocation.pdf (visited October 2007).

[42] See the Final Order and Judgment of the court approving the Settlement Agreement of 26 July 2000 (as corrected on 2 August 2000), available at www.swissbankclaims.com/PDFs_Eng/FinalOrder.pdf (visited October 2007).

[43] Plan of Allocation and Distribution, proposed by Special Master Judah Gribetz and approved by Judge Korman on 22 November 2000, available at www. swissbankclaims. com/PDFs_Eng/VolumeIPlan.pdf (visited October 2007).

[44] Settlement Agreement, Section 8.2(a). The term 'Releasee' includes all Swiss banks, all Swiss governmental bodies, and several Swiss business entities.

accounts, and (5) to distribute the appropriate amounts to the current owners.[45]

The institutional nature of CRT-II is entirely different from CRT-I and has been defined as a 'court-sponsored alternative dispute resolution process in which both banks and claimants agree to a set of procedures for resolution of claims and have certain rights and obligations'.[46] CRT-II received 33,496 claims from Nazi victims or their heirs to assets deposited in Swiss banks in the period before and during the Second World War.[47] As of July 2006, a relatively modest number of 2,139 awards had been certified by the Tribunal and approved by the Court.

The Housing and Property Claims Commission (HPCC)

The property rights crisis in Kosovo started long before the 1999 conflict and has its origins in the post-Autonomy period, when thousands of Kosovo Albanians were discriminated against and lost their rights to socially owned apartments. In most cases, these apartments were allocated to Serbian employees and subsequently privatised. Moreover, in 1991, the Serbian Parliament restricted the sale of property by Serbs to Albanians in order to stem Serb emigration. In practice, however, sales continued through secret, informal or unregistered contracts and rendered the property registration system obsolete, making the determination of property title extremely difficult.

The 1999 conflict gave rise to massive displacements. In the general climate of violence and lawlessness that prevailed after the conflict, many Albanians saw the opportunity to re-take possession of the apartments they had previously occupied. Instances of forced transactions were reported throughout the province.[48]

UN Security Council resolution 1244 (1999), which establishes the United Nations Interim Administration Mission in Kosovo (UNMIK), emphasises the right of all refugees and displaced persons to return to their homes in safety.[49] On 15 November 1999, UNMIK established

---

[45] Plan of Allocation, at 13.
[46] Roger P. Alford, 'The Claims Resolution Tribunal and Holocaust Claims Against Swiss Banks', *Berkeley Journal of International Law* 20(1) (2002), 250, 265–6.
[47] See www.crt-ii.org/index_en.phtm. (visited October 2007).
[48] Report of the Secretary-General on the United Nations Interim Administration Mission in Kosovo, 12 July 1999, UN Doc. S/1999/779, para. 77 and 78.
[49] UN Security Council Resolution 1244, S/RES/1244 (1999), 10 June 1999, *International Legal Materials* 34 (1999), 1451, para. 11 (j) and (k).

the Housing and Property Directorate (HPD) with a quasi-judicial independent branch, the Housing and Property Claims Commission (HPCC), in order to resolve three specific categories of residential property claims: claims from owners or other right holders who lost property after 23 March 1989 as a result of discrimination; claims for the regularisation of informal property transactions; and claims from refugees and displaced persons who have lost possession of their properties as a result of the 1999 conflict.[50] HPCC decisions were final and could not be reviewed by any other judicial or administrative authority in Kosovo.[51]

Severe financial constraints limited the outreach and claims registration capacity of the HPD and HPCC.[52] While initially a caseload of over 60,000 claims was expected, only 29,160 properties have been claimed. The vast majority of these claims were claims from refugees and IDPs. Decision making by the HPCC has been slowed down by the requirement that all parties affected by the claim need to be notified, by financial constraints and by the 2000–1 political crisis in Serbia.[53] Despite these difficulties, all claims have been resolved.

In March 2006, UNMIK established the Kosovo Property Agency (KPA)[54] as an administrative agency functioning independently pursuant to Chapter 11.2 of the Constitutional Framework of Kosovo.[55] It is mandated to facilitate the resolution of claims that followed the armed conflict between 27 February 1998 and 20 June 1999 in respect of private

---

[50] Both institutions were created through the UNMIK Regulation No. 1999/23 on the Establishment of the Housing and Property Directorate and the Housing and Property Claims Commission, 15 November 1999, available at www.unmikonline.org/regulations/unmikgazette/index.htm (visited October 2007). UNMIK Regulations are promulgated by the Special Representative of the Secretary-General of the United Nations and have the force of law. They override provisions of domestic law insofar as these are inconsistent.

[51] UNMIK Regulation No. 1999/23, Section 2.7. Unlike the Bosnian CRPC, the HPCC and HPD are also responsible for the implementation of the decisions issued by the HPCC. See Das, 'Restoring Property Rights', 440.

[52] Alan Dodson and Veijo Heiskanen, 'Housing and Property Restitution in Kosovo', in Scott Leckie, *Returning Home: Housing and Property Restitution Rights of Refugees and Displaced Persons* (Ardsley, NY: Transnational, 2003), 241.

[53] Dodson and Heiskanen, 'Housing and Property Restitution in Kosovo', 236.

[54] See UNMIK Regulation No. 2000/60 on Residential Property Claims and The Rules of Procedure and Evidence of the Housing and Property Directorate and the Housing and Property Claims Commission, 31 October 2000, available at www.unmikonline.org/regulations/unmikgazette/index.htm (visited October 2007).

[55] For further information, See www.kpaonline.org/ (visited October 2007).

immovable property (including agricultural and commercial property). It has three main functions: (a) to receive, register and assist the courts in resolving specific claims on private immovable property; (b) to enforce final decisions; and (c) to administer abandoned properties. The staff and assets of the HPD are part of the KPA. The KPA therefore assumes responsibility for the implementation of all residential property claims that were pending with the HPD on 4 March 2006 and has to resolve them in an effective and expeditious manner. The HPCC will continue to decide the small number of remaining residential claims.

The IOM Claims Process under the German Forced Labour Compensation Programme (GFLCP)

On 2 August 2000, Germany created a Foundation, entitled 'Remembrance, Responsibility and Future' to grant financial compensation to former forced labourers and those affected by other injustices from the National Socialist period.[56] The Foundation is funded by the German State and the companies joined in the Foundation Initiative of German Industry.[57] Seven partner organisations are responsible for processing certain categories of individual claims. The International Organization for Migration (IOM) was designated as the partner organisation responsible for non-Jewish claimants from the so-called 'rest-of-the-world' category.[58]

Several groups of people may claim compensation. First, the so-called 'slave labourers' are persons who were held inside or outside their own country in a concentration camp, ghetto or another place of confinement under comparable conditions.[59] Second, 'forced labourers' encompasses persons who were deported from their own country to Germany or a German-occupied area and were subjected to forced

---

[56] Law on the Creation of the Foundation 'Remembrance, Responsibility and Future', 2 August 2000, as amended on 4 August 2001 (Federal Law Gazette BGBl. 2000 I 1263 and BGBl. 2001 I 2036), Section 2(1) (commonly known as the 'German Foundation Act').

[57] 'German Foundation Act', Sections 3(2) and 9(2).

[58] The 'rest-of-the-world' category covers all countries except Poland, Ukraine, Moldova, the Russian Federation, Latvia, Lithuania, Belarus, Estonia and the Czech Republic. 'German Foundation Act', Section 9(2).

[59] 'German Foundation Act', Section 11(1)1. For examples of comparable conditions, see Peter Van der Auweraert, 'The Practicalities of Forced Labor Compensation. The Work of the International Organisation for Migration as One of the Partner Organisations under the German Foundation Law', in Peer Zumbansen (ed.), *NS-Forced Labor: Remembrance and Responsibility* (Wiesbaden: Nomos, 2002), pp. 304–5.

labour for a commercial enterprise or public authority and were held in conditions resembling imprisonment or similar extremely harsh living conditions.[60] The third category covers certain property losses suffered under the Nazi regime as a result of direct participation of German companies, for which the IOM has been designated as the sole partner organisation to process claims. For the latter category, the IOM established a specific Property Claims Commission, composed of three arbitrators.[61]

The IOM received approximately 409,000 claims from individuals in over 60 countries. Relatively strict eligibility requirements resulted in a substantial number of negative decisions. In the slave and forced labour category, some 332,000 claims were filed. Of these, a total of 327,000 claims were resolved: compensation was awarded in over 90,000 claims and 236,000 negative decisions were issued. With respect to property losses, more than 35,200 claims were received and resolved. Again, the vast majority of these decisions were negative; only 30 per cent of the claimants received a positive decision. Virtually all of the 42,000 personal injury claims were decided, with only 1,800 positive decisions. By the end of 2005, more than 28,000 appeals had been lodged.

The IOM Claims Process under the Holocaust Victim Assets Programme (HVAP)

In November 2000, the IOM was designated as one of the organisations participating in the implementation of the Settlement Agreement reached in the Holocaust Victim Assets Litigation before the US Eastern District Court of New York.[62] In addition to compensating for deposits in Swiss banks, the US $1.25 billion settlement fund also served to pay compensation to former slave labourers and certain other victims of the National Socialist Regime. In accordance with the Special Master's Proposed Plan of Allocation and Distribution, IOM established the Holocaust Victim Assets Programme (HVAP) in order to process these claims and to pay compensation.

---

[60] 'German Foundation Act', Section 11(1)2.
[61] The procedures are set out in the IOM Property Claims Commission, Supplemental Principles and Rules of Procedure, 5 June 2001, Section 20.1, available at www.compensation-for-forced-labour.org/ (visited October 2007).
[62] See the Settlement Agreement.

Three groups of claimants could claim under the HVAP:

- Slave Labour Class I, i.e. persons who were persecuted or targeted for persecution because they were or were believed to be Roma, Jehova's Witness, homosexual, or physically or mentally handicapped, and who performed slave labour for German companies or for the Nazi regime[63];
- Slave Labour Class II, i.e. persons who performed slave labour for certain Swiss companies or their affiliates, whether or not such persons were victims or targets of Nazi persecution[64];
- The Refugee Class, i.e. persons who were persecuted or targeted for persecution because they were or were believed to be Roma, Jehova's Witness, homosexual, or physically or mentally handicapped, and who (a) sought entry into Switzerland, or were admitted into but subsequently expelled from Switzerland, or (b) after gaining entry, were detained, abused or otherwise mistreated as refugees in Switzerland, during the period 1 January 1933 to 9 May 1945.

By July 2004, the IOM had received 33,036 claims in Slave Labour Class I. More than 20,000 of these claims were resolved. Approximately 15,000 claims were filed under Slave Labour Class II, of which approximately 5,000 claims were decided. Finally, in the Refugee Class, 1,130 claims were received and resolved.

The International Commission on Holocaust Era Insurance Claims (ICHEIC)

Policies insuring life and education were common forms of investment in pre-war Europe. Since the end of the Second World War, thousands of insurance policies have remained hidden, unaccounted for and unpaid to their rightful owners, i.e. the survivors and heirs of victims of the Holocaust. After several insurance companies were brought to court in the US, negotiations started with Jewish and survivor organisations and the State of Israel, resulting in the signing of a Memorandum of

---

[63] Under the Settlement Agreement, members of Slave Labor Class I must have laboured for 'companies or entities that actually or allegedly deposited the revenues of proceeds of that labor with, or transacted such revenues or proceeds through, the Releasees'. (Settlement Agreement, Section 8.2(c)).

[64] Slave Labour Class II claimants must demonstrate that they performed slave or forced labour for a Swiss entity that was a party to the Holocaust Victim Assets Litigation. On 2 April 2001, the Court published a list with the names of these companies.

Understanding in 1998.[65] The Memorandum created the ICHEIC with the purpose of establishing 'a just process [. . .] that will expeditiously address the issue of unpaid insurance policies issued to victims of the Holocaust'.[66]

The Memorandum tasks the ICHEIC with investigating the current status of the insurance policies issued to Holocaust victims during the period 1920 to 1945 and with the establishment of a claims and valuation process to settle and pay individual claims. The ICHEIC concluded implementation agreements with some insurance companies.[67] Moreover, agreements and arrangements with Governmental restitution and compensation organisations and with insurance industry associations gradually expanded its activities. For instance, in the agreement between the German and the US Governments concerning the German Foundation 'Remembrance, Responsibility and Future', it was agreed that insurance claims that came within the scope of the ICHEIC claims procedures and that were made against German insurance companies would be processed by the companies and the German Insurance Association in accordance with and on the basis of the ICHEIC procedures.[68]

The ICHEIC is composed of twelve members, plus the Chairperson, and a number of observers.[69] The ICHEIC itself did not evaluate claims. This task rested with the companies, which should process claims in accordance with ICHEIC claims processing and valuation guidelines. The ICHEIC's role is to receive claims and to ensure that (1) claims that

---

[65] Memorandum of Understanding, 25 August 1998, available at www.icheic.org/pdf/ICHEIC_MOU.PDF (visited October 2007). The companies included Allianz Insurance, AXA Insurance Group, Basler Leben, Winterthur and Zurich Group. Shortly afterwards, Basler pulled out. Generali joined on 10 September 1998.

[66] Memorandum of Understanding, para. 1.

[67] In November 2000, the ICHEIC and the World Jewish Restitution Organization signed an implementation agreement with the Italian insurer Generali. In April 2003, an agreement was reached with AXA, Winterthur and Zurich. See ICHEIC, Holocaust Era Insurance Claims Processing Guide, 22 June 2003, at 9–10, available at www.icheic.org/pdf/ICHEIC_CPG.pdf. (visited October 2007).

[68] Agreement between the Government of the United States of America and the Government of the Federal Republic of Germany concerning the Foundation 'Remembrance, Responsibility and the Future', signed in Berlin on 17 July 2000, *International Legal Materials* 39 (2000), 1298, Art. 1(4).

[69] See the Memorandum of Understanding, para. 2. Six members were designated by the US regulators and the World Jewish Restitution Organization, together with the Claims Conference and the State of Israel. Six others were appointed by the European insurance companies and regulators. ICHEIC appointed former US Secretary of State Lawrence Eagleburger as Chairperson.

name a company are sent to the named company and are reviewed there; (2) claims that do not name a company are checked by those companies associated with the Commission which did business in the country where the claimant lived; and (3) all decisions on ICHEIC claims are made in accordance with all ICHEIC guidelines. The ICHEIC claims process gives ICHEIC claimants the opportunity to appeal against a company's decision in certain instances. Two independent and impartial appeal bodies have been established: an Appeals Tribunal and an Appeals Panel.[70]

Since the start of the claims resolution process in early 2000, the ICHEIC received over 91,500 claims. By August 2007, more than 48,000 offers had been made. Approximately 2,200 appeals were lodged.

---

[70] The Tribunal has adopted specific Rules of Procedure and comprises a President, a Vice President and independent Arbitrators. ICHEIC, Appeals Tribunal Rules of Procedure, 15 July 1999, Art. 1.1, available at www.icheic.org/pdf/ICHEIC_Appeals.pdf (visited October 2007). The Panel consists of three members, one of whom is appointed as Chairperson. The Appeals Guidelines are set out in Annex E to the German Foundation Agreement.

3

Conceptual framework

The above overview allows us to define the notion of mass claims and specify the objectives and characteristic features of mass claims programmes. It should be noted that the concept of mass claims, as examined in this study, is unrelated to the well-defined technical concepts of class actions and mass torts known in some common law countries.[1]

Defining mass claims

The term 'claim' is generally understood as a right to seek remedy arising from a wrong or injury suffered.[2] But when can claims be considered mass claims? Only one of the above described programmes has given a definition of the term 'mass claims process'. In a Resolution of April 2003, the Housing and Property Claims Commission referred to a 'mass claims process' as a 'process designed to deal with a high number of claims that arise out of the same extraordinary situation or event and are filed with the decision-making body within a limited period of time'.[3] This corresponds perfectly to the two distinctive features that can be inferred from the above overview.

---

[1] For a brief review of class actions, see Jack H. Friedenthal, Mary Kay Kane and Arthur R. Miller, *Civil Procedure* (St Paul MN: West, 1999), 3rd edn, p. 736–74 and Olivier De Schutter, *Fonction de juger et droits fondamentaux: Transformation du contrôle juridictionnel dans les ordres juridiques américain et européen* (Bruxelles: Bruylant, 1999), p. 907–42. For an account of mass torts, see Mark A. Peterson and Molly Selvin, *Resolution of Mass Torts: Toward a Framework for Evaluation of Aggregative Procedures* (Santa Monica, CA: Rand Corporation, 1988), RAND Note N-2805-ICJ, p. 12.

[2] In certain mass claims processes, the term 'application' is occasionally (though not consistently) used instead of 'claim'. An application can be understood as a 'request for action or relief' or 'a form used to make such a request'. This different terminology reflects a fundamental distinction between two groups of mass claims programmes, i.e., those in which claimants are asserting a legal right under international law and those which result from a class action settlement and in which payments are made ex gratia.

[3] HPCC, Resolution No 7, 11/04/2003, para. 1.4.

Numerosity[4]

Trite though this observation may be, the principal distinctive feature of mass claims is the high number of claims involved. In the mass claims programmes included in the research, the caseload ranges from 4,000 (in the case of the Iran–US Claims Tribunal) to 2.6 million claims (in the UNCC).

There appears to be no critical threshold number marking the transition from 'claims' to 'mass claims'. According to Heiskanen, the minimum number required depends on the 'complexity and similarity of the claims'.[5] He suggests that normally a caseload of at least 2,000 to 5,000 claims is sufficient to label a claims process as 'mass'.[6]

More importantly, the use of the single phrase 'mass claims' tends to obscure a critical difference between two types of process. The first consists of programmes with a few thousand claims. It includes the Iran–US Claims Tribunal and the CRT-I. The second consists of programmes such as the UNCC, the CRPC and the IOM-administered programmes, involving hundreds of thousands of claims. In the first type of mass claims process, it is possible – though not necessarily beneficial – to employ traditional procedures to process the claims. While the settlement could benefit from employing specialised mass claims procedures, the use of such procedures is no absolute necessity with this kind of caseload. In the second type, the sheer number makes traditional settlement proceedings prohibitive. The size of the claimant population dictates that 'something be done to make processing such claims manageable' and leaves no choice but to adopt specific mass claims procedures.[7]

---

[4] In the context of class action proceedings in the US, the term 'numerosity' refers to one of the prerequisites for a class action to proceed in the federal courts, i.e., the class must be so large that joinder of all its members would be impracticable. See for instance Friedenthal, Kane & Miller, *Civil Procedure*, p. 742. We use the term 'numerosity' (or 'numerousness') in its general, non-technical sense, i.e., the state of being numerous.

[5] Veijo Heiskanen, 'Innovations in Mass Claims Dispute Resolution: Speeding the Resolution of Mass Claims Using Information Technology', *Dispute Resolution Journal* 58 (2003), 79.

[6] Heiskanen, 'Speeding the Resolution of Mass Claims', 79.

[7] For a similar argument with respect to mass torts in the US, see Kenneth S. Abraham and Glen O. Robinson, 'Aggregative Valuation of Mass Tort Claims', *Law and Contemporary Problems* 53 (1990), 137, 138.

Commonality of legal and factual issues[8]

The concept of mass claims requires not only numerous claimants; it also presupposes that the issues raised by their claims are sufficiently similar so that it is more efficient to adjudicate the claims in a single claims process than in a series of individual proceedings.[9]

In a mass claims situation, all claims arise out of one basic set of facts, i.e. a war, a revolution or any other event causing widespread harm. Practically all of the claims 'arise at around the same time and are very similar in terms of the legal and factual issues that they raise'.[10] This does not mean that all questions of law or fact need to be common. In many cases, there will be a pattern of harmful conduct, consisting of separate though related incidents, rather than one particular harmful event. For instance, the losses of property before the CRPC in Bosnia and the HPCC in Kosovo were all based upon separate facts and attributable to different individuals. However, the taking of property followed a general pattern so that the claims all raised very similar legal issues.

It is clear, however, that this pattern might have affected various claimants in different ways, leaving considerable scope for individual issues to arise in mass claims. The commonality requirement does not require that the common issues of law or fact predominate over the individual aspects of the claims.[11] However, if numerous claims arise from isolated incidents, with no discernible relationship between them, they would not be regarded as 'mass claims'.

For some commentators, the claims before the Iran–US Claims Tribunal were of a diverse nature.[12] While this is undoubtedly true for the large commercial claims, at least the 1,500 individual claims based on alleged wrongful expulsion were highly similar claims raising common legal and factual issues.

---

[8] Again, the term 'commonality' is used in its ordinary sense and not in the technical legal sense of American class action practice.

[9] See for instance HPCC, Resolution No 7, para. 1.4: 'claimants in a mass claims process are generally in the same situation, having suffered the same or similar losses within the same period of time'. See also Heiskanen, 'Speeding the Resolution of Mass Claims', 67.

[10] Heiskanen, 'Speeding the Resolution of Mass Claims', 67; Holtzmann, 'Mass Claims Settlement Systems', 1; UNCC, Report "A" claims, 4th inst., para. 9.

[11] Note the difference with class actions under Federal Rule 23(b)(3) in the US. So-called 'common question' class actions require that common questions of law or fact predominate over questions that only affect individual class members. Friedenthal, Kane and Miller, *Civil Procedure*, pp. 749–50.

[12] See for instance Reed, 'The Iran–United States Claims Tribunal', 12.

Other features

In addition, international mass claims usually share three other features that are relevant to the study of evidentiary and claims resolution techniques.

First, a large portion of claims on the docket of a mass claims programme may be of a moderate or low economic value. In CRT-I, for instance, many bank accounts had rather small value. Likewise, the UNCC received approximately 920,000 claims in the so-called Category "A" claims, i.e. claims for a fixed sum of either US $2,500 (for individuals), or US $5,000 (for families).

A second feature is that mass claims processes usually place a large group of claimants opposite a single respondent or a small group of respondents. Typically, the claimants are individuals, either natural or legal persons. The respondent is usually a sovereign State or a corporation. While this is not a general rule – in the UNCC, claims were submitted by individuals, corporations as well as Governments and organisations, and in the CRPC and the HPCC the respondents were individuals – it is the most common situation in mass claims programmes.

Third, with the exception of the Iran–US Claims Tribunal, all present-day mass claims processes cover claims arising out of an armed conflict. Again, this is not a conceptual requirement. It is conceivable that similar types of claims would arise from environmental disasters, causing widespread damage or injury[13], or from systematic human rights violations in peacetime.

Objectives of international mass claims processes

If mass claims are simply numerous claims sharing common issues, a mass claims process is not necessarily different from any other claims process. The overview nevertheless suggested that mass claims systems depart from ordinary claims processes in significant ways. Their specificity, it is suggested, stems from the particular requirements they must meet. This section identifies the specific goals of mass claims programmes on the basis of their founding documents and procedural rules.

---

[13] See for instance Kenneth F. McCallion, 'Institutional and Procedural Aspects of Mass Claims Litigation and Settlement: The Exxon Valdez and Bhopal Gas Disaster Cases', in The International Bureau of the Permanent Court of Arbitration (ed.), *Institutional and Procedural Aspects of Mass Claims Settlement Systems* (Kluwer: The Hague, 2000), p. 57.

Substantive goals

While a detailed review of the substantive goals of mass claims processes is well beyond the scope of this study, a few general observations are called for.

All present-day mass claims processes seek to provide restitution or compensation for losses, damage or injuries caused – either directly or indirectly – by the respondent. They can be easily distinguished from needs-based allocation processes with a predominantly humanitarian or social character. Although humanitarian considerations may affect the design of the process – e.g. by establishing a priority in which individual claims are processed, as was the case in the UNCC[14] – the purpose of mass claims processes does not lie in the social or economic rehabilitation of war victims, nor in community development or post-war recovery. Unlike more broadly distributive processes, mass claims processes are not concerned with merely allocating resources among a particular group of individuals.

Rather, they aim at restoring the equilibrium that existed between the wrongdoer and the victim before the 'wrong' occurred. Most mass claims processes rely on relatively strict eligibility criteria, aimed at distinguishing between those who have suffered specific harms and others. Significant efforts are also made to offer an amount of compensation that is as close as possible to the true value of the losses, damage or injuries. While the ideal of perfect approximation can rarely be achieved in practice, mass claims processes still *aim* to offer compensation in relation to the harm or loss. By obliging the respondent to pay exactly or approximately this amount to the claimant, most mass claims processes appear to place themselves in a corrective justice framework.[15] Admittedly, corrective or remedial justice theory does not explain all variations that exist among mass claims processes, some of which depart from traditional corrective justice ideals in significant ways. This is the case, for instance, for those mass claims processes in which compensation

---

[14] Fred Wooldridge and Olufemi Elias, 'Humanitarian Considerations in the Work of the United Nations Compensation Commission', *International Review of the Red Cross* 85 (2003), 555, 562–71.

[15] The origins of corrective justice are often traced to Aristotle. See for instance Dinah Shelton, *Remedies in International Human Rights Law* (Oxford: Oxford University Press, 1999), p. 38. On corrective justice as the basis for mass tort claims in the US, see in particular Robert G. Bone, 'Statistical Adjudication: Rights, Justice, and Utility in a World of Process Scarcity', *Vanderbilt Law Review* 46 (1993) 561, 605–14.

payments are drawn from a compensation fund that is replenished by several donors.[16] With respect to the fund created by the German Foundation Law, for instance, German companies bear only half of the costs of the compensation payments, with the other half provided by the German Federal Government. In such cases it is the fund, rather than the particular respondent responsible for the losses, which pays compensation to the claimant; this does not fit well with corrective justice theory and seems to lean more towards 'compensatory justice'.[17]

Moreover, corrective justice clearly requires a 'wrong'.[18] While in some processes the respondents have recognised their moral and/or legal responsibility,[19] payments under the Holocaust Victim Assets Process, for instance, constitute voluntary payments. Indeed, in this settlement agreement, the parties agreed that neither this agreement nor any payment made under the agreement 'shall constitute, be construed as, or be offered or received in evidence as an admission of any claim or any fact'.[20] These payments are made ex gratia rather than as a recognition of responsibility.[21]

Despite these differences, the common theme in all mass claims processes remains fairly simple: (1) a large number of claimants have suffered losses, damage or injury; (2) which can be attributed to the behaviour of a distinct group of respondents; and (3) restitution or compensation is awarded to correct, to the extent feasible, the harm done and to restore the balance.

The situation is sometimes further complicated by the fact that, in post-conflict situations, the corrective objective of mass claims resolution coincides with specific public policy goals. This is most clearly illustrated by the work of the CRPC in Bosnia, where the goal of restoring lost property rights was closely linked to the broader political objective of creating the conditions for the return of refugees and

---

[16] See 'German Foundation Act', Section 3(2).

[17] For a description of compensatory justice, see Gary T. Schwartz, 'The Ethics and Economics of Tort Liability Insurance', *Cornell Law Review* 75 (1990), 313, 328–31.

[18] Shelton, *Remedies in International Human Rights Law*, p. 39; Bone, 'Statistical Adjudication', 606.

[19] An example of acceptance of moral responsibility is found in the preamble of the German Foundation Act. See also Rudolf Dolzer, 'The Settlement of War-Related Claims: Does International Law Recognize a Victim's Private Right of Action? Lessons after 1945', *Berkeley Journal of International Law* 20(1) (2002), 296, 306.

[20] Settlement Agreement, Art. 2.1.

[21] As will be shown below, the ex gratia nature of the payments in some programmes helps explain the choice of particular techniques.

displaced persons and the restoration of a multi-ethnic Bosnia. Restoring property title was a prerequisite for an orderly and legal return process. While the CRPC's mandate was limited specifically to the restoration of property rights, some interaction with the larger political process was inevitable.

Mass claims processes may also serve other public policy objectives, such as advancing public control over the conduct of states or enterprises or deterring future wrongful behaviour. In this sense, remedies serve social as well as individual needs.[22] Since mass claims processes affect many individuals and vast economic and social interests, public policy concerns will inevitably play a role in their creation and design. These societal objectives are rarely made explicit, however, and the principal aim in all cases appears to be the corrective justice ideal of righting past wrongs.

Specific process goals

The founding documents give mass claims processes particularly demanding agendas. Apart from ensuring 'fair' or 'just' remedies for mass victims, mass claims processes are expected to meet a number of specific procedural objectives.

Speed

Because of the number of claims involved, time is a critical concern. Mass claims processes have to resolve numerous claims quickly.[23]

Both the founding documents and the procedural rules explicitly instruct the adjudicators to resolve claims promptly. In his Report of 2 May 1991, for instance, the UN Secretary-General stated that the UNCC's primary objective is 'to settle compensation claims within a reasonable period of time'.[24] The UNCC Rules specify that the Commissioners are to organise the work 'so as to ensure the expeditious

---

[22] See Daniel Bodansky, John R. Crook and Dinah Shelton, 'Righting Wrongs: Reparations in the Articles on State Responsibility', *American Journal of International Law* 96 (2002), 833, 845.

[23] See for instance Christopher S. Gibson, 'Mass Claims Processing: Techniques for Processing over 400,000 Claims for Individual Loss at the UNCC', in Richard B. Lillich, *The United Nations Compensation Commission – Thirteenth Sokol Colloquium* (Irvington, NY: Transnational, 1995), p. 156; Wühler, 'A New Contribution', 266.

[24] Report of the Secretary-General of 2 May 1991, para. 13.

processing of claims'.[25] They provide 'expedited procedures' for claims in Categories "A", "B" and "C", which the Council has specifically deemed 'urgent'.[26] In their reports, the UNCC Commissioners frequently refer to the need to reconcile fairness and speed. In 1998, for instance, a Panel stated that '[...] the vast number of claims before the Commission, and the time limits adopted by the Rules, necessitated the employment of legal standards and valuation methods that were administrable and which carefully balanced the twin objectives of speed and accuracy'.[27]

Likewise, Article 37 of the CRT-I Rules, entitled '*Time is of the essence*', leaves little to the imagination.[28] Similarly, the CRT-II Rules are designed to 'provide claimants with the benefits of an expeditious claims process'.[29] In fact, the CRT-II Rules 'are the result of a compromise between two requirements of equally high importance – a rapid resolution of all claims to Victim accounts combined with a thorough and fair judicial examination of the entitlement of each person filing a claim [...]'.[30]

According to the Special Master's Plan of Allocation and Distribution in the Holocaust Victim Assets Litigation, '[...] a lengthy and cumbersome process of individual eligibility determinations must be avoided'.[31] Likewise, the Memorandum of Understanding establishing the ICHEIC provides in its first paragraph that 'a just process shall be established that will expeditiously address the issue of unpaid insurance policies issued to victims of the Holocaust'.[32]

---

[25] UNCC, Provisional Rules, Art. 29. Moreover, the UNCC Rules foresee very short review periods within which the panels must complete the consideration of claims submitted to them. See Veijo Heiskanen, 'The United Nations Compensation Commission', *Collected Courses of the Hague Academy of International Law* 296 (2002), 255, 368–9; Wühler, 'A New Contribution', 266.

[26] UNCC, Provisional Rules, Art. 37; UNCC Governing Council, Decision No. 1: Criteria for Expedited Processing of Urgent Claims, S/AC.26/1991/1, 2 August 1991, *International Legal Materials* 30 (1991), 1712.

[27] UNCC, Report and Recommendations Made by the Panel of Commissioners Concerning the First Instalment of "E3" Claims, 17 December 1998, UN Doc. S/AC.26/1998/13, para. 6.

[28] CRT-I, Rules of Procedure, Art. 17 and 37.

[29] CRT-II, Rules Governing the Claims Resolution Process (As Amended), p. 4 (Introduction), available at www.crt-ii.org/_pdf/governing_rules_en.pdf (visited October 2007).

[30] Sylvain Beauchamp, 'The New Claims Resolution Tribunal for Dormant Accounts in Switzerland: Distribution Organ, Mass Claims Adjudicative Body or Sui Generis Entity?', *Journal of World Investment* 3(6) (2002), 999, 1001.

[31] CRT-II, Plan of Allocation and Distribution, p. 10.

[32] Memorandum of Understanding, para. 1.

Without doubt, these provisions encompass the right to a remedy within a reasonable period of time, which is recognised and guaranteed by virtually all human rights instruments.[33] Arguably, some of these provisions go beyond the traditional requirement of timeliness by conveying a special sense of urgency. In the Holocaust-related programmes, for instance, claims resolution is thought particularly urgent because the victim population is elderly and it is feared that many of them might die before their claims are resolved. In the case of the property claims commissions in the Balkans, the displacement crisis after the respective wars – combined with the humanitarian situation of the refugees – demanded prompt solutions. Likewise, in the UNCC, humanitarian considerations made the processing of individual claims urgent.[34]

While the traditional right to a timely remedy requires decision making without *undue* delay, mass claims processes need to offer remedies with *minimal* delay, i.e. at greater speed than is usually required. If timeliness is merely a mean between the extremes of haste and dilatoriness,[35] the requirement of expeditious decision making imposes an additional duty to decide claims *promptly*. The dire situation in which many claimants find themselves demands swift action.[36]

The only exception in this respect is the Iran–US Claims Tribunal. Despite the large number of individual claims, the Claims Settlement Declaration makes reference to the requirement of expeditiousness only with respect to the composition of the Tribunal, not with respect to the procedures.[37]

---

[33] See for example African Commission on Human Rights and People's Rights, Principles and Guidelines on the Right to a Fair Trial and Legal Assistance in Africa, November 1999, principle A 2 (i) (recognising 'an entitlement to a determination of their rights and obligations without undue delay'), available at www.achpr.org (visited October 2007); American Law Institute/UNIDROIT, Draft Principles and Rules of Transnational Civil Procedure, April 2003, available at www.unidroit.org (visited October 2007). The European Court of Human Rights, for instance, has a long-standing jurisprudence on the issue. For examples, see ECHR, *Case of König* v. *Germany*, 28 June 1978, No. 6232/73, para. 100 and *Milasi* v. *Italy*, 25 June 1987, No. 10527/83, para. 18.

[34] David D. Caron and Brian Morris, 'The UN Compensation Commission: Practical Justice, Not Retribution', *European Journal of International Law* 13(1) (2002), 183, 188.

[35] Michael D. Bayles, *Procedural Justice: Allocating to Individuals* (Dordrecht: Kluwer, 1990), p. 133.

[36] Caron and Morris, 'The UN Compensation Commission', 188.

[37] See Iran–US Claims Tribunal Settlement Declaration, Art. III(1): 'The Tribunal shall consist of nine members or such larger multiple of three as Iran and the United States may agree are necessary to conduct its business expeditiously.'

Economy

Mass claims processes are established to provide compensation and restitution to numerous claimants at lower cost than ordinary individual proceedings. Since the claims are numerous, the costs could easily become staggering. To be both practicable and fair, a mass claims programme 'must minimize transaction costs, be relatively easy to administer and involve relatively simple, understandable and objective eligibility criteria, while maximizing protection of those said to have suffered'.[38]

Again, the founding documents and procedural rules of most mass claims processes leave no question as to the need for economy. In his Report setting out the proposed compensation mechanism for Kuwait, for instance, the UN Secretary-General identified 'maximum [. . .] efficiency [. . .] and economy' as principal requirements for a successful mass claims process.[39] Likewise, in their reports, the UNCC Commissioners frequently relied on efficiency arguments to justify specific approaches or methodologies. One Panel stated that traditional procedures, if applied to mass claims, 'would result in unacceptable delays and substantially increase the burden of costs for such claimants and more so for the respondents'.[40] According to the Special Master's Plan of Allocation and Distribution in the Holocaust Victim Assets litigation, one of the main concerns in mass claims resolution is that '[. . .] administrative expenses must be minimized, particularly where, as here, the settlement fund is limited and the class members are numerous'.[41] The CRT-II Rules are 'designed with considerations of economy given an important place'.[42] The ICHEIC Appeals Tribunal Rules give the arbitrators the authority to adopt any procedural rule 'necessary to the efficient processing of Appeals'.[43]

The economy requirement serves various rationales, depending on how the restitution or compensation scheme is set up. The operational expenses of the CRPC and the HPCC, for instance, were borne by the international donor community and both institutions experienced significant difficulties in securing sufficient levels of funding.[44] In other

---

[38] *In re Agent Orange*, 611 F. Supp. 1396 (E.D.N.Y. 1985), 1410.
[39] Report of the Secretary-General of 2 May 1991, para. 2.
[40] UNCC, Report "A" claims, 4th inst., para. 9.
[41] CRT-II, Plan of Allocation and Distribution, p. 10.
[42] CRT-II, Rules of Procedure, p. 4 (Introduction).
[43] ICHEIC, Appeals Tribunal Rules of Procedure, Art. 1(4).
[44] See Garlick, 'Protection for Property Rights', 72 and 80.

cases, the administrative expenses are paid from a compensation fund, from which the individual compensation payments to claimants are also drawn. High administrative costs then risk consuming a substantial portion of the compensation resources, thereby reducing the net benefits for successful claimants. Finally, when the administrative costs are borne entirely by the respondent, expensive procedures might burden the respondent with transaction costs that are disproportionate to its liability.

As McGovern points out, there is a risk that low operational expenses might lead to over-use by claimants: 'If the claims resolution facility becomes so routinized that undeserving claimants view it as a public good, thereby making application for funds costless to themselves while incurring costs for legitimate parties, the effect may be counterproductive.'[45]

Consistency

Though seldom explicitly mentioned, the creation of mass claims processes is also motivated by the desire to ensure consistency in the treatment of similarly situated claimants. As stated by the HPCC, because of the high number of claims and their similarity, a mass claims process 'must be organized in a fair and efficient manner to ensure that claimants are treated equally and all the claims are resolved within a reasonable period of time'.[46] A specific reference to consistency is also found in the UNCC Rules: 'Chairmen of the panels will organize the work of their respective panels so as to ensure the expeditious processing of the claims and the consistent application of the relevant criteria and these Rules.'[47]

The concern for consistency may take many forms. In its most elementary form, it simply cautions against the risks of disparate outcomes if mass claims are tried individually. Indeed, if mass claims are resolved through a multiplicity of small individual suits before national courts in different countries, there is little or no protection against inconsistent outcomes.

In this sense, the mere establishment of a mass claims process, providing one single avenue for all claimants, contains a promise of increased consistency. To deliver on this promise, however, the mass claims process

---

[45] McGovern, 'Claims Resolution Facilities', 2.
[46] HPCC, Resolution No 7, para. 1.6. See also Gibson, 'Mass Claims Processing', 169; Wühler, 'A New Contribution', 264.
[47] UNCC, Provisional Rules, Art. 29.

must organise its proceedings in such a way that equal treatment of all claims is guaranteed. With a large number of claims and numerous decision makers involved, maintaining consistency in mass claims resolution is a significant challenge.[48]

Process characteristics

In addition, three general characteristics distinguish mass claims processes from other types of international claims resolution.

First, mass claims programmes are usually self-contained ad hoc regimes.[49] They have their own founding documents, which typically provide them with the authority to develop their own procedural and substantive rules. If appeals or reconsideration of decisions are possible, they are usually handled within the system rather than outside. Spill-over effects are therefore limited. Once the claims are processed, the system withers away.[50] As Heiskanen notes, the CRT 'appears to be the only existing mass claims program that has been assigned another related task after completing its initial assignment'.[51]

Second, since mass claims programmes serve large groups of individuals, easy access to the claims process is imperative. Most mass claims processes do not rely on the traditional espousal and diplomatic protection doctrines, and allow individual claimants to submit their claims directly to the mass claims facility. Some actively reach out to the public. Most programmes use standard claim forms and assist claimants with the preparation and registration of claims. Apart from minimising administrative expenditure, mass claims processes also aim to reduce the private costs to claimants to a minimum. They usually do not charge registration fees[52] and do not require representation by an attorney or counsel.[53]

Lastly, unlike international commercial arbitration, mass claims resolution processes are not driven by the parties.[54] In the interest of

---

[48] Wühler, 'A New Contribution', 267.
[49] Heiskanen, 'Speeding the Resolution of Mass Claims', 81.
[50] Heiskanen, 'Speeding the Resolution of Mass Claims', 81.
[51] Heiskanen, 'Speeding the Resolution of Mass Claims', 81.
[52] See for instance ICHEIC, Appeals Tribunal Rules of Procedure, Art. 32. See also Memorandum of Understanding, para. 5 (establishing a claims process 'that will be of no cost to claimants'). With respect to the GFLCP, see Van der Auweraert, 'The Practicalities of Forced Labor Compensation', 307.
[53] See for instance ICHEIC, Appeals Tribunal Rules of Procedure, Art. 15(1).
[54] Heiskanen, 'Speeding the Resolution of Mass Claims', 81; Heiskanen, 'The United Nations Compensation Commission', 302–3 and 370 (arguing that the UNCC 'was

efficiency and speed, those responsible for administering the process must take firm control of all procedural issues. In mass claims programmes with adversarial procedures, this authority is vested in the adjudicators. In mass claims programmes of an administrative character, the secretariat is usually in charge of the efficient organisation of the process.[55] Since the adjudicators are often not employed full-time by the mass claims facility, it is the secretariat that has to develop fair and efficient processing techniques. Referring to the UNCC, Gibson explains that 'the Secretariat is not only the "glue" holding the UNCC together on a number of levels; it is necessarily [...] the workhorse for generating the substantive ideas, methodologies and criteria for evaluating, processing and compensating the claims'.[56] This includes in particular an active role with respect to the design of computer-supported claim verification methodologies, the gathering of evidentiary records and the consistent handling of claims.

forced to adopt a more proactive and inquisitorial role and develop verification procedures that were less dependent on the role and contributions of the parties').
[55] Heiskanen, 'Speeding the Resolution of Mass Claims', 81.
[56] Gibson, 'Mass Claims Processing', 200.

4

Study in diversity

If mass claims were tried individually through the existing courts and tribunals, they would immensely burden the judicial system itself. They would clog the courts' dockets for decades, consume a considerable portion of the judicial resources and disturb the proper administration of justice for other claimants. Inconsistent outcomes would be inevitable. Or worse, some claims would never be tried and justice would be denied. Specific mass claims programmes have therefore been established to channel all related claims through one facility and provide a single route to justice for all claimants. These mass claims processes are expected to meet a number of specific process goals, including speed, economy and consistency. They should strive, as some have suggested, for 'practical justice: that is, a justice that would be swift and efficient, yet not rough'.[1]

While all mass claims programmes share the same objective of delivering effective remedies to a large number of claimants within a reasonable period of time, there is significant diversity in how they pursue this goal. While some programmes rely on typical 'judicial' procedures, others utilise proceedings of an 'administrative' or 'quasi-judicial' nature. Some programmes employ adversarial procedures, while others are structured as single-party proceedings. Moreover, the circumstances leading to their creation were radically different. Some were established by international agreement. Others were 'imposed' by the international community, acting through the United Nations. Several recently established mass claims processes resulted from a class action settlement before US courts. This diversity calls for a specific analytical approach.

Analytical approach

Any comparison of mass claims processes must take into account the different dynamics and circumstances that have led to their genesis and

---

[1] Caron and Morris, 'The UN Compensation Commission', 188.

that have helped shape their respective procedures. A contextual view is imperative.

Indeed, the context from which a particular claims process arises will determine, at least to some extent, its ability to develop and utilise novel and creative techniques. Depending on the origins and circumstances, the use of specific evidentiary and procedural techniques may be obvious in certain programmes and infinitely more controversial in others. The relevant context therefore needs to be taken into account throughout the analysis. For instance, the Iran–US Claims Tribunal and the UNCC took a radically different approach to many procedural and evidentiary issues because of the different circumstances in which both programmes were established. As Brower observed:

> In certain respects [the Iran–US Claims Tribunal] has not functioned as it should and I should say at the outset that [these problems] were inevitably the result, or the inevitable result, of the structure of the Tribunal and the circumstances of its genesis. Unlike virtually every other bilateral claims commission in history, our Tribunal had its origin not in the resounding defeat by one State Party of the other in war, but rather in the compromise known as the Algiers Accords. The United States did not defeat Iran. [. . .] They reached an agreement on the basis of sovereign equality, as equal negotiating partners. They struck a bargain and in this process established a Tribunal which is distinctly judicial, or adjudicatory, in character. And it is the fact of this equality that almost ensured that the Tribunal could not be operated with the high degree of administrative rationality that one would like.[2]

Moreover, mass claims should not be merely compared to individualised proceedings. Analysing mass claims processing techniques against the backdrop of existing procedural law, as it has been developed in individualised proceedings, for instance, is too narrow an approach. The specificity of mass claims procedure, as argued above, lies in the challenge of resolving numerous claims at greater speed and at lower cost than traditional individualised approaches. Meeting this challenge presupposes the liberty of calling into question traditional procedural dogmas and popular beliefs about the value of individualised justice. An exclusively positivist legal analysis is not sufficiently flexible to yield meaningful results.

[2] Charles N. Brower, 'Lessons to be Drawn from the Iran–US Claims Tribunal', *Journal of International Arbitration* 9(1) 1992, 51–2.

Instead, mass claims processing techniques should be evaluated on the basis of their impact upon the substantive goals of the settlement process and the values at stake.[3] In a value-based analysis, the question to be addressed is not whether these techniques meet the test of existing procedural law, but whether they are capable of furthering the values the claims process seeks to serve and, if so, at what cost. In particular, it allows identification of the trade-offs between competing interests and values present in the use of any given technique.

Admittedly, this instrumentalist rather than 'proceduralist' approach is primarily concerned with the effect of evidentiary and procedural techniques on the underlying substantive issue and is less concerned with their impact upon the judicial system in general.[4] In this approach, evidence and procedure are not an end in themselves, but as Davis notes, they give 'purpose and promise to the goals the substance seeks to accomplish'.[5]

Mapping the procedural landscape

Before taking a closer look at the key values to be considered in this analysis, it is worthwhile examining the broad contours of the procedural landscape. Building upon existing classifications of claims resolution facilities in the United States,[6] this section presents a general analytical framework that encompasses all the institutional and procedural variations within international mass claims programmes. Indeed, for analytical purposes, we can think of each mass claims facility as falling somewhere between the classic adjudicative model and the administrative model. This can be done both for the procedures that are used to determine eligibility and for the techniques utilised for assessing the value of eligible claims.

The framework suggested here is bipolar. It makes reference to two traditional decision-making models, i.e. the adjudicative or litigation

---

[3] Such approach is typically used when designing procedures for mass tort claims in the US. See McGovern, 'Claims Resolution Facilities', 2.

[4] See also Mary J. Davis, 'Toward the Proper Role for Mass Tort Class Actions', *Oregon Law Review* 77 (1998), 157, 158 and 160.

[5] Davis, 'Mass Tort Class Actions', 160.

[6] See in particular Mark A. Peterson, 'Giving Away Money: Comparative Comments on Claims Resolution Facilities', *Law and Contemporary Problems* 53 (1990), 113 and Deborah R. Hensler, 'Assessing Claims Resolution Facilities: What We Need to Know', *Law and Contemporary Problems* 53 (1990), 175, 181–4. With regard to procedures for the allocation of burdens and benefits to individuals, see Bayles, *Procedural Justice*, pp. 163–89.

model, on the one hand, and the administrative or bureaucratic investigation model, on the other. As such, it omits at least two alternative decision-making models that seek mutual voluntary acceptance of an outcome[7] – i.e. negotiation and mediation – and have been successful in other contexts. These alternative models have been excluded because the processes of negotiation and mediation are both time-consuming and labour-intensive. The direct costs are usually high. Therefore they are less appropriate in a programme that involves large groups of claimants. Moreover, since negotiation and mediation imply the participation and input of the parties, they usually require the presence of the parties in the same location, which is rarely feasible for international mass claims involving large groups of claimants spread over many different countries and continents. For instance, in the UNCC, the claimants were spread over ninety different countries and the CRT-I received claims from individuals in some seventy countries. Furthermore, the technique of negotiation is more effective when the parties' interests rather than their legally recognised rights are at stake: parties may have more scope to make mutual concessions with respect to their interests than when the recognition of their right is involved. For the foreseeable future, international mass claims practice are therefore likely to focus on adjudicative or administrative techniques rather than on negotiation and mediation.[8]

Determining eligibility

Each mass claims facility falls somewhere between the classic adjudicative or litigation model, on the one hand, and the administrative or bureaucratic investigation model, on the other.

Administrative model

In the administrative model, eligibility is typically determined by reference to strict and objective criteria that require minimal exercise of discretionary judgment.[9] Compensation or restitution is awarded to all claimants who present specific types of evidence and meet well-defined eligibility requirements. If the eligibility criteria are formulated with

---

[7] Bayles, *Procedural Justice*, p. 177.
[8] Mediation has been tried in the context of the Housing and Property Directorate in Kosovo. See UNMIK Regulation No. 2000/60, Section 10(1).
[9] Hensler, 'Assessing Claims Resolution Facilities', 182.

sufficient detail and precision and if they are objectively verifiable, the processing of claims becomes a more or less mechanical activity. This enables the decision maker to delegate claims review or claims assessment to administrative staff. In all cases, however, the model requires strict hierarchical control to ensure that all those involved in the decision making properly apply the criteria and norms. This control is in the hands of a few people at the top – usually called 'commissioners' – who have the authority to set the goals and standards and to determine whether these have been properly implemented.[10]

Moreover, in the administrative model, claims are typically divided into clearly defined and mutually exclusive categories of claims. In some instances, categorisation simply serves operational or organisational purposes, e.g. to maximise the expertise of personnel working on specific categories of claims. In other cases, especially when the caseload is large, the grouping of claims is a first step towards the design and the use of aggregative claims processing methodologies such as sampling or statistical modelling.

Furthermore, the administrative model is typically non-adversarial. As Bayles observes, the model does not structure claims as conflicts between two contesting parties.[11] It reduces disputes to factual questions requiring appropriate classification and categorisation. Moreover, in the administrative model, the claims processing facility has an inquisitorial nature, whereby the decision maker has the primary responsibility for developing the evidence for a decision.[12] Usually the claimant is required to provide information as well as evidence, but the decision maker is not restricted to that information or documentation. The decision maker has access to all the facts, not just those that the parties decide to present.[13] The administrative model does not require the separation of functions: the decision maker acts as the primary investigator.[14] There need not be a ban on *ex parte* communications.[15] The focus is usually on written evidence with little or no opportunity for the presentation of oral evidence. Representation by counsel is often not required, sometimes not even permitted.

Finally, administrative procedures are more flexible than court proceedings. While the decision makers in adjudicative procedures tend

[10] Bayles, *Procedural Justice*, p. 170.   [11] Bayles, *Procedural Justice*, p. 171.
[12] Bayles, *Procedural Justice*, p. 170.   [13] Bayles, *Procedural Justice*, pp. 171–2.
[14] Bayles, *Procedural Justice*, p. 171.   [15] Bayles, Procedural Justice, p. 171.

to be generalists lacking specialised expertise, administrative procedures are often organised in such a way that technical expertise is promoted.[16]

Adjudicative or litigation model

The adjudicative or litigation model typically employs looser, more subjective eligibility rules.[17] Based on the uniqueness of each claim and claimant, the treatment of claims and claimants is individualised.[18] Each claim is treated in isolation of the other claims and decisions are to be based upon the particularities of each individual situation.[19] Adjudicative procedures therefore often demand more extensive evidence.

The model usually depends on an adversarial process and presupposes that opposing parties have to put forward their respective arguments. As Cramton notes, '[t]he model of individualized justice posits that each claimant should make all relevant decisions with respect to [his/her] claim'.[20] The adjudicator is considered 'a neutral, relatively passive arbiter of conflicting private interests who rules on questions of law and supervises the conduct of the litigation'.[21] Delegation of adjudicative power is in principle not allowed.

In practice, many mass claims programmes mix characteristics of the administrative and adjudicative model. They employ administrative processing techniques for certain types of claims and use adjudicative rules for others. In this way, they seek to maximise the benefits of both the administrative and adjudicative models while minimising their costs.[22]

Examples in international mass claims practice

The adjudicative and the administrative archetypes provide convenient points of reference to classify international mass claims processes.

The Iran–United States Claims Tribunal, for instance, adopted procedures that conform neatly to the litigation model. The Claims

---

[16] B.G. Garth, 'Improvement of Civil Litigation by Lessons Derived from Administrative Procedures: General Report', in W. Wedekind (edn), *Justice and Efficiency: General Reports and Discussions. The Eighth World Conference on Procedural Law* (Deventer: Kluwer Law and Taxation, 1989), p. 265.

[17] Hensler, 'Assessing Claims Resolution Facilities', 182.

[18] Hensler, 'Assessing Claims Resolution Facilities', 183.

[19] Bayles, *Procedural Justice*, p. 169.

[20] Roger C. Cramton, 'Individualized Justice, Mass Torts, and 'Settlement Class Actions': An Introduction', *Cornell Law Review* 80 (1995), 811, 817.

[21] Cramton, 'Individualized Justice', 814.

[22] Hensler, 'Assessing Claims Resolution Facilities', 183.

Settlement Declaration refers to the institution as an 'international arbitral tribunal' that adjudicates claims through 'binding third-party arbitration' in accordance with the UNCITRAL arbitration rules as modified by the Parties or the Tribunal.[23] The Tribunal adjudicates claims on an individualised or case-by-case basis. Its proceedings are adversarial, involving *inter alia* the exchange of written pleadings (statement of claim, statement of defence, reply, rejoinder) and oral hearings.

The CRT-I also operated in a largely adjudicative posture. It was created as an arbitral process, adjudicating claims on an individual basis. The proceedings – in which the relevant bank acted as the respondent party[24] – had a largely adversarial character. In a number of ways, however, the Tribunal's decision-making process departed from the adjudicative model. The proceedings were conducted 'in an informal manner and under relaxed procedural rules that are convenient for the claimants and take into account their age, language and residence'.[25] Article 17 gave the arbitrators discretion to conduct the proceedings and emphasised the need 'to ensure an expeditious and equitable determination of all claims'.[26] It was a documents-only arbitration, with oral hearings only held when strictly necessary.[27] The arbitrators had extensive fact-finding powers.[28] In short, although the CRT-I procedures largely remained adjudicative, some procedural features made it lean toward the administrative investigation model.

The nature of the second Claims Resolution Process was different. CRT-II was no longer an arbitral tribunal governed by Swiss law.[29] Although the banks continued to cooperate by making certain information available, they were no longer parties to the proceedings.[30] While claims to deposited assets were still adjudicated on an individual basis, the procedures used to determine eligibility involve data matching and research, a type of process that appears to be administrative rather than adjudicative.[31] Moreover, in June 2002, the Special Masters announced a restructuring of the CRT with institutional and procedural changes aimed at 'increasing the

---

[23] Iran–US Claims Tribunal Settlement Declaration, Art. I, II (1) and III (2).
[24] Although the possibility was used by some banks, in practice, most banks rarely made use of their participatory opportunities.
[25] CRT-I, Rules of Procedure, Art. 17 (i).   [26] CRT-I, Rules of Procedure, Art. 17.
[27] CRT-I, Rules of Procedure., Art. 17 (iv).   [28] CRT-I, Rules of Procedure., Art. 17 (ii).
[29] Alford, 'The Claims Resolution Tribunal', 265.
[30] CRT-II, Rules of Procedure, at B-1 (Introduction).
[31] CRT-II, Rules of Procedure, Arts 19–21.

efficiency of the claims resolution process'.[32] All of the CRT-I arbitrators resigned from the institution and a new decision-making procedure was created. The CRT-II attorneys drafted the decisions, which were then forwarded through the Special Masters to the US Court for approval.[33] In short, CRT-II moved further away from the litigation model and was much closer to the administrative model than CRT-I.

The UNCC also had a mixed nature, effectively combining elements of the administrative and the litigation models. However, since the Commission applied radically different claims processing methodologies to different claims categories, these different categories have to be assessed separately.

For the resolution of the small individual claims in Categories "A", "B" and "C", the Governing Council established relatively precise eligibility criteria, which were further refined by the Panels. Most claims review tasks were delegated to the secretariat. Similar claims were grouped together. Proceedings were inquisitorial rather than adversarial. It was the responsibility of the Commissioners 'to establish the facts and evaluate the claims, and it [was] up to the panels to seek the information and documentation required'.[34] Except for periodic reports on the claims, the proceedings for these claims involved little or no opportunity for Iraq to participate. No oral hearings were held. The UNCC secretariat actively gathered evidence. Evidently, these procedures have all the hallmarks of the administrative model.

The larger individual, corporate and government claims in Categories "D", "E" and "F" were resolved in a different way. They were subject to an individualised review. Iraq was granted more opportunities to participate in the proceedings. The Panel could decide to make claim files available to the Government of Iraq and to request additional written submissions. It could also invite Iraq to present its views in oral proceedings. Although such occurrences were rare in the initial phases of the UNCC's work, at a later stage oral proceedings were more often used, especially in sensitive cases.[35] Nevertheless, the process remained inquisitorial rather than adversarial and it was still up to the

---

[32] CRT-II, Press release, 3 June 2002. The release states *inter alia* that the 'participation of high level Senior Claims Judges active in CRT will no longer be required' and that 'CRT staff attorneys will now be responsible for drafting decisions'.

[33] Beauchamp, 'The New Claims Resolution Tribunal', 1035.

[34] Wühler, 'A New Contribution', 267.

[35] UNCC Governing Council, Decision No. 114: Review of Current UNCC Procedures, 7 December 2000, UN Doc. S/AC.26/Dec.114 (2000), para. 14.

Commissioners to seek the information and documentation required to arrive at a fair determination of the claims. In short, although these procedures incorporated a few elements of the litigation model, they remained predominantly administrative.

In the IOM-led programme under the GFLCP, the claims were registered through the IOM field offices and entered into a central database by a professional data-entry company. The reason given for the decentralisation of claims registration was 'the need to be close to the claimants in a phase of the claims processing cycle when many claimants would undoubtedly require some form of assistance or guidance. It was also hoped that lowering the barrier for claimants to seek information and help from IOM, would lead to a higher quality of claims and a more efficient and cheaper claims verification process later on'.[36] This was possible only through the 'use of internet based technology, which allows for the simultaneous registration of claims by the IOM field offices in a central claims database kept at the IOM headquarters in Geneva'. The actual processing and verification of claims was carried out by staff at IOM-Geneva and involved data matching and archival research.[37] Every three to four months, the IOM submitted to the Foundation a list with claims recommended for compensation. The Foundation had four weeks to carry out an audit of the claims. The audit was usually performed on a sample group of claims. The Foundation could approve the list, reject certain recommendations or suspend approval of certain claims.[38] Once the list was approved, the Foundation transferred the necessary funds to pay compensation to all the claimants included in the list. This largely administrative procedure was complemented by an appeals procedure before an Appeals Body, comprising three independent members.[39] The Appeals Body determined appeals on the basis of written information and available evidence. Even in this stage, however, there were no oral hearings of appellants.[40]

Similarly, the IOM claims process under the HVAP was largely based on archival searches, plausibility reviews and computerised data

---

[36] Van der Auweraert, 'The Practicalities of Forced Labor Compensation', 309.
[37] Van der Auweraert, 'The Practicalities of Forced Labor Compensation', 311.
[38] Van der Auweraert, 'The Practicalities of Forced Labor Compensation', 311.
[39] 'German Foundation Act', Section 19. On the scope of the appeals process, see Van der Auweraert, 'The Practicalities of Forced Labor Compensation', 316.
[40] IOM Appeals Body for Forced Labour Claims, Principles and Rules of Appeals Procedure, 7 February 2003, Art. 16(D), available at www.compensation-for-forced-labour.org/ (visited October 2007).

matching. Since the claimants were of age, speed and efficiency in decision making were essential.

The CRPC came close to the administrative model. The Commission made decisions on the basis of a sophisticated set of eligibility rules and employed single-party proceedings. The Commissioners delegated a significant part of their claims review to the internationally supervised secretariat. At the peak of its activities, the secretariat employed over 400 staff members, the vast majority of whom were locally recruited. The CRPC did not provide for oral evidence or public hearings. Neither the current occupant of the claimed property nor the local authorities were invited to participate in the proceedings. Single-party proceedings could be envisaged because the Dayton Peace Agreement itself had already determined that every refugee or displaced person who owned property before the conflict could return to their pre-war property. Since property transactions that took place during the war were presumed to be affected by duress, the CRPC simply had to investigate the individual claimant's rights over the claimed property as of 1 April 1992 (i.e. the date on which the hostilities started) and to confirm their entitlement under the Dayton Peace Agreement. Fact-finding and evidence gathering was undertaken primarily by the Commission itself, rather than by the claimants. Because many claimants lost their title documents, the CRPC legal staff checked each individual claim against the available records. Together with other international agencies, the CRPC was able to recover and reconstruct most of the computerised cadastre data, which was used as a verification database. The CRPC could also make use of the 1991 census database that contained the main place of residence of all citizens. It could also consult registers of the local courts and administrative bodies for additional evidence on property rights. Multi-ethnic teams of local lawyers, supervised by an international staff member, screened the computerised claims, checked them against the available records and prepared decision proposals. A working group of three commissioners reviewed a sample of the decisions and the whole batch of decisions was submitted to the full Commission at its monthly Plenary Sessions. After approval by the Commission, individual certificates of the decisions were issued.

Lastly, the Kosovo programme was modelled after the Bosnian and South African precedents[41] and effectively combined elements of both.

---

[41] In South Africa, the land restitution process is implemented by an administrative body and a specialised court. These are, respectively, the 'Commission on the Restitution of

The claims process was administered by an administrative body, the HPD, which registered claims and tried to mediate between the parties. A quasi-judicial body, the HPCC had exclusive jurisdiction to adjudicate the property claims referred to it by the HPD. Both HPD and HPCC operated under the auspices of UNMIK.[42] The HPCC consisted of a single panel with one local and two international commissioners, all of whom were appointed by the Special Representative of the Secretary-General.[43] Although predominantly of an administrative nature, the Kosovo programme contained some adversarial and judicial elements. The current occupant and other parties with a legal interest in the claimed property were given notice of the claims and invited to participate in the procedures and to submit written evidence.[44] Given the minorities' security risks and limited freedom of movement, the HPCC did not conduct public hearings or receive oral evidence unless there was a specific need. The Commission was also authorised to consider uncontested refugee claims in a fast-track summary procedure.[45] For the expeditious processing of claims, the HPCC could 'use computer databases, programs and other electronic tools in order to expedite its decision-making' and 'consider claims raising common legal and evidentiary issues together'.[46] As Dodson and Heiskanen noted, the 'rules of evidence are flexible and aimed at doing justice rather than at unnecessary formality'.[47]

Assessing claims values

A mass claims process may very well employ adjudicative processes to determine eligibility, but standardised processes for the assessment of the value of the claim, or vice versa. Two alternative models should again be distinguished when considering the techniques used to determine the value of the claimed losses or damages. At one extreme, the process used

Land Rights' and the 'Land Claims Court'. See Monty J. Roodt, 'Land Restitution in South Africa', in Scott Leckie, *Returning Home: Housing and Property Restitution Rights of Refugees and Displaced Persons* (Ardsley, NY: Transnational, 2003), pp. 243–71.

[42] UNMIK Regulation No. 1999/23, Section 2.1: the HPCC will function 'until the Special Representative of the Secretary-General determines that local courts are able to carry out the functions entrusted to the Commission'.

[43] UNMIK Regulation No. 1999/23, Section 2.2.

[44] UNMIK Regulation No. 2000/60, Section 9.

[45] UNMIK Regulation No. 2000/60, Section 23.

[46] UNMIK Regulation No. 2000/60, Section 19.5.

[47] Dodson and Heiskanen, 'Housing and Property Restitution in Kosovo', 235.

to value mass claims may resemble the standardised grid approach. At the other extreme, a system of individualised assignment of values can be used as in tort law.

In a standardised grid approach, the losses and damages are valued on the basis of a predetermined grid with mutually exclusive and inflexible categories.[48] Individual claims are categorised and assigned a fixed amount of compensation corresponding to the grid location. Typically, the criteria for placement in one category or another are fairly simple and require minimal proof by the claimant and minimal analysis by the facility.[49]

In an individualised valuation system, on the other hand, each claim is examined in detail in order to assign a specific value tailored to that, and only that, claim. This model assumes that 'information has infinite value and that each incremental piece of data is potentially worthwhile for a decision maker [. . .] to use in customizing an award'.[50] Each claim has to be thoroughly examined in order to determine its precise value. The valuation is based on the evidence presented by the claimant and is made through a careful weighing of all information available to the adjudicator.

Again, some valuation processes combine standardised and individualised valuation and maximise the benefits of both approaches while reducing their costs.

The UNCC used the standardised grid approach for Categories "A" and "B", where the Governing Council established fixed compensation sums for all claimants who were eligible. Evidence for these fixed compensation amounts were kept minimal. In Category "C", the amount of compensation was in principle based on the real value of the losses suffered as a result of the Iraqi invasion and occupation of Kuwait. As the precise value of certain losses proved difficult or impossible to ascertain, the "C" Panel valued these losses through averaging and statistical modelling. These techniques can be seen as mixed systems. For larger claims, the UNCC employed individualised valuation methods.

Likewise, the IOM-administered Property Claims Commission under the GFLCP adopted a method of valuation, which classified each compensable item within a grid of standardised amounts based on the nature

---

[48] McGovern, 'The Intellectual Heritage', 189; Hensler, 'Assessing Claims Resolution Facilities', 182.
[49] McGovern, 'The Intellectual Heritage', 190.
[50] McGovern, 'The Intellectual Heritage', 190.

and size of the property and its location. In its individual decisions, the Commission justified the use of the grid as follows:

> The Commission [. . .] chose this methodology in view of: its aim of standardizing amounts to eliminate arbitrary differences in property values from one region to another and from one time period to another; the difficulty in making case-by-case valuations given the often scarce, subjective, or inconsistent valuation information available to claimants because of the passage of time and the circumstances in which the losses occurred; and the importance of nonetheless recognizing and evaluating whatever specific information claimants have provided.[51]

Social choices at stake

General overview

The choice of a particular decision-making model impacts on a number of different values. Efficiency and speed, for instance, are generally recognised benefits of the administrative decision-making model and the standardised grid approach.[52] Direct costs are at a minimum in these models. Based on strict eligibility criteria with minimal exercise of judgment and the possibility of delegation, decisions can be made quickly.[53] Moreover, as Garth notes, the administrative model also tends 'to emphasize accessibility and informality to allow ordinary people to pursue their claims'.[54] These features make them particularly suitable for handling large volumes of claims.

At the other extreme, direct costs appear to be at a maximum in the litigation model and the individualised valuation approach. These processes are generally slower than administrative processes and seem less capable of processing large numbers of claims quickly. Why then are these procedures used and sometimes preferred over standardised and administrative procedures? Clearly, their use is based on the popular belief that fairness in claims processing is better served by individualised adjudicative procedures. According to this perception, individualised systems lead to more accurate outcomes than standardised approaches.

---

[51] This is a standard formula in individual awards of the IOM Property Claims Commission.

[52] See for instance, Deborah R. Hensler and Mark A. Peterson, 'Understanding Mass Personal Injury Litigation: A Socio-Legal Analysis', *Brooklyn Law Review* 59 (1993), 961, 1059–60; Bayles, *Procedural Justice*, p. 172.

[53] Bayles, *Procedural Justice*, p. 172.   [54] Garth, 'Improvement of Civil Litigation', 272.

In particular, proponents of individualised systems argue that claims are not interchangeable and, consequently, that standardised systems cannot ensure the desired level of outcome accuracy: '[A] forced categorization of claims results in manifest unfairness at the margins where artificial and arbitrary lines demand an inclusion of claims that are incompatible and separate claims that are closely related'.[55]

Proponents of standardised non-litigation systems, on the other hand, emphasise the importance of consistency among claim outcomes. Standardised and administrative systems are said to enhance 'collective fairness':

> Although each individual may not receive precisely the 'correct' amount, the 'fairness' to the group as a whole is enhanced because the awards are consistent and because the overall awards correspond correctly to our sense of justice. In other words, the error costs under a standardized approach are higher for individuals, but the consistency errors are low. The [individualised and adjudicative] tort system has higher consistency errors and lower individual errors.[56]

In the administrative model, the underlying values are certainty and consistency. The norms must be precise and cover all cases. Little or no room is left for discretion. As Bayles observes, whether they promote outcome accuracy in individual cases will largely depend on the subject matter: rules-based systems are only appropriate when 'factual features are quite reliably correlated with appropriate decision outcomes'.[57] If the correlations are weak, Bayles explains, the outcomes will be less optimal and the error costs greater.

From a behavioural perspective, finally, it has been argued that values of dignity, autonomy and participation are under-represented in standardised and administrative approaches.[58] Bayles argues that, in the administrative model, participation is less than with adversary adjudication because parties have less control over the presentation of their views. Although they are usually given the opportunity to present what information and documentation they have, it is the decision maker who ultimately controls the presentation of the facts and the evidence. Such systems risk depriving individuals of 'meaningful control over their own legal claims, pushing them involuntarily into compensation grids and

---

[55] McGovern, 'The Intellectual Heritage', 190.
[56] McGovern, 'The Intellectual Heritage', 190.   [57] Bayles, *Procedural Justice*, p. 172.
[58] Bayles, *Procedural Justice*, p. 172.

administrative claims-handling processes to whose ministrations they have not consented'.[59] Claimants tend to be dissatisfied when they can present only limited information and do not have their 'day in court' or the opportunity to express their story. In the adjudicative model, each claimant receives – at least in theory – an equal opportunity to present their claim and each claimant is in control of all strategic and other relevant decisions with respect to that claim.[60]

Values at stake

The classic debate between the different decision-making models enables us to identify the main values that are at stake when choosing one procedural technique over another. They are efficiency (encompassing both the time element and the cost element), outcome accuracy, consistency and party participation. The overview also demonstrates that these four values are related and that compromise and trade-offs are inevitable.

These four values provide the framework according to which this study will analyse and assess the various evidentiary and decision-making techniques used in international mass claims programmes. The selection of these values presents the additional advantage that they can be measured more or less objectively, thus providing a sound basis for comparison. More abstract values – such as justice and equity – have not been used, although they are indirectly present in some of the discussions.

Efficiency

Efficiency – a central concept in law and economics[61] – is an obvious criterion for the analysis of procedural and evidentiary techniques in mass claims procedure. It is a specific goal in mass claims procedure and is a relatively objective and apolitical indicator, providing a sound basis for analysis.

In an economic approach, procedures are generally considered efficient if they minimise the sum of two types of costs, namely direct costs and error costs. The direct costs are those of running the decision-making system. They include public costs such as the adjudicators' time,

[59] Cramton, 'Individualized Justice', 821.   [60] Cramton, 'Individualized Justice', 817.
[61] For an introduction to the concept of efficiency, see Robert Cooter and Thomas Ulen, *Law & Economics* (Reading, MA: Addison-Wesley, 2000), 3rd edn, p. 12.

the salaries of officials, the costs of organising hearings, equipment, facilities and so on. They also include private costs, e.g. the parties' time, their costs in hiring lawyers, obtaining evidence or expert testimony, etc.[62] Error costs arise when an incorrect decision is made, i.e. a decision awarding compensation or restitution to an 'undeserving' claimant or a decision that fails to award compensation or restitution to a 'deserving' claimant. Indeed, '[e]ach incorrect decision results in an inefficient use of resources and an inappropriate expense, because it is not furthering the substantive purposes'.[63]

Direct costs and error costs are related to and interact with each other.[64] If one tried to minimise the direct costs of the claims process, the error costs might become excessive.[65] Similarly, if one aimed to achieve greater accuracy by using expensive procedures, at some point the increase in direct costs will become greater than the savings in reduced error costs. The minimisation of either direct or error costs alone, without taking into account their interaction, may therefore yield unexpected or undesirable overall results. This is why efficiency requires the minimisation of the *sum* of direct and error costs, rather than the minimisation of each cost separately.

Outcome accuracy

An outcome is accurate if it correctly determines the facts and the law, and if it correctly applies the law to the facts.[66] The law of evidence and procedural law inevitably 'involve an effort to strike a balance between accuracy and legal costs'.[67] Accuracy takes a central place in the evaluation of the various mass claims processing techniques.

The determination of the facts requires particular attention. While outcome accuracy is a highly valued goal, it is important to be aware

---

[62] Bayles, *Procedural Justice*, p. 119.   [63] Bayles, *Procedural Justice*, pp. 118–19.

[64] Bayles, *Procedural Justice*, p. 118. See also, Hector Fix-Fierro, *Courts, Justice and Efficiency: A Socio-Legal Study of Economic Rationality in Adjudication* (Oxford and Portland: Hart Publishing, 2003), p. 36. See also, with respect to litigation and settlement in a national context, Richard A. Posner, 'An Economic Approach to Procedure and Judicial Administration', *Journal of Legal Studies* 2 (1973), 399, 441.

[65] Michael J. Saks, 'Enhancing and Restraining Accuracy in Adjudication', *Law and Contemporary Problems* 51 (1988), 243, 245.

[66] Bone, 'Statistical Adjudication', 577.

[67] Louis Kaplow, 'The Value of Accuracy in Adjudication: An Economic Analysis', *Journal of Legal Studies* 23 (1994), 307, 307–8; Michael J. Saks and Peter D. Blanck, 'Justice Improved: The Unrecognized Benefits of Aggregation and Sampling in the Trial of Mass Torts', *Stanford Law Review* 44 (1990), 815, 829 and 833.

that, in reality, perfect accuracy in fact-finding is largely illusory. As Carbonneau observes, '[u]nequivocal precision and exactitude are not the order of the day in justice determinations'.[68] This follows directly from the realisation that accuracy-increasing measures rarely come without costs. As Saks notes in his study on accuracy in decision making, at some point truth-finding processes could exact costs 'that exceed any benefit the parties or society could gain from the effort. At some point the game is not worth the candle. The law must impose some limitation on the development of its truth-finding methods before the litigation system becomes bogged down in its own efforts to do its job well.'[69]

Moreover, perfect accuracy in fact finding is not always required for claims adjudication. For Saks, '[f]inding facts is merely instrumental to the larger purpose of the legal process; it plays a supporting and not a leading role. The legal process is a truth-seeking enterprise only insofar as truth is needed to resolve disputes'.[70] If the parties agree on a particular issue, for instance, or if a party does not dispute a factual assertion made by the other party, a tribunal will usually not verify on its own motion the accuracy of the assertion. Nor is the tribunal expected to verify the correctness of the assertion, because the function of the tribunal is to settle disputes and if there is no dispute, there is nothing to settle. In this sense, the concept of truth adopted in adjudication is conventional rather than material.

As a consequence, fact-based accuracy may be more important in some claims resolution programmes than in others depending on the nature of the claims and the specific context of the process.

First, the importance of accuracy depends on whether the claims include predominantly cognitive conflicts, which are best resolved through fact finding, or distributional conflicts that require making other kinds of judgments.[71] In practice, most claims include a mixture

---

[68] Thomas E. Carbonneau, 'Darkness and Light in the Shadows of International Arbitral Adjudication', in Richard B. Lillich (ed.), *Fact-Finding Before International Tribunals – Eleventh Sokol Colloquium* (Ardsley-on-Hudson, NY: Transnational, 1992), pp. 153, 159.

[69] Saks, 'Enhancing and Restraining Accuracy', 244.

[70] Saks, 'Enhancing and Restraining Accuracy', 244. See also Carbonneau, 'International Arbitral Adjudication', 159; Mirjan Damaska, 'Truth & Its Rivals: Evidence Reform and the Goals of Evidence Law', *Hastings Law Journal* 49 (1998), 289, 289.

[71] Saks, 'Enhancing and Restraining Accuracy', 244.

of both, which may 'help explain some of the choices the law makes in structuring its procedures and deciding what kinds of evidence to admit'.[72] Saks rightly notes that '[t]he resources one is willing to devote to finding materially relevant facts may depend upon how pivotal those facts are to the case. In resolving disputes involving mixed questions of cognitive uncertainty and distributional conflict, still other considerations may dominate the process and the decisions reached'.[73]

Second, the concrete circumstances in which the claims process operates may determine the relative importance of accuracy. A claims resolution process has to be satisfying to its users, including the losing parties and the society at large. According to Saks, '[a]t various stages of our society's development, that may mean preferring one set of procedures rather than another, even if the favoured rule reduces rather than increases the system's fact-finding capability'.[74]

The specific nature of mass claims processes requires particular attention in this regard. The traditional system of conventional justice and truth, as outlined above, is based on the ideal of two equal parties and the freedom of contract. In mass claims situations, the relationship between the individual claimant and the respondent is somewhat different, and intervention may be required. Indeed, as Part II will demonstrate, various mass claims processes have shifted the fact-finding function from the parties to the tribunal or claims commission, reflecting a shift from the concept of conventional truth towards the concept of material or scientific truth.

In sum, accurate fact finding plays an important yet limited role in claims resolution.[75] In the face of uncertainties, less than perfect accuracy is – willingly or unwillingly – accepted. Consequently, as Bone suggests, it may be more appropriate to define outcome accuracy in mass claims settlement in terms of 'error risks' rather than 'errors'. One outcome is then considered more accurate than another 'if the error risk associated with the former is less than the error risk associated with the latter'.[76]

---

[72] Saks, 'Enhancing and Restraining Accuracy', 244.
[73] Saks, 'Enhancing and Restraining Accuracy', 244.
[74] Saks, 'Enhancing and Restraining Accuracy', 244.
[75] See also Carbonneau, 'International Arbitral Adjudication', 159.
[76] Bone, 'Statistical Adjudication', 577.

Consistency

Rational and fair decision making requires consistency.[77] Decisions that are inconsistent are arbitrary and, consequently, unfair or unjust.[78]

Consistency, which can be defined as the absence of contradictions, is closely related to equality[79], which requires that 'like cases should be treated alike and unlike cases should be treated not alike in proportion to their unlikeness'.[80] Some have considered this Aristotelian maxim to be purely formal and empty.[81]

One can argue that, at least for our present purposes, the real question is not whether like cases should be decided alike – few would disagree – but what we mean by 'like cases'. No two cases being identical in every respect, the relevant question is whether we should 'base our decision-making norm on relatively large categories of likeness, or by contrast leave a decision maker more or less at liberty to consider any possible way in which this particular array of facts might be unique'.[82]

The issue illustrates the tension that inevitably arises between outcome accuracy and consistency. If consistency is achieved by grouping together large categories of claims, i.e. by making abstraction of minor differences between claims, it may end up sacrificing the level of outcome accuracy that individuals expect. In the opposite sense, it is also clear that if one leaves the decision makers free to consider even the slightest differences between claims, the result may be a loss of consistency. This is especially true in mass claims resolution, with multiple

---

[77] On the relationship between consistency and justice, see for instance N. MacCormick, *Legal Reasoning and Legal Theory* (Oxford: Clarendon, 1978), p. 75; Chaïm Perelman, *Justice et raison*, (Bruxelles: Ed. de l'Université de Bruxelles, 1972), 2eme édn, p. 21; and Frederick Schauer, 'Precedent', *Stanford Law Review* 39 (1987), 571, 596.

[78] On the need for a normative principle of consistency, see MacCormick, *Legal Reasoning and Legal Theory*, pp. 76–7.

[79] John E. Coons, 'Consistency', *California Law Review* 75 (1987), 59, 59–60 and 65–75.

[80] Aristotle, *Nicomachean Ethics* (Indianapolis (Ind.): Hackett, 1985), translated by Terence Irwin, pp. 122–8.

[81] See for instance, Peter Westen, 'The Empty Idea of Equality', *Harvard Law Review* 95 (1982), 537, 551:

> It is true that rules should be applied equally, consistently, and impartially, if by 'equally', 'consistently' and 'impartially' one means the tautological proposition that the rule should be applied in all cases to which the terms of the rule dictate that it be applied. But it is wrong to think that, once a rule is applied in accord with its own terms, equality has something additional to say about the scope of the rule [. . .]

[82] Schauer, 'Precedent', 596.

decision makers. It is important to realise, therefore, that consistency – however desirable and undisputed in the abstract – comes only 'by giving up some of our flexibility to explore fully the deepest corners of the events now before us'.[83]

Process values

Parties to procedures are particularly sensitive to procedural fairness.[84] However, procedural justice theorists disagree on the specific components of procedural fairness. Some have suggested that party control over the process and the case outcome is the crucial factor in the perception of procedural fairness.[85] For others, the perceived fairness of a procedure depends largely on whether a person receives dignified and respectful treatment.[86]

Regardless of these differences, the general proposition emerging from procedural justice research is that the process for reaching decisions has a value of its own for participants and 'this value is independent, to a degree that can be subject to measurement, from the value of the outcome for such participants'.[87] As a minimum requirement, the procedure needs to offer the parties some meaningful form of participation.

Process values nevertheless play an extremely limited role in mass claims procedures, where participation by the parties is particularly limited. Very few mass claims processes provide for oral hearings. Some go as far as granting claimants only one opportunity to 'tell their story', i.e. through the submission of the written claim. This is the case, for instance, in the CRPC and for Category "A", "B" and "C" claimants in the UNCC.

This lack of participatory rights is an inevitable consequence of the 'numbers problem' in mass claims. While some form of meaningful participation may be feasible for a few thousands of claimants, organising even a limited form of participation for hundreds of thousands of

---

[83] Schauer, 'Precedent', 602.

[84] Allan E. Lind et al., 'In the Eye of the Beholder: Tort Litigants' Evaluations of Their Experiences in the Civil Justice System', *Law and Society Review* 24 (1990), 953, 957.

[85] John Thibaut and Laurens Walker, 'A Theory of Procedure', *California Law Review* 66 (1978), 541. See also Lind et al., 'In the Eye of the Beholder', 957–8; Tom R. Tyler, 'A Psychological Perspective on the Settlement of Mass Tort Claims', *Law and Contemporary Problems* 53 (1990), 199, 201.

[86] See Lind, 'In the Eye of the Beholder', 958. The link between dignity and fair process is also found in legal theory. See the references in Bayles, *Procedural Justice*, p. 130.

[87] Fix-Fierro, *Courts, Justice and Efficiency*, p. 57.

claimants would entail excessive costs in terms of both resources and time, and would inevitably conflict with the right to a timely remedy. Moreover, even if hearings were organised, only a few claimants would in practice be able to make use of their participatory rights. Many more would have to wait years, or even decades, before receiving their day in court.[88] Likewise, when the claimants are spread all over the globe, it is illusory to think that many of them will be able to make effective use of their participatory rights.

The argument goes beyond merely stating that there is a trade-off between process values and efficiency. Rather, it is submitted that both values are mutually exclusive in a mass claims context: one cannot be achieved without abandoning the other. If the process wants to be efficient, it cannot offer meaningful participation to all claimants. If the process seeks to promote participation, on the other hand, it will do so by sacrificing all sense of efficiency. Faced with this dilemma, most mass claims programmes, such as the UNCC and the CRPC, have opted for efficiency for humanitarian reasons: the socio-economic condition of the claimants required speedy decisions. Put differently, it was assumed that claimants would generally prefer material and timely remedies over participation in the process.[89]

It can also be argued that, after armed conflicts, the victims' desire to 'tell their story' and to face their opponents is better met in another type of process. Truth or reconciliation commissions are arguably better equipped to deal with these concerns than legal processes, which are primarily aimed at adjudicating claims.

---

[88] See also Saks and Blanck, 'Justice Improved', 839.

[89] In the absence of a clear humanitarian need, the choice may be far more difficult. Studies concerning mass tort claims in the US appear to indicate that claimants prefer slow claims processes with meaningful participation over efficient procedures with little or no participation. See generally Tyler, 'A Psychological Perspective', 202–3.

PART II

Evidentiary techniques in international mass claims adjudication

Developing fair and practical rules of evidence – i.e. rules that determine what information may be provided to the adjudicator and how it is to be provided[1] – is a key challenge in most international adjudication. International tribunals often have to decide claims on the basis of scanty, incomplete or otherwise inadequate evidence.[2] As a consequence, they regularly have to rely upon circumstantial evidence, call upon experts, use presumptions and draw inferences from the circumstances. As Thomas Carbonneau rightly notes, '[t]here are [...] no facts without judgment any more than there are judgments without facts'.[3]

This is even more so in the context of mass claims arising from armed conflict, where a complex combination of interrelated problems tends to make the administration of evidence a particularly challenging task. Contemporary mass claims processes have therefore further relaxed the already flexible evidentiary rules applicable in international procedure.

This Part examines whether and how the rules on evidence can be relaxed without jeopardising the integrity and fairness of the claims process. If evidentiary support is known to be scanty, should the normal evidentiary requirements be relaxed and if so, how can the claims resolution process ensure that legitimate claims are upheld but that false, fraudulent or otherwise invalid claims are excluded?

This question will be addressed by examining three distinct areas of the administration of evidence. Chapter 6 examines whether and when the allocation of the burden of proof can be used to ease the claimants' task of presenting evidence. Chapter 7 analyses whether the standard of

---

[1] Definition provided by Richard A. Posner, 'An Economic Approach to the Law of Evidence', John M. Olin Law & Economics Working Paper No. 66 (1999), 1.

[2] Durward D. Sandifer, *Evidence Before International Tribunals* (Charlottesville, NY: University Press of Virginia, 1975), p. 22.

[3] Carbonneau, 'Darkness and Light', 158.

evidence can be relaxed and, if so, how this impacts outcome accuracy. Finally, Chapter 8 focuses on presumptions and inferences in international mass claims procedure. First, however, the introductory Chapter 5 discusses the nature of the evidentiary difficulties that commonly arise in international mass claims processes.

5

Need for special rules of evidence

Main evidentiary problems

The adjudication of mass claims arising from armed conflicts or similar events raises a wide range of evidentiary problems. Some are unique and relate to a specific conflict or a particular type of claim; others are generic and arise in other contexts as well.[1] Those hereinafter discussed seem the most critical ones requiring particular attention.

War conditions

Except for the Iran–US Claims Tribunal, all international mass claims programmes have been established in response to armed conflicts.[2] The conditions of war restrict in various ways the claimants' ability to produce evidence.

First, many of the documents and other items that could be used to substantiate claims may be destroyed, lost or looted. As it would be unreasonable to require claimants to produce evidence that no longer exists, most mass claims processes take into account the claimants' difficulty to prove their claim. In the UNCC, for instance, one Panel of Commissioners noted that 'the looting, vandalism and destruction of property was extensive. Many homes were gutted or left in complete disarray. Thus, some or all of the documents and other items that could be used to substantiate a claim may have been looted or destroyed, or lost subsequently during efforts to clean-up the damage and debris'.[3]

---

[1] For an overview of the general difficulties in obtaining and evaluating evidence in international proceedings, see Sandifer, *Evidence Before International Tribunal*, p. 22.

[2] With respect to the Iran–US Claims Tribunal, it can be argued that the conditions in Iran at the time of the revolution had a similar impact on the claimants' access to evidence.

[3] UNCC, Report and Recommendations Made by the Panel of Commissioners Concerning the First Instalment of Individual Claims for Damages up to $100,000 (Category "C" Claims), UN Doc. S/AC.26/1994/3, 21 December 1994, p. 27.

Similarly, under the ICHEIC Rules, a claimant must show that it is plausible 'in the light of all the special circumstances involved, including but not limited to the destruction caused by World War II [. . .]' that they are entitled to the claimed insurance policy.[4]

Second, in some armed conflicts, the deliberate destruction or concealment of evidentiary records is part and parcel of the military strategies of the warring factions. If the respondent adheres to a deliberate policy of destroying, concealing or tampering with evidentiary records, it would be unreasonable to keep the burden of proof upon the claimants. In Bosnia, for instance, the official property records in many areas were destroyed, removed or tampered with in an attempt to prevent the return of minorities after the conflict. With respect to compensation for dormant accounts (CRT), on the other hand, the Volcker Report established that, although there was 'confirmed evidence of questionable and deceitful actions by some individual banks in the handling of accounts of victims, there was no evidence of systematic destruction of records of victims' accounts'.[5]

Third, armed conflicts often cause people to flee without securing the documents that later could be used to prove their losses. The ethnic cleansing campaign in Bosnia and the ensuing displacement crisis in the region are a case in point. Similar problems were faced in the context of the UNCC:

> The circumstances in which the claimants' losses occurred, specifically those in Iraq or Kuwait, may have had a significant impact on claimants' abilities to provide evidence in support of their claims. Thus, for example, consideration was given to the general emergency conditions prevailing in Kuwait and Iraq under which many thousands of individuals were forced to flee or hide or were held captive, without safely securing their possessions or retaining documents that later could be used to substantiate their losses. In addition, consideration was given to the fact that many claimants could not return to Iraq or Kuwait, or chose not to return, and therefore had difficulty producing primary evidence of their losses. The invasion took place at the height of the Gulf summer. Accordingly, many persons were outside Kuwait and Iraq on vacation, and would have

---

[4] See ICHEIC, Relaxed Standards of Proof Guide, available at www.icheic.org/docs-documents.html (visited October 2007).

[5] Independent Committee of Eminent Persons, Report on Dormant Accounts of Victims of Nazi Persecution in Swiss Banks (commonly known as the 'Volcker Report'), 6 December 1999, p. 13.

had no reason to take documentation relevant to establishing their claim with them.[6]

Finally, a climate of fear, reprisals and violence can severely hinder not only the claims process in general, but also the production of evidence. It may discourage potential witnesses and claimants from stepping forward and dissuade officials from cooperating in the search for evidence. Obtaining and producing evidence will be more difficult for claimants from minorities that have specifically been targeted. In post-war Bosnia and Kosovo, for instance, there was limited freedom of movement for ethnic minorities, causing difficulties for those individuals to file claims, collect official documentation or to undertake other steps to collect and present evidence.

Lapse of time

While some restitution and compensation programmes were launched in the immediate aftermath of an armed conflict, others started only half a century after the end of the hostilities. The Second World War-related compensation programmes, in particular, became politically feasible only in the nineties, after the end of the Cold War. While long delays are not without precedent in international practice,[7] the establishment of a claims process some fifty years after a conflict appears to be a first.

This time lapse brings about a range of delicate evidentiary problems. Evidence which might easily have been obtained at the time is now lost or extremely difficult to collect. Many of those involved have died. First-hand information is becoming rare. Statements taken from witnesses such a long time after the event are not always fully credible. Records are lost and cannot be replaced.

Quality of the relevant records

Regardless of the war conditions, the claimants' ability to produce documentation is also a function of the existence, quality and comprehensiveness of evidentiary records.[8] For some types of property

---

[6] UNCC, Report "C" claims, 1st inst., p. 27. See also UNCC, Recommendations Made by the Panel of Commissioners Concerning Individual Claims for Serious Personal Injury or Death (Category "B" claims), UN Doc. S/AC.26/1994/1, 26 May 1994, pp. 33–4.
[7] For examples, see Sandifer, *Evidence Before International Tribunals*, p. 24.
[8] Sandifer, *Evidence Before International Tribunals*, p. 22.

losses – e.g. personal property or artworks – there is no central registry in which ownership or possession are recorded. For others, such as real property claims, there is usually some type of repository of titles and/or possessory rights. The existence, state and quality of these records needs to be taken into account. If the records are poorly prepared, inadequately updated or otherwise lacking in quality and reliability, it will be difficult, if not impossible, to establish entitlements with a sufficient level of confidence.

Again, the CRPC may serve as an example. Bosnia and Herzegovina's dual registration system, based on the Austrian–Hungarian tradition, was composed of cadastre registers and property books (or *zemljisna knjiga*), with the latter recording ownership rights over real property. Already before the conflict, the dual system was severely neglected by the State and not or improperly used by its citizens. Many property transactions were never registered in the property books. Moreover, around 30 per cent of the country's original property books had already been destroyed during the Second World War and had never been replaced. Even without the damage the property books sustained during the 1992–5 conflict, the Bosnian property books proved to be an unreliable and incomplete source of evidence.

Parties' access to evidentiary sources

As explained above, the parties to mass claims proceedings are usually individuals, on the one hand, and an institutional respondent, on the other.[9] As far as access to evidentiary sources is concerned, the individual will often find themself in a disadvantageous position. Records held by State bodies, for instance, will be easily accessible to the agents of the State party, but they may be impossible, costly or simply difficult to access for individuals.

While the cost of collecting all relevant materials can be prohibitive for an individual claimant, especially after a humanitarian crisis, the respondent will not necessarily be hindered by such financial constraints. In a mass claims situation opposing one respondent to numerous individuals, the respondent is in a position to exploit economies of scale by spreading the private investments made for proving

---

[9] As explained above, this is not necessarily the case. The CRPC and the HPCC are exceptions in this respect.

one claim across all claims.[10] Moreover, since the stakes are higher for the respondent than for a single claimant, the respondent has a clear economic incentive to invest more than an individual claimant.[11]

Socio-economic situation of the claimants

The socio-economic situation of the claimants also affects the preparation of the claims and the submission of the evidence. Different levels of income, literacy and education may result in significant discrepancies in the quality of presentation of the claims and in the relevance and materiality of the evidence submitted. While this is true for all litigation, it is especially pertinent for claims arising out of a war that has disrupted the social and economic development of an entire population.

Especially in large mass claims programmes, the difference between various claimant groups needs to be carefully weighed. For poorer claimants, the proper filing of the UNCC claim form may have been a very difficult exercise, especially when they received no guidance or assistance from their Government. Bearing in mind the inequalities between claimants from different countries, the UNCC secretariat prepared 'country reports' detailing the socio-economic backgrounds of claimants from particular countries and explaining the national claims programmes and other forms of assistance available to them. These reports had to facilitate the Commissioners' understanding of the factual and legal issues raised by the claims from a particular country and to make them aware of existing inequalities between different claimant groups.[12]

Nature and type of claims

Certain types of claims, such as claims for personal property or looted art, are difficult to prove even in normal circumstances. How exactly is one expected to demonstrate ownership and loss of particular items of household furnishings, clothes, utensils etc.? Establishing the value

---

[10] This proposition holds for the presentation of evidence on all 'common issues' that arise in various individual claims. See for instance Peterson and Selvin, *Resolution of Mass Torts*, p. 12.

[11] For an analogy with mass torts in the US, see for instance David Rosenberg, 'Mass Tort Class Actions: What Defendants Have and Plaintiffs Don't', *Harvard Journal On Legislation* 37 (2000) 393.

[12] See Gibson, 'Mass Claims Processing', pp. 169–71.

of such items is, even in fair weather conditions, an arduous and imprecise task.

Examples are found even in early international jurisprudence. In the *Amabile case* before the Italian–US Claims Commission, for instance, the claimant argued that *ex parte* evidence was the only evidence available to her and that 'the very nature of the property itself [i.e. 120 items of personal property] accounted for the claimant's inability to produce other types of documentary evidence to establish the existence, ownership and value of the personal property which had been lost'.[13] Although the argument eventually failed because of internal contradictions in the evidence, the Italian–US Conciliation Commission appeared willing to accept this line of reasoning: 'It is obvious that *the nature of the property* and the circumstances surrounding the loss or damage will be determinative in most instances of the type and quantity of evidence which the claimant can furnish to document his claim.'

Basic dilemma

Each of the present-day mass claims processes has faced some or all of the above-mentioned problems. In the CRPC, approximately 30 per cent of the claimants were not able to submit *any* reliable proof of their pre-war property rights. In the UNCC and the Iran–US Claims Tribunal, the trying circumstances in which most expatriates left their country of residence made it difficult for these claimants to submit supporting evidence of the losses they incurred. All the Second World War-related compensation programmes likewise received numerous claims lacking supporting documentation.[14]

Moreover, this scarcity of evidentiary support is inextricably linked to the conditions in which the losses were sustained and is at least partly caused by the harmful events upon which the claims are based.

This creates a basic dilemma, which is present in all mass claims processes. On the one hand, victims with a genuine claim for compensation deserve to be awarded an effective remedy, even if the war or related conditions prevent them from presenting full documentary

---

[13] Italian–US Conciliation Commission, *Amabile Claim*, 25 June 1952, *International Law Reports* 22 (1955), 852.

[14] For the IOM-administered programmes, see IOM – Press Release 2/2002, 'Many claimants lack sufficient documentation', Geneva, 7 February 2002. The CRT and ICHEIC Rules make special provision for inadequately supported claims.

evidence of their losses. Clearly, a claimant cannot be expected to provide documents which no longer exist. Likewise, it would be difficult to justify evidentiary rules that require claimants to produce documents which are not at their disposal and which they cannot access. Moreover, to the extent that the massive scale of the harms caused by the respondent complicates the collection and handling of evidence and makes these activities extremely costly, it would again be unfair to accept this as a reason for not awarding compensation to some claimants. Finally, to the extent that the evidentiary difficulties are directly or indirectly attributable to the respondent, it would be fundamentally unfair to exclude claimants from the compensation or restitution process on the basis of a failure to meet the evidentiary requirements.[15]

On the other hand, the evidentiary standards should not do injustice to the respondent and should effectively exclude fraudulent, false or otherwise invalid claims. Relaxing the evidentiary requirements in favour of the claimant may place an unjustified burden on the respondent party, which would be forced to prove that the claims are untrue, and may encourage and effectively reward fraudulent or false claims.[16]

This dilemma explains the need for specialised rules of evidence in international mass claims processes. If the evidentiary support is scarce, and if this is not attributable to the claimants, then the design of an evidentiary framework must take into account this reality.[17] In such circumstances, strict rules of evidence would inevitably lead to a high proportion of rejected claims, cause high levels of frustration and dissatisfaction amongst claimants and generally prevent the claims process from achieving its goals. It is probably in this sense that Theo Van Boven's guidelines on Restitution, Compensation and Rehabilitation for Victims of Gross Violations of Human Rights and Fundamental Freedoms recommended that '[a]dministrative or judicial tribunals

---

[15] A similar reasoning is found in a different context in the Inter-American Court of Human Rights, *Velasquez Rodriguez* Case, Judgment of 29 July 1988, Inter-Am.Ct.H.R. (Ser. C) No. 4 (1988), para. 124.

[16] Mojtaba Kazazi, *Burden of Proof and Related Issues: A Study on Evidence before International Tribunals* (The Hague: Kluwer Law International, 1996), p. 352.

[17] For a similar approach, see the Convention on the Settlement of Matters Arising Out of the War and the Occupation, signed at Bonn on 26 May 1952 (as amended by Schedule IV to the Protocol on the Termination of the Occupation Regime in the Federal Republic of Germany, signed at Paris on 23 October 1954), *United Nations Treaty Series* No. 4762 (1959), chapter IV, para. 2(c).

responsible for affording reparations should take into account that records or other tangible evidence may be limited or unavailable'.[18]

Fair decision making requires a delicate balancing of both the claimants' and respondent's interests. Three main techniques are available to the designers of mass claims processes to overcome the problems raised by this dilemma: the claimant's burden of proof can be eased; the standards of evidence can be relaxed; and presumptions and inferences can be developed to fill the evidentiary gaps. Each of these techniques has been used to varying degrees in the different mass claims processes. Each of them presents advantages and disadvantages, as the following chapters will demonstrate.

---

[18] Theo Van Boven, Study Concerning the Right to Restitution, Compensation and Rehabilitation for Victims of Gross Violations of Human Rights and Fundamental Freedoms, UN Doc. E/CN.4/Sub.2/1993/8, 2 July 1993, para. 137 (1993). The Special Rapporteur added that '[i]n the absence of other evidence, reparations should be based on the testimony of victims, family members, medical and mental health professionals'. These techniques, however, are not particularly practicable in the context of mass claims.

6

Burden of proof

This chapter discusses the burden of proof rules in international mass claims processes. A first section discusses the principal features of the burden of proof and identifies the general rules governing its distribution in general international procedure. Subsequently, a few historical claims commissions will be contrasted with present-day mass claims processes. A final section suggests guidelines to determine when the traditional rules on burden of proof should be amended.

Concept and general rules

Concept and terminology

The burden of proof in international proceedings, however important to practitioners, has received limited academic attention to date. A prominent exception is Mojtaba Kazazi's overview of judicial and arbitral practice, which also explores the concept and terminology in French and English legal language.[1] The phrase 'burden of proof' in English and '*la charge de la preuve*' or '*le fardeau de la preuve*' in French generally mean 'the obligation to prove' or 'the necessity of affirmatively proving a fact or facts in dispute'.[2] As Kazazi explains, however, the legal connotations and scope of these terms are not exactly the same in Anglo-American and French law.

In common law countries, the 'burden of proof' covers two different notions.[3] It refers to the 'burden of persuasion', i.e. the 'legal burden', which is not meant to shift from one party to the other at any stage of the

---

[1] Kazazi, *Burden of Proof.*
[2] Bryan A. Garner (ed.), *Black's Law Dictionary* (St Paul: West Group, 1990), 6th edn, p. 196.
[3] See generally James Fleming and Geoffrey C. Hazard, *Civil Procedure*, paras 7.5–8 (Boston, 2nd edn, 1977); Edmund M. Morgan, *Some Problems of Proof Under the Anglo-American System of Litigation* (New York: Columbia University Press, 1956), pp. 72–86.

proceeding.[4] This burden, related to substantive law, concerns 'the onus on the party with the burden of proof to convince the trier of fact of all elements of his case'.[5] The party having the burden of persuasion will lose the case if the fact-finder's mind is undecided after considering all the relevant evidence.[6]

'Burden of proof' also refers to the 'burden of going forward with the evidence' (also referred to as the 'burden of producing evidence' or simply 'the burden of evidence'). This burden shifts back and forth between the parties as the proceedings progress. Contrary to the legal burden, this burden is already relevant at an early stage of the trial.[7]

The burdens of production and persuasion may or may not be allocated to the same party.[8] In principle, it is not necessary to produce two different sets of evidence to discharge each of the burdens; the same evidence may serve both purposes. Nevertheless, discharging the burden of producing evidence does not necessarily mean that the legal burden is also discharged.[9]

In French law, the phrase '*la charge ou le fardeau de la preuve*' refers only to the burden of persuasion.[10] It does not cover the shifting burden of producing evidence, as it is known in common law countries.[11]

There is no such difference between the meaning of the French and English terminology in international law, where the aforementioned

---

[4] See for example Charles V. Laughlin, 'The Location of the Burden of Persuasion', *University of Pittsburgh Law Review* 18 (1956), 3.

[5] Laughlin, 'The Burden of Persuasion', 3. See also J.D. Heydon, *Cases and Materials on Evidence* (London: Butterworths, 1975), p. 13; Kazazi, *Burden of Proof*, p. 24.

[6] Robert Belton, 'Burdens of Pleading and Proof in Discrimination Cases: Toward a Theory of Procedural Justice', *Vanderbilt Law Review* 34 (1981), 1205, 1216.

[7] Kazazi, *Burden of Proof*, p. 25. See also Belton, 'Toward a Theory of Procedural Justice', 1216.

[8] Kazazi, *Burden of Proof*, p. 25. See also Belton, 'Toward a Theory of Procedural Justice', 1216.

[9] Kazazi, *Burden of Proof*, p. 25.

[10] Kazazi, *Burden of Proof*, p. 26. For a thorough account of the burden of proof in French law, see Jean Devèze, 'Contribution à l'étude de la charge de la preuve en matière civile' (Grenoble: Service de reproduction des thesis de l'Université des sciences sociales de Grenoble, 1980).

[11] Peter Herzog and Martha Weser, *Civil Procedure in France* (The Hague: Nijhoff, 1967), p. 310. See also J.-C. Witenberg, 'Onus probandi devant les juridictions arbitrales', *Revue Générale de Droit International Public* 55 (1951), 321, 324 and J.-C. Witenberg, 'La théorie des preuves devant les juridictions internationales', *Recueil des Cours de l'Académie de Droit International de La Haye* 56 (1936), 1, 43.

expressions and their Latin equivalent *onus probandi* are used indiscriminately, depending on the language of the proceedings.[12]

In international arbitration, with its flexible procedural rules, 'the burden of producing evidence' has no strict meaning.[13] According to Kazazi, international tribunals follow the pattern of civil law countries, where it is only at the end of the proceedings that the court decides whether or not the burden of proof has been discharged.[14] Or, as Sandifer concludes:

> [t]he broad basic rule of burden of proof adopted, in general, by international tribunals resembles the civil law rule and may be simply stated: that the burden of proof rests upon him who asserts the affirmative of a proposition that if not substantiated will result in a decision adverse to his contention. This burden may rest on the defendant, if there be a defendant, equally with the plaintiff, as the former may incur the burden of substantiating any proposition he asserts in answers to the allegations of the plaintiff.[15]

General rules on the burden of proof in international procedure

The allocation of the burden of proof in international procedure is determined by the respective roles and duties of the claimant, the respondent and the arbitral tribunal.

First, the well-known rule of *actori incumbit probatio* generally applies: each party, regardless of its procedural position as claimant or respondent has to prove its claims and contentions.[16] Article 24 (1) of the UNCITRAL Arbitration Rules, for instance, explicitly provides that '[e]ach party shall have the burden of proving the facts relied on to support his claim or defence'.[17] Under this principle, a tribunal or

---

[12] Kazazi, *Burden of Proof*, pp. 22–3.

[13] The fact that the concept is not clearly distinguished from the 'burden of proof' in international procedure does not mean, however, that it does not exist. See the discussion of the 'presentation of pleadings and evidence' in Kazazi, *Burden of Proof*, p. 33.

[14] Kazazi, *Burden of Proof*, p. 32.

[15] Sandifer, *Evidence Before International Tribunals*, p. 127.

[16] Kazazi, *Burden of Proof*, p. 378; Witenberg, 'Onus probandi', 327; Charles N. Brower, 'Evidence Before International Tribunals: The Need for Some Standard Rules', *The International Lawyer* 28(1) (1994), 47, 49.

[17] UNCITRAL Arbitration Rules, G.A. Res. 31/98, 31 U.N.GAOR, Supp. No. 17, UN Doc. A/31/17 (1976), *International Legal Materials* 15 (1976), 701, 710.

claims commission has to dismiss a claim for which the claimant has failed to produce sufficient evidence, even though the respondent likewise fails to support his denial by evidence. In *International Ore*, for example, the Iran–US Claims Tribunal held that '[. . .] the mere fact that the Respondents have not offered any evidence in support of their denial of the Claimant's allegations does not suffice to shift the burden of proof and to relieve the claimants from their duty to evidence their own contentions'.[18]

Second, the parties are under a duty to cooperate in submitting to the tribunal the relevant facts. The tribunal should base its decision on as many facts and as much information as possible.[19] As a supplement to the first rule, this duty of cooperation, explicitly mentioned in the rules of several international tribunals, requires the respondent not to conceal the truth and to actively cooperate in disclosing the facts. Article 34 (3) of the ICSID Rules of Procedure for Arbitration Proceedings, for instance, provides that the parties shall cooperate with the Tribunal in the production of evidence and that the Tribunal 'shall take formal note of the failure of a party to comply with its obligations under this paragraph and of any reasons given for such failure'.[20] The obligation implies in particular a duty to produce documents that are exclusively in the repondent's possession. According to Kazazi, this duty arises when 'the claimant has apparently done his best and all in his power to secure evidence and has actually produced some *prima facie* evidence in support of his case'.[21]

Third, international tribunals have fact-finding authority, meaning that they can themselves initiate steps to establish the relevant facts.[22] They also have the power to determine which party carries the burden of proof and they enjoy discretion and freedom in weighing and evaluating evidence.[23] While the scope and limits of their fact-finding authority

---

[18] Iran–US Claims Tribunal, *International Ore* v. *Razi Chemical Company*, 29 February 1988, Iran Award 351–486–3, reprinted in 18 *Iran–US Claims Tribunal Reports* 98, para. 10.

[19] Kazazi, *Burden of Proof*, p. 119.

[20] ICSID, Rules of Procedure for Arbitration Proceedings, ICSID Basic Documents, pt. D (1985), available at www.worldbank.org/icsid/ (visited October 2007).

[21] Kazazi, *Burden of Proof*, p. 149.

[22] For an overview of the fact-finding activities of various courts and tribunals, see Richard B. Lillich (edn), *Fact-Finding Before International Tribunals – Eleventh Sokol Colloquium* (Ardsley-on-Hudson, NY: Transnational, 1992).

[23] See for instance Rule 34 (1) of the ICSID Rules of Procedure for Arbitration Proceedings. With respect to the Iran–US Claims Tribunal, see Article 25(6) of the Tribunal Rules,

may be subject to differences of opinion, the concept itself and its impact on the burden of proof are generally accepted.[24] As a consequence, international tribunals are generally not content to base a decision simply upon the failure of a party to maintain the burden of proof: 'If a party fails to bring forward satisfactory proof, tribunals in practice customarily exercise the discretion vested in them by requiring a further production of evidence by one or both parties or by appointing experts to make appropriate inquiries or making researches on their own initiative.'[25] Obviously, tribunals have to exercise their fact-finding authority with full impartiality and 'with due regard to the fundamental principles of equality of parties and the necessity of providing parties with full opportunity to present their claims and defences'.[26]

These three principles in international practice are generally accepted.[27] Their precise inter-relationship is less clear and international tribunals or commissions need to find a proper balance between them. For Kazazi:

> [. . .] the only overriding rule with respect to the burden of proof in international procedure is the rule which results from the application of the three above-mentioned rules together, each to the extent necessary, in an international proceeding. The proper application of this overriding principle is an important duty of international tribunals and constitutes a measure on which basis their efficiency can be judged.[28]

As a consequence, the respective importance of each of these three specific rules may differ from tribunal to tribunal, depending on the

---

available at www.iusct.org/tribunal-rules.pdf. With respect to the Inter-American Human Rights Court, see Thomas Buergenthal, 'Judicial Fact-finding: Inter-American Human Rights Court', in Richard B. Lillich (ed.), *Fact-Finding Before International Tribunals – Eleventh Sokol Colloquium* (Ardsley-on-Hudson, NY: Transnational, 1992), pp. 261, 270.

[24] Kazazi, *Burden of Proof*, p. 379. See also Paul Reuter, *Le développement de l'ordre juridique international: Écrits de droit international* (Paris: Economica, 1995), p. 541: 'Le juge a un rôle actif ; il doit rechercher lui aussi tous les éléments qui permettront d'établir les faits ou les règles essentielles pour la solution du litige.'

[25] Sandifer, *Evidence Before International Tribunals*, p. 131. See also Howard M. Holtzmann, 'Fact-Finding by the Iran–United States Claims Tribunal', in Richard B. Lillich (ed.), *Fact-Finding Before International Tribunals – Eleventh Sokol Colloquium* (Ardsley-on-Hudson, NY: Transnational, 1992), pp. 101, 109.

[26] Kazazi, *Burden of Proof*, p. 155.

[27] Gérard Niyungeko, *La preuve devant les juridictions internationales* (Bruxelles: Université Libre de Bruxelles, 1988), p. 18.

[28] Kazazi, *Burden of Proof*, p. 235.

circumstances, the nature of the caseload, the relationship between the parties and the objectives of the tribunal. For our purposes, it will be submitted that the adjudication of mass claims after armed conflicts requires a specific balance between the three basic rules. Indeed, the specificity of these claims and procedures may require that, in the interest of fairness and efficiency, the second and/or third rule preponderate over the first.

Between rigour and flexibility in traditional practice

As a general rule, historical claims commissions and arbitral tribunals have taken a strict and uncompromising approach to the burden of proof. They did not hesitate to reject claims for the sole reason that the claimant failed to discharge the burden of proving the facts they relied upon to claim compensation.

In a few specific cases, however, the same commissions were persuaded to be more flexible and tried to develop a reasonable solution that was appropriate under the circumstances of the case. This was done on the basis of the so-called *probatio diabolica* doctrine. In its most elementary form, this doctrine maintains that the party who carries the burden of proof, though responsible for discharging that burden, cannot be expected to provide documents that no longer exist or that are not at its disposal and to which it cannot have access.[29] The doctrine can affect either the burden of proof or the standards of evidence.

One of the best-known illustrations of this principle is the ICJ's decision to allow the UK to rely on indirect evidence in the *Corfu Channel Case*. According to the ICJ, the exclusive control exercised by a State within its frontiers may make it impossible to furnish direct proof of facts which would involve its responsibility in case of a violation of international law.[30] The victim State must in that case be allowed a more liberal recourse to inferences of fact and circumstantial evidence.[31]

Although the notion of *probatio diabolica* was originally limited to situations in which it was materially impossible to present the required documentation, it has been applied also in cases where it was merely

---

[29] Kazazi, *Burden of Proof*, p. 352.

[30] ICJ, *Corfu Channel Case (UK v. Alb.)*, Judgment of 9 April 1949 (merits), *ICJ Reports* 1949, 18.

[31] ICJ, *Corfu Channel Case*, p. 18. Such indirect evidence must be regarded as of special weight when based on a series of facts, linked together and leading logically to a single conclusion.

difficult for the claimant to produce the required documentation. The following examples illustrate the practice of mixed arbitral tribunals and claims commissions.

Mixed arbitral tribunals

Mixed arbitral tribunals established after the First World War between each of the Allied and Associated Powers, on the one hand, and each of the Central Powers, on the other,[32] required claimants to prove all the facts that they relied on to claim compensation or restitution. Failure to discharge the burden of proof resulted in the rejection of the claim, regardless of the difficulties the claimant may have faced to access, produce or submit evidence. In the *Paul Lang Case*, for instance, the French–German tribunal rejected the claim for failure to establish the causal relationship between the claimant's internment during the war and the damages he suffered.[33]

The categorical dismissal of this claim, with no consideration for the claimant's difficulties to establish the required link, marks a sharp contrast with the surprisingly liberal approach taken by the same Tribunal in the *Janin Case*, where the *probatio diabolica* doctrine played a major role, albeit an implicit one. The claimant, a French national, owned a house in Germany, which was first requisitioned for the purpose of housing soldiers and subsequently placed under sequestration. Upon his return, the claimant found his wine cellar plundered and his furniture damaged. The claimant successfully established the loss of the wine stock and certain damages, as well as the soldiers' responsibility in this respect. As to the other items, e.g. disappearance of silverware, however, Germany argued that the claimant had failed to establish that the theft and damage occurred during the period of requisitioning and sequestration. The Tribunal did not accept this reasoning, stating that: '*il serait injuste d'exiger que le requérant, nécessairement absent pendant toute la guerre, prouve* à quelle époque *le vol a été commis et les dégâts ont été causés*'.[34] Having established

---

[32] For an overview and a general introduction to the functioning of the Mixed Arbitral Tribunals, see Norbert Wühler, 'Mixed Arbitral Tribunals', in Rudolf Bernhard (ed.), *Encyclopedia of Public International Law* (Amsterdam: North-Holland, 1997), Vol. III, p. 433.

[33] Tribunal arbitral mixte Franco–allemand (1re section), *Paul Lang c. Etat allemand*, 7 octobre 1924, *Recueil des décisions des tribunaux arbitraux mixtes*, Tome VI, p. 166.

[34] Tribunal arbitral mixte franco–allemand, *Janin c. Etat allemand*, 4 février 1922, *Recueil des décisions des tribunaux arbitraux mixtes*, Tome I, p. 777 (emphasis added). For a

that the wine cellar was plundered by soldiers, the Tribunal moreover presumed that they also took the other items that were kept in the cellar: '*[E]n présence du fait non contesté que les soldats ont pillé la cave et fracturé des armoires, il y a lieu d'admettre la présomption qu'ils se sont également emparés d'autres objets, enfermés dans ces armoires*'.[35] This inference results in an effective reversal of the burden of proof.[36] In a final step, the Tribunal added that 'it is probable' that these cupboards contained the items of silverware and lingerie that the claimant alleged they contained and the disappearance of which was confirmed by a witness.[37]

In short, the Tribunal required no proof as to the period in which the theft took place. It presumed that the persons responsible for the breaking of the cupboards also stole the objects that were kept in the cupboards and finally assumed that the objects that were in the cupboards were the ones that the claimant maintained were stolen.

The *Banque d'Orient Case*, adjudicated by the Turkish–Greek Mixed Arbitral Tribunal, is one of the rare instances in which an arbitral tribunal elaborated on the *probatio diabolica* theory and identified the requirements for its application:

> [...] il serait inéquitable, voire même inique, que l'obligation du demandeur de faire la preuve fût portée au delà de la limite où il lui devient impossible ou extrêmement difficile de s'acquitter de sa charge, alors que par contre il est facile – ou en tout cas beaucoup plus facile – pour le défendeur d'établir des circonstances qui, si elles sont prouvées, peuvent faire écarter la demande. Dans une pareille situation, les rôles doivent être renversés, et à partir de ladite limite le fardeau de la preuve tombe sur l'adversaire de celui qui au début en avait la charge. Ce principe est particulièrement incontestable au cas où le défendeur a lui-même créé les difficultés qui s'opposent à l'administration de la preuve par le demandeur.[38]

---

similar case and approach, see Tribunal arbitral mixte franco–bulgare, *De Chèvremont c. Etat bulgare*, 23 juin 1924, *Recueil des décisions des tribunaux arbitraux mixtes*, Tome IV, p. 458.

[35] TAM franco–allemand, *Janin c. Etat allemand*, p. 777.

[36] In fact, the German agent established that some items were stolen by individuals after the soldiers left and before sequestration started and that these items were later retrieved. In other words, for these specific items, the defendant successfully discharged the burden of proving that they were not stolen by the German soldiers. This portion of the claim was consequently rejected.

[37] TAM franco–allemand, *Janin c. Etat allemand*, p. 777.

[38] Tribunal arbitral mixte turco–grec, *Banque d'Orient c. Gouvernement turc*, 9 février 1928, *Recueil des décisions des tribunaux arbitraux mixtes*, tome VII, p. 973.

This paragraph is interesting for three reasons. First, the Tribunal applied the *probatio diabolica* theory not only in a situation of impossibility, but also where it was 'extremely difficult' for the claimant to prove the facts. Second, the difficulty for the claimant was weighed against the ease with which the respondent could prove the opposite, which implies that the burden of proof would have remained on the claimant if it had been equally difficult for the claimant and the respondent to prove their respective positions. As it was easier for the respondent, however, the burden of proof shifted to this party. Finally, the reversal of the burden was considered particularly appropriate when the respondent had created or contributed to the difficulties that the claimant experienced in presenting the required proof.

Italian Conciliation Commissions

The Italian Conciliation Commissions, established after the Second World War between Italy and several Allied Powers,[39] dealt with disputes concerning *inter alia* the restitution of property, the restoration of legal rights and interests of United Nations nationals or persons treated as enemies, and compensation for property losses caused by the war.[40] In spite of the reference to 'conciliation' in their name, the Commissions were given powers analogous to those of arbitral tribunals.

The practice of the Conciliation Commissions was in accordance with the basic rule that the claimant should prove the facts upon which they relied. Failure to do so resulted in the rejection of the claim, irrespective of the difficulties experienced by the claimant to provide evidence. In the *Batchelder Claim*, for instance, a US national claimed compensation for the loss of household furnishings and other personal property which was allegedly removed from his villa during the war. In its decision, the Italian–US Conciliation Commission dismissed the claim for lack of sufficient evidence, recalling that the claimant should 'submit proof that such loss occurred as a result of the war or, at least, [. . .] submit sufficient evidence of a causal connection between the war

---

[39] See Article 83 of the Treaty of Peace between the Allied and Associated Powers and Italy, signed at Paris on 10 February 1947, 49 *United Nations Treaty Series* 1.

[40] For general information, see Ignaz Seidl-Hohenveldern, 'Conciliation Commissions Established Pursuant to Art. 83 of the Peace Treaty with Italy of 1947', in Rudolf Bernhard (ed.), *Encyclopedia of Public International Law* (Amsterdam: North-Holland, 1992), Vol. I, p. 725.

and the loss that the burden of rebuttal would be shifted to the Italian Government'.[41]

In the *Graniero Claim*, the claimant requested compensation in respect of damage to real property that she owned in Italy. The US Agent alleged that Mrs Graniero, who was a national of both Italy and the US, had been treated as an enemy under the laws in force in Italy during the war and that she was placed in a concentration camp and otherwise ill-treated. The Commission placed the burden of proof with the claimant:

> In any event, the claimant has the burden of establishing treatment as enemy and she must do so by clear and convincing proof. Even if she were not able to produce any document of her internment she should have explained her failure to do so. Even if it is assumed that she was placed in a concentration camp, there is no evidence that she was so placed because of her American nationality. At the very most there is a remote and very dubious inference that that was the reason.[42]

In other cases, however, the Conciliation Commissions was far more lenient. The decision of the Anglo–Italian Conciliation Commission in the *Grant-Smith Claim* is illustrative.[43] In this case, the Commission reversed the burden of proof on the basis of a *probatio diabolica* argument. During the war, Mrs Grant-Smith's yacht had allegedly been seized by the Italian Navy at Antibes, France. In 1948, the British Government applied on behalf of the owner to the Italian Government for the return of the yacht. When the Italian Government replied that the yacht had been destroyed, the claimant submitted a claim for compensation to the Commission. The Italian Government argued that the burden was on the claimant to prove that the yacht had been subjected to measures of control by Italy:

> Although the Italian Government admits that it was the Italian Navy which took possession of the yacht at Antibes and brought it to Italy, it is argued that such seizure would not in itself satisfy the conditions of Article 78, para. 9(c), since they also require that Italy should in her territory have subjected the yacht to a specific measure of control; it would, therefore, be for the British Government, according to the general

---

[41] Italian–United States Conciliation Commisison, *Batchelder Claim (The Kirinkuoiska and The Thele)*, 26 July 1954, 22 *International Law Reports* 865.

[42] Italian–United States Conciliation Commission, *Graniero Claim*, 20 January 1959, 30 *International Law Reports* 453.

[43] Anglo–Italian Conciliation Commission, *Grant-Smith Claim (the Gin and Angostura)*, 4 March 1952, 22 *International Law Reports* 967.

principles of law, to furnish proof that such a measure had been imposed. Moreover, according to the Italian Government, the fact that the property could not be found would not suffice to found an action under Article 78, para. 4(a), but proof that destruction took place as a result of the war would also be required.[44]

The Commission did not accept this reasoning, emphasising that the yacht had been 'seized in French waters by the Italian Navy and brought by them to Italian waters' and 'was not there placed by the Italian authorities at the free disposal of the owner'.[45] Based on the circumstances of the case, the Commission shifted the burden of proof from the claimant to the respondent:

> The circumstances in which the ship was captured and later disappeared justify, in the present case, according to the general principles of law, a reversal of the onus of proof as to the cause of its not being found [seeing that the Treaty cannot possibly have intended] that such onus of proof should be thrown upon the owner of the ship. It was therefore for the Italian Government, whose Navy captured the yacht [. . .] to prove that the ship, contrary to all the probabilities, was not a victim of an act of war.[46]

Two considerations motivated the Commission's decision. First, it was manifestly difficult for the claimant to bring proof of what happened to the yacht after it had been seized. Second, the Tribunal appears to rely on what it considers to be the most probable scenario and consequently places the burden of proof on the party whose contentions are less probable. As such, the decision stands in sharp contrast with the rigid approach taken in many other cases. Unfortunately, the Commission failed to clarify why the circumstances in the present case are so radically different from those relied on by other claimants.

The Iran–US Claims Tribunal

Although the Iran–US Claims Tribunal is a contemporary claims tribunal, its procedures and evidentiary rules resemble conventional

---

[44] Anglo–Italian Conciliation Commission, *Grant-Smith Claim (the Gin and Angostura)*, 972.

[45] Anglo-Italian Conciliation Commission, *Grant-Smith Claim (the Gin and Angostura)*, 972.

[46] Anglo-Italian Conciliation Commission, *Grant-Smith Claim (the Gin and Angostura)*, 972.

arbitral approaches rather than modern mass claims procedures. It is therefore dealt with in this section rather than in the following one.[47]

Article 24(1) of the Tribunal Rules – unchanged from the UNCITRAL Rules – provides that '[e]ach party shall have the burden of proving the facts relied on to support his claim or defence'.[48] The rule played a key role in many Tribunal awards.

The issue of *probatio diabolica* surfaced in a number of cases. Indeed, many US investors and contractors were forced to leave Iran after the 1979 revolution without gathering the documents and records relating to their business. The Tribunal was willing to take into account such evidentiary problems.[49] This was for instance reflected in the Tribunal's use of adverse inferences[50], which it qualified as follows: 'When a party [. . .] has access to relevant evidence, the tribunal is authorized to draw adverse inferences from the failure of that party to produce such evidence.'[51] *A contrario*, if a party does not have access to the relevant evidence, such adverse inference should not be drawn.[52]

In practice, however, *probatio diabolica* arguments appear to have been rarely accepted as a sufficient basis for altering the burden of proof. In the *Levitt Case*, for instance, the Tribunal determined that the respondents had failed to produce a number of documents that had been requested by the Tribunal. The respondents' explanations, according to the Tribunal, suggested deliberate non-compliance rather than an inability to produce. The Tribunal reiterated that adverse inferences may be drawn from the failure of a party to produce evidence that is 'likely to be at its disposal'. However, the Tribunal continued that the respondents' failure 'does not relieve the Claimant of his obligation to muster all

---

[47] Kazazi, *Burden of Proof.* See also Holtzmann, 'Fact-Finding by the Iran–US Claims Tribunal', 101 et ff.

[48] Article 24 of the Iran–US Claims Tribunal, Rules of Procedure.

  The Tribunal is also offered the discretion to 'conduct the arbitration in such a manner as it considers appropriate provided that the parties are treated with equality and that at any stage of the proceedings each party is given a full opportunity of presenting his case' (Article 15 of the Iran–US Claims Tribunal, Rules of Procedure).

[49] See Aldrich, *The Jurisprudence of the Iran–US Claims Tribunal,* p. 334.

[50] Aldrich, *The Jurisprudence of the Iran–US Claims Tribunal,* pp. 339–41.

[51] Concurring Opinion of Richard Mosk in *Ultrasystems Inc.* v. *Islamic Republic of Iran,* Award No. 27–84–3, 4 March 1983, *Iran–US Claims Tribunal Reports* 2 (1983), 114, 115.

[52] Holtzmann, 'Fact-Finding by the Iran–US Claims Tribunal', 127: 'The necessary predicate for the inference is the Tribunal's reasonable certainty that the party against whom the inference is to be drawn has possession of, or access to, the missing evidence.'

the evidentiary support at his disposal'.[53] In the *Sea-Land Case*, the Tribunal dealt with the issue of damages in respect of moveable property. Although the Tribunal accepted the claimant's assertion that some equipment was left in Iran, it dismissed the claim for compensation because the claimant had not been able to prove that the respondents had access to or benefited from the equipment.[54] It is questionable whether such proof can reasonably be expected from the claimant, given the circumstances surrounding the loss. As the American arbitrator, Howard M. Holtzmann, stated: '[t]o require Sea-Land to do more than prove that the material was taken into the PSO Port and could not be brought out is to place upon it a virtually impossible burden of proof, considering the nature of the equipment and the circumstances surrounding its loss'.[55]

In some cases, particularly with respect to jurisdiction, the Tribunal took an active role in investigating the facts.[56] This fact-finding role has become much more prominent in the other mass claims processes, discussed in the following section.

Present-day mass claims practice

In present-day mass claims processes, insufficient or inadequate evidence has substantially affected the allocation of the burden of proof and the precise balance between the three general rules.

The United Nations Compensation Commission

Many UNCC claims, and in particular the millions of small claims submitted by individuals, lacked supporting evidence. In recognition of

---

[53] Iran–US Claims Tribunal, *William J. Levitt v. Islamic Republic Of Iran*, Award No. 520–210–3, 29 August 1991, para. 57–66, 27 *Iran–US Claims Tribunal Reports* 145, 162–5.

Iran–US Claims Tribunal, *William J. Levitt v. Islamic Republic Of Iran.*, para. 109. See the criticism in the Dissenting and Concurring Opinion of Judge Allison, in 27 *Iran–US Claims Tribunal Reports* 187, 188–9.

[54] Iran–US Claims Tribunal, *Sea-Land Service, Inc. v. The Government of the Islamic Republic of Iran, Ports and Shipping Organization*, Award No. 135–33–1, 20 June 1984, 6 *Iran–US Claims Tribunal Reports*, 149, 173.

[55] Opinion of Howard M. Holtzmann, Dissenting as to Award on the Claims and Concurring as to the Dismissal of Counterclaims, *reprinted in* 6 *Iran–US Claims Tribunal Reports*, 175, 178.

[56] Holtzmann, 'Fact-Finding by the Iran–US Claims Tribunal', 107.

these problems, the UNCC developed specific evidentiary rules, which are characterised by an active fact-finding role of the institution itself, varying evidentiary standards depending on the category of claim and an extensive use of presumptions and inferences.

With respect to the burden of proof, Article 35 of the Provisional Rules for Claims Procedure provided that '[e]ach claimant is responsible for submitting documents and other evidence which demonstrate satisfactorily that [his or her claim] is eligible for compensation pursuant to Security Council resolution 687 (1991)'.[57] Although this provision appears to be consistent with traditional practice, there are three important differences, which were necessitated by the specificity of the UNCC's mandate and the volume of claims it received.

First, Article 35 of the UNCC Rules requires the submission of documents and other evidence, which 'demonstrate satisfactorily' that a claim is eligible for compensation.[58] Although the phrase 'demonstrate satisfactorily' is somewhat vague and subjective, it establishes a lesser standard than the traditional requirement that 'each party shall have the burden of proving the facts relied on to support his claim or defense', which is found in the UNCITRAL Arbitration Rules and various other rules.[59]

Second, the claimants' burden of proof has been simplified significantly by the fact that Iraq's liability for direct losses, damages or injury had already been established by the Security Council and formally accepted by Iraq.[60] Individual claimants were therefore 'relieved from the otherwise heavy burden of proving the liability of a sovereign state'[61] and were only expected to establish the existence of a loss, the value of the loss and the causal link with the invasion and occupation of Kuwait. Even for the establishment of these elements, however, the burden of proof was mitigated. In Categories "A" and "B", fixed compensation sums were introduced and no proof of the precise value of the loss was required. Similarly, in the small claims categories, the causal link

---

[57] UNCC, Provisional Rules, Art. 35(1).

[58] This element relates to the standard of evidence rather than the burden of proof. See below.

[59] Art. 24(1) of the UNCITRAL Arbitration Rules.

[60] See UN Security Council Resolution 687 (1991), para. 16; Identical letters from the Permanent Representative of Iraq to the United Nations, addressed respectively to the Secretary-General and the President of the Security Council, 6 April 1991, UN Doc. S/22456.

[61] Mojtaba Kazazi, 'An Overview of Evidence Before the UNCC', *International Law Forum* 1 (1999), 219, 221.

between certain facts, such as a departure from Kuwait within a specified time period and the Iraqi invasion and occupation, was presumed.

Third, the UNCC itself gathered relevant information and documentation to help establish the facts underlying the claims. The UNCC secretariat collected, checked and in some cases computerised a vast number of evidentiary records against which individual claims could be compared. Especially for Category "A" claims – i.e. claims submitted by individuals who had to leave Iraq or Kuwait between the date of the invasion of Kuwait, 2 August 1990, and the date on which the Iraqi occupation came to an end, 2 March 1991 – computerised data-matching techniques were designed and utilised to check hundreds of thousands of individual departure claims against evidentiary records that were judged reliable and credible. Therefore, the UNCC secretariat gathered a vast volume of evidence on departures from Iraq and Kuwait in the relevant time period, including lists of residents in Kuwait and Iraq as of 2 August 1990, flight manifests, border control records, lists of evacuees kept by international organisations, etc. The "A" Panel verified and assessed the evidentiary value of these records. The data in the claims forms were then checked through specially designed matching software against the information in these records. Where a perfect match was found, the claims were considered verified and no further investigation was required.[62] It was thus perfectly feasible that a claimant who had not submitted any evidence of their departure-related losses was nevertheless found in the evidence collected by the UNCC.

For the determination of Category "A" claims, the vast volume of evidentiary documentation gathered by the institution itself has been more decisive and efficient than the scarce, often confused or tattered documentation submitted by the claimants. This reflects a changing balance: for the masses of small and urgent individual claims, the institution's own role in evidence collection and fact finding has become more important than the strict enforcement of the *actori incumbit probatio* rule. This particularly active fact-finding role of the UNCC is consistent with its general nature and the intentions of the drafters of the UNCC's mandate. As the UN Secretary-General stated in his Report of 2 May 1991, the Commission is not an arbitral tribunal before which

---

[62] See UNCC, Report and Recommendations Made by the Panel of Commissioners Concerning the First Instalment of Claims for Departure From Iraq or Kuwait (Category "A" claims), 21 October 1994, UN Doc. S/AC.26/1994/2, para. 24. For a more extensive analysis, see Chapter 10.

parties appear; rather it performs 'an essentially fact-finding function of examining claims, verifying their validity, evaluating losses, assessing payments and resolving disputed claims'.[63]

The Claims Resolution Tribunal for Dormant Accounts (CRT-I)

Article 22 of the CRT-I Rules of Procedure, consistent with the general *actori incumbit probatio* principle, places the burden of proof primarily upon the claimant: 'The claimant must show that it is plausible in [the] light of all the circumstances that he or she is entitled, in whole or in part, to the dormant account.'[64] Acknowledging the difficulties to prove a claim fifty years after the end of the Second World War, however, the CRT-I Rules of Procedure moderate this burden considerably.

In the CRT-I procedures, claims were first sent to the bank where the relevant account was held in order for the bank to disclose the identity of the account holder and the amount held in the account. If the bank did not disclose this information, an initial screening procedure determined whether such disclosure was warranted despite the bank's refusal. For the purposes of the screening procedure, the threshold of evidence to be met by claimants was extremely low.[65] Coherent and convincing 'information' was sufficient for the acceptance of a claim for further processing. Disclosure was only refused in two situations: (1) if the claimant has not submitted any information on his or her entitlement to the dormant account, or (2) if it is apparent that the claimant is not entitled to the dormant account.[66] In the further processing, the so-called 'same name claims' raised a particular problem, i.e. claims filed by a claimant who recognised a surname on the list of published accounts without knowing whether the listed account holder was actually a relative. For instance, a claimant by the name of Fischer sees an account published under the name of Hermann Fischer.[67] Although he does not know who Hermann Fischer was, he files a claim based on the argument that a person by the name of Fischer *could* be related to his family. If the

---

[63] Report of the Secretary-General of 2 May 1991, para. 20.

[64] CRT-I, Rules of Procedure, Article 22.

[65] On the evidentiary requirements in the screening procedure, see also Jacomijn J. van Haersolte-van Hof, 'Issues of Evidence in the Practice of the Claims Resolution Tribunal for Dormant Accounts', *International Law Forum* 1 (1999), 216.

[66] CRT-I, Rules of Procedure, Art. 10. Interestingly, the terms evidence, proof or documentation do not even appear in the relevant part of Article 10.

[67] See CRT-I, Final Report, p. 37.

claimant could not identify a specific relative, however, CRT-I denied the claim on the grounds that a shared surname between the claimant and the account holder was, without more detailed information about the claimant's relationship to the account holder, insufficient.

Second, once the claimant passed the initial screening procedure, they were given the name of the bank and the bank was instructed to provide all available bank documentation. Without doubt, this placed the claimant in a much better situation. The bank documents helped the claimants focus their claim and provided corroboration of relevant issues.[68] This procedure was in fact a concrete application of the second general rule governing the burden of proof, i.e. the respondent's duty to cooperate in the production of evidence.

Third, as to the fact-finding authority of the tribunal, Article 17 of the CRT-I Rules of Procedure granted broad powers to the Claims Panels or Sole Arbitrators. In particular, they were entitled to 'conduct on their own such factual and legal inquiries as may appear necessary to assess as comprehensively as possible all submitted claims' and to 'order the parties to submit any relevant documents or other evidence in their possession or under their control pertaining to the assets at issue'.[69]

The Commission for Real Property Claims

CRPC claimants were expected to present all evidence that was available to them,[70] which was substantially less than the traditional requirement of 'proving the facts'. For reasons of efficiency, fairness and integrity of the claims process, the fact-finding authority of the Commission effectively replaced the traditional burden on the claimants to establish the facts. Indeed, 'if no evidence is available to a claimant or if the evidence presented is of doubtful credibility, the Commission will initiate evidence collection or evidence verification procedures', using *inter alia* 'the bodies and services where records on real property owners are kept'.[71]

The CRPC itself actively collected and verified the necessary documentation. The Commission took the initiative of collecting all existing

---

[68] Van Haersolte-van Hof, 'Issues of Evidence', 216–7.
[69] CRT-I, Rules of Procedure, Art. 17.
[70] CRPC, Book of Regulations on Real Property, Art. 32. See also Section 8.2 of UNMIK Regulation No. 2000/60.
[71] CRPC, Book of Regulations on Real Property, Art 33 and 36.

pre-war cadastral and census records and entered these data into an easily accessible database. CRPC verified the credibility and accuracy of these records and concluded that they had sufficient evidentiary weight to support claims. All private property claims were then matched against this database. Moreover, the CRPC dispatched verification officers to all courts, cadastre offices and housing companies to collect and verify official documents and to check the information and/or documentation submitted by the claimant. As a consequence, decisions were rarely – if ever – made on the basis of the documentation submitted by the claimant alone.

The IOM claims process under the German Forced Labour Compensation Programme

In the IOM-GFLCP, entitlements to compensation were to 'be demonstrated by the applicant by submission of documentation'.[72] This burden of proof was attenuated in three ways.

First, the IOM performed a fact-finding role by 'bring[ing] in relevant evidence'.[73] It systematically checked claims data with the Red Cross International Tracing Service (ITC) in Bad Arolsen and, if no evidence was found there, with the Foundation-funded *Archivverbund* and other archives.[74] To find supporting evidence, the IOM also cooperated closely with victims' associations, the Central Council for German Sinti and Roma, the Yugoslav and the Polish Red Cross and other regional and local organisations. Targeted historical research has become an important feature of the claims procedure. For instance, the IOM Property Claims Commission undertook, where possible, historical research for groups of claims or circumstances of loss.

Second, applicants had the right to 'request information from enterprises in Germany for which or for whose legal predecessors they performed forced labour, insofar as this is requisite for determining their eligibility for awards'.[75] Even though, formally speaking, the enterprises were not respondent in the proceedings, they were under a duty to cooperate in the production of evidence.

---

[72] German Foundation Act, Section 11 para. 2.
[73] German Foundation Act, Section 11 para. 2.
[74] Van der Auweraert, 'The Practicalities of Forced Labor Compensation', 312.
[75] German Foundation Act, Section 18.

Third, the last sentence of Section 11 (2) provides a safety net, by stating that '[i]f no relevant evidence is available, the claimant's eligibility can be made credible in some other way'.[76] In reality, this safety net proved to be critical to the resolution of the majority of the claims. As explained in an IOM newsletter, '[m]any of the claims that were resolved [. . .] were not accompanied by documentary evidence nor did archival searches yield positive results. But they have been decided through credibility assessments. Prior to these assessments, the IOM had to develop fair and consistent standards and criteria to ensure that the decision-making process was consistent and objective. It also had to work with the Foundation to ensure that the methods and standards applied are accepted'.[77]

The Supplemental Principles and Rules of Procedure of the Property Claims Commission include the following basic rule: 'Claims should be supported by written evidence. If a claimant is unable to provide written evidence in support of the claim, the claimant must explain why written evidence cannot be submitted'.[78] Section 22 further clarifies that '[a] fact shall be considered established if it has been credibly demonstrated' and that '[a] claim cannot be rejected on the sole ground that it is not supported by official documentary evidence'.[79] Put differently, the Supplemental Rules explicitly rule out the possibility of rejecting a claim solely on the basis of a claimant's failure to submit official documentation.

The International Commission on Holocaust Era Insurance Claims

The ICHEIC similarly relaxed the claimants' burden of proof. A claimant had to submit all relevant documentary and non-documentary evidence in their possession or under their control that may reasonably be expected in view of the circumstances and the years that elapsed. This evidence included but was not limited to the history of the claimant

---

[76] German Foundation Act, Section 11(2). This relates to the standard of evidence rather than the burden of proof. See Chapter 7.

[77] IOM, 'Slave and Forced Labour: Past Achievements and Challenges Ahead', *Compensation News*, Issue 1–2003, p. 3.

[78] IOM Property Claims Commission, Supplemental Principles and Rules of Procedure, 5 June 2001, Section 11, available at www.compensation-for-forced-labour.org/ (visited October 2007).

[79] IOM Property Claims Commission, Supplemental Principles and Rules of Procedure, section 22(2).

and the claimant's family, the history of the policy-holder/beneficiary/ insured (if they are not the claimant), and whether or not the policy-holder, insured person or claimant was a victim of Nazi-persecution[80].

The claimant had to submit 'a copy or reproduction of any original document about the insurance contract within the claimant's possession or control'.[81] The participating insurance companies then 'review[ed] claims pursuant to relaxed standards of proof based on the information provided by the claimant as well as information discovered during the insurer's investigation of its files, records and archives, together with documents and records recovered during the ICHEIC's search of appropriate archives'.[82] Although the insurers did not act as 'respondents' in the first phase of the ICHEIC proceedings, they were required to cooperate in the search for evidence. The Commission itself was to supplement the evidence submitted by the claimant.

Analysis

Introduction

The burden of proof allocates among the parties the task of gathering and presenting evidence. In the hands of creative adjudicators, the burden of proof is also a strategic instrument capable of affecting claims outcomes and generating incentives for procedural behaviour. Three trends emerge from the practice reviewed above.

First, while historical claims commissions occasionally relied on the *probatio diabolica* doctrine to shift or relax the burden of proof, they have done so sparingly and on a strictly ad hoc basis. They hesitated between rigour and flexibility. Contemporary mass claims practice has abandoned this ad hoc approach. They developed written rules, which apply consistently to all similarly situated claims. Such a structural approach is clearly preferable, since it promotes equality among claimants and consistency in decisions.

Second, rather than requiring claimants to shoulder the burden of proof alone, present-day mass claims facilities have assisted claimants in the collection of relevant documentation.[83]

---

[80] ICHEIC, Relaxed Standards of Proof Guide, rule A(2).
[81] ICHEIC, Relaxed Standards of Proof Guide, rule A(3).
[82] ICHEIC, Relaxed Standards of Proof Guide, introductory paragraph.
[83] See also Heiskanen, 'The United Nations Compensation Commission', 358.

In specific cases, finally, mass claims processes have reinforced the duty of the respondent to cooperate in the production of evidence. Although none of the recently established mass claims processes has gone as far as shifting the burden of proof in a general way, some processes have strengthened the respondent's duty to share evidence with the claimants or to disclose it to the claims tribunal.

Moreover, as Chapter 8 will demonstrate, all mass claims processes have made extensive use of presumptions and inferences in order to shift the burden of proof on particular issues.

With respect to the relationship between the three general rules governing the burden of proof in international procedure, it can therefore be concluded that modern mass claims practice places more emphasis on the roles of the respondent and the adjudicator than would ordinarily be the case. The burden of proof is effectively shared between the three players, i.e. the claimant, the respondent and the adjudicator. Both the strengthening of the respondent's duty to cooperate in the production of evidence and the reinforcement of the adjudicator's fact-finding authority are evidentiary techniques designed to relieve claimants of the duty of proving their claims or at least to significantly 'relax' this duty. In this sense, both techniques involve a departure from the general rule that the claimant must prove the facts upon which they rely to claim compensation or restitution.

This section discusses when it is justified to depart from the general rule and how this is best achieved. It is partly based upon a 'law and economics' analysis of the allocation of the burden of proof. By identifying the various parameters that determine the costs of giving the burden of proof to either one of the three players, it is also possible to determine when departures from the general rule are warranted. The possible rationales for these alternative burden allocations will be discussed on the basis of the model developed by Hay and Spier.[84]

This analysis concentrates primarily on mass claims situations in which there is a respondent party that participates in the proceedings. As explained in Part I, some recently established mass claims processes, such as the CRPC, involve single-party proceedings. In other mass

---

[84] Bruce L. Hay and Kathryn E. Spier, 'Burdens of Proof in Civil Litigation: An Economic Perspective', *Journal of Legal Studies* 26 (1997), 413. In a separate article, Hay has further refined the economic analysis by explaining the effect of certain additional parameters on the costs of a given allocation. See Bruce L. Hay, 'Allocating the Burden of Proof', *Indiana Law Journal* 72 (1997), 651.

claims processes (e.g. the UNCC), the participation of the respondents in the proceedings has been reduced to a bare minimum. Obviously, in such situations, the task of presenting evidence needs to be borne either by the claimants, by the tribunal or by both.

Justifying the general rule
Philosophical argument

As stated above, the allocation of the burden of proof in international procedure generally requires that each party proves its claims and contentions. This means that the claimant has the initial burden of proving their entitlement to a remedy and producing sufficient evidence to make it credible.[85] A number of philosophical arguments support this general rule, three of which are particularly relevant to our purposes.

First, the principle of social conservatism requires 'special justification for engaging the machinery of the law to effect a change in the status quo'.[86] The argument has intuitive plausibility, as Robinson observes: it is hard to imagine a rational legal system in which claimants could obtain judicial intervention without at least 'offering both a tenable argument for intervention and information sufficient to support an inference that the argument is factually credible in the particular case'.[87]

Second, 'social efficiency' requires that a claimant should not initiate a lawsuit without bearing the costs of making a minimal showing. Otherwise the judicial system would become excessively costly both to the judiciary and to the respondents who would be forced to search for and present evidence in order to rebut meritless claims.[88]

Fairness, finally, requires that claimants 'should not be allowed to place undue burdens on defendants by the mere act of instituting a lawsuit'.[89]

However sympathetic one might be to the victims of a wrong, it would be manifestly unfair to force a respondent to bear the burden of producing exonerating evidence without some justification for doing so.[90]

---

[85] Glen O. Robinson, 'Multiple Causation in Tort Law: Reflections on the DES Cases', *Virginia Law Review* 68 (1982) 713, 729.

[86] Robinson, 'Multiple Causation', 730.　　[87] Robinson, 'Multiple Causation', 730.

[88] Robinson, 'Multiple Causation', 730.　　[89] Robinson, 'Multiple Causation', 731.

[90] Robinson, 'Multiple Causation', 731, footnote 71.

Economic argument

In an economic analysis of the burden of proof, the direct costs[91] are those of gathering, presenting and processing evidence. They include the private costs for the parties in attempting to secure the preferred outcome as well as the resources spent by the claims facility either to gather the evidence itself or to process the evidence presented by the parties. The error costs in this specific context are the disadvantageous results produced by an outcome that favours one party while the evidence supports the other party.[92] If the burden is assigned to the claimant, most erroneous decisions will be 'false negatives', i.e. decisions that fail to award compensation to the claimant even though the claim is meritorious. If the burden is cast upon the respondent, on the other hand, most errors will be 'false positives', i.e. decisions that erroneously award compensation even though the claim is meritless. Both types of errors prevent mass claims resolution facilities from achieving their objectives.

The central question is to determine who should bear the burden of proof if 'the social objective is to minimize the total social costs associated with dispute resolution'.[93] The economic approach is best explained on the basis of a simple hypothesis: a claim in which a contested issue is whether some event X occurred, with the claimant alleging that X occurred and the respondent saying that it did not.[94]

The two main parameters to be considered are (1) each party's costs of presenting evidence and (2) the probability that X occurred. The parties' respective costs must be considered since one party may have better access to the evidence, meaning that they can gather the necessary evidence at lower cost than the other party. If the adjudicator is concerned with minimising the total costs of the legal process, therefore, the parties' relative costs of presenting evidence should be taken into account. As Hay and Spier note, 'other things being equal, the lower one party's relative costs, the stronger the argument for giving him the burden of proof'.[95] The probability element needs to be taken into account since the parties will make strategic decisions when introducing

---

[91] In this context, direct costs are sometimes referred to as 'process costs'. See Hay, 'Allocating the Burden of Proof', 654.
[92] Hay, 'Allocating the Burden of Proof', 654.
[93] Hay, 'Allocating the Burden of Proof', 651.
[94] Hay & Spier, 'Burdens of Proof in Civil Litigation', 414.
[95] Hay & Spier, 'Burdens of Proof in Civil Litigation', 419.

evidence. Indeed, the party with the burden of proof will present the evidence if, and only if, the evidence supports their position.

On the basis of these two parameters, Hay and Spier developed a basic economic model. To minimise the expected costs of presenting evidence on whether X occurred, the adjudicator should assign the burden to the claimant if the following formula holds:[96]

| Probability that X occurred | $\times$ | Claimant's costs of showing X occurred | $<$ | Probability that X did not occur | $\times$ | Respondent's costs of showing X did not occur |

The left-hand box indicates the expected costs of giving the burden to the claimant. The right-hand box indicates the expected costs of assigning the burden to the respondent. The adjudicator should give the claimant the burden of proof whenever (1) his costs of gathering and presenting evidence on a contested issue are not substantially greater than the respondent's costs, and (2) the probability that the claimant is correct is not disproportionately greater than the probability that the respondent is correct.[97]

Both conditions are usually met in civil litigation and the economic model therefore supports the conclusion that, as a general rule, the adjudicator should give the claimant the burden of proving the facts that the claimant alleges.[98] However, if either of these two conditions is not met, departures from this general rule are justified.

Hay refined the above model with three additional parameters: the amount at stake for the party; the party's expectations of winning if evidence is presented; and the social cost of erroneous outcomes.[99] For Hay 'the greater the magnitude of these factors, [...] the greater the costs of giving that party the burden of proof'.[100] Hay's analysis of the five parameters again confirms that, as a general rule, the burden of proof on contested issues should remain with the claimant.[101]

---

[96] Hay and Spier, 'Burdens of Proof in Civil Litigation', 418. For a more elaborate formulation of the basic rule, see 423.

[97] Hay and Spier, 'Burdens of Proof in Civil Litigation', 424–5.

[98] For a more detailed review of this point, see Hay, 'Allocating the Burden of Proof', 655–660.

[99] Hay, 'Allocating the Burden of Proof', 663.

[100] Hay, 'Allocating the Burden of Proof', 652. Only the significance of an increase in the party's optimism is inconclusive.

[101] Hay, 'Allocating the Burden of Proof', 677.

Justifying exceptions to the general rule

Based on the above model, it can be suggested that any of the three following features, if present and sufficiently strong, would give mass claims adjudicators a potential rationale for not giving the claimant the burden of proving the facts.[102]

High probability that the claim is meritorious

The probability to be considered includes both the unconditional probability that X will occur and the likelihood that the adjudicator would observe certain 'signals' (i.e. receive certain information) if X in fact occurred:

- Unconditional probability: Put simply, this term represents how frequently X occurs. For instance, if X refers to the expulsion of an expatriate from their country of residence, this probability represents the likelihood that the claimant was wrongfully expelled. The less frequently expatriates are expelled unlawfully, the less likely it is that it occurred in this particular case. If unlawful expulsion is a highly infrequent event, then – all else being equal – the adjudicator should believe that it probably did not occur in this particular case.
- Conditional probability: While adjudicators have only limited information about a case before the evidence has been presented, they always begin with some information about the case and receive some 'signals' about the probability that X occurred.[103] In the same example of the unlawful expulsion, the adjudicator may know, for instance, that the relevant facts occurred during an armed conflict, that the claimant is a national of an enemy country and that most nationals of this country were expelled. These signals then increase the likelihood that X occurred in this case.

The effect of an increase in the probability that the claim is meritorious, with all other parameters being equal, can be explained by considering the following hypothetical example. An adjudicator receives a hundred claims for compensation, each arising out of a similar type of event X.

---

[102] The fourth parameter examined by Hay, i.e. the amount at stake for each party, is arguably not relevant in most mass claims situations. At least for analytical purposes, it can be assumed that the individual claimant and the respondent have the same amount at stake in each individual case.

[103] Hay, 'Allocating the Burden of Proof', 674.

There exists no evidence in any of the hundred claims with respect to the occurrence of X. The absence of proof means that the party on whom the burden of proof is cast, loses the case. What would then be the optimal way of assigning the burden of proof and deciding the cases?

Let us assume first that the type of event that X refers to is extremely rare and occurs only in the most exceptional circumstances, e.g. in roughly one out of every hundred cases. If the adjudicator decides to give the claimant the burden of proof, then it can be assumed that ninety-nine awards are likely to be correct and only one decision is likely to be erroneous, i.e. a false negative. If the burden of proof goes to the respondent, however, the result will be ninety-nine false positives and only one correct decision.

The situation changes if we assume, on the other hand, that X refers to a very frequent event and the adjudicator has already the impression from certain data, called Y, that the occurrence of X in this case is very likely. Let us assume, for instance, that the adjudicator knows that in 99 per cent of the cases in which data Y are present, event X in fact occurs. In this scenario, giving the claimant the burden of proof will yield very high error costs. In fact, by giving the burden of proof to the claimants, the adjudicator can expect that ninety-nine out of a hundred decisions will be false negatives and only one decision will be correct. If the respondent carries the burden of proof, however, the opposite will occur: ninety-nine decisions are likely to be correct and only one will be a false positive.

The example shows that, if there is a scarcity of evidence, giving the claimant the burden of proof despite a high probability that their claim is meritorious inevitably increases the chances that the decision will be erroneous. The same reasoning applies where evidence of X is extremely costly or difficult to obtain. Because of the costs or difficulties, many will fail to present the evidence, leading to similar results as described above.[104] When the claimant bears the risk of losing the case if they fail to present the evidence and when the claim is probably meritorious, the error costs are likely to be higher than when this risk is borne by the respondent.

---

[104] Arguably, the proposition even holds when the evidence is available to both parties. Indeed, the Hay and Spier analysis is based upon the assumption that evidence exists and that it is available to the parties. See Hay, 'Allocating the Burden of Proof', 653; Hay & Spier, 'Burdens of Proof in Civil Litigation', 416.

Put differently, any increase in the probability that the claimant is correct, also increases the error costs associated with giving that party the burden of proof.[105] A high probability that the claim is meritorious – with all other parameters being equal – therefore furnishes an economic rationale for not giving the claimant the burden of proof.

Probability assessment, though rarely made in explicit terms, is not uncommon in national legal practice. Courts sometimes give the respondent the burden of proof when, given the information available to the court, the probability is high that the claimant is correct. The *res ipsa loquitur* rule in tort law is a good example.[106] The burden-shifting effect of most (rebuttable) presumptions and of prima facie evidence can also be explained on this ground.

International claims practice has also accepted this rationale as sufficient to relieve the claimant from the duty of establishing the facts underlying the claim. The above quoted decision of the Anglo–Italian Conciliation Commission in the *Grant Smith Claim* is illustrative. The Commission assigned the task of proving the cause of the disappearance of the ship to the respondent party, based upon the high probability that the ship was a victim of an act of war.

In present-day mass claims practice, probability is most relevant for presumptions and inferences. The UNCC presumed for instance that departures from Iraq or Kuwait during the relevant time period were caused by the Iraqi invasion and occupation of Kuwait. Undisputed statistical data indeed showed that virtually all expatriates residing in Iraq and Kuwait left the region between the date of Iraq's unlawful invasion of Kuwait and the end of the occupation. The fact that the mass departures took place at the time of the invasion and occupation made it highly probable that there was some causal relationship between these departures and the invasion and occupation of Kuwait. If individual claimants would have had the burden of proof on this causality, despite the high probability that any departure during this time period was caused by the unlawful invasion and occupation, error costs would have significantly increased, especially because claimants left in chaos and danger, which made it difficult for them to have evidence on the reasons for their departure. The UNCC therefore introduced a presumption that any departure during the relevant time period was caused by the

---

[105] Hay, 'Allocating the Burden of Proof', 662.
[106] See also Hay and Spier, 'Burdens of Proof in Civil Litigation', 425–6.

unlawful invasion and occupation of Kuwait, thereby relieving claimants from the task of presenting evidence on this issue.

In conclusion, allocating the burden of proof in a cost-minimising way requires the adjudicator to estimate the probable merits of the claim. A precise judicial evaluation of the probabilities will not always be possible, but, as Hay concluded, 'if the court is concerned with minimizing the costs of the legal system, even a rough assessment is better than none at all'.[107] In this sense, the probability factor underscores the importance of objective and undisputed historical or factual research and statistical data in mass claims situations. If such research succeeds in increasing the probability that particular claims are meritorious, it furnishes a rationale for not giving individual claimants the burden of proof, or at least for mitigating the burden on the claimants.

Parties' respective costs

In determining the optimal allocation of the burden of proof, the parties' relative costs of gathering and presenting evidence on the contested issue are a second factor that needs to be taken into account. The general rule that each party must prove the facts that they allege is based on the assumption that both parties have equal access to the evidence. In reality, however, one party may have easier access to evidence than the other.

If the burden is allocated to the party with the highest relative costs, the total costs associated with the presentation of evidence will naturally rise. In some cases, it might increase the error costs as well. For instance when this party's costs of presenting evidence exceed the stakes they have in the claim, they will not present the evidence and will prefer to lose the case. Consequently, as Hay and Spier suggest, 'the lower one party's relative costs, the stronger the argument for giving him the burden of proof'.[108]

Domestic law frequently assigns the burden of proof to the party with easiest access to the evidence.[109] For instance, property delivered in good

---

[107] Hay, 'Allocating the Burden of Proof', 679.

[108] Hay and Spier, 'Burdens of Proof in Civil Litigation', 419. See also Belton, 'Toward a Theory of Procedural Justice', 1218: 'Considerations of fairness [. . .] are concerned with the possibility that evidence on a particular element may lie more within the knowledge or control of one party than another. A court's concern for fairness, then, may lead it to allocate the [burden of proof] on the question to the more knowledgeable party.'

[109] Hay, 'Allocating the Burden of Proof', 678.

condition to a bailee, but returned in a damaged state or not returned, is presumed to have been damaged or lost through the bailee's negligence.[110] Likewise, in employment-related discrimination cases, a prima facie case is often sufficient to cast the burden of proof upon the respondent,[111] because it is presumably much easier for the employer to demonstrate through its personnel records that a particular measure was taken for reasons other than discrimination than it is for the claimant to establish that discrimination took place.

The same reasoning has occasionally surfaced in international claims practice. For instance, the Turkish–Greek Mixed Arbitral Tribunal in the *Banque d'Orient Case* weighed the respective difficulties (or costs) for each party to prove the facts. It found that it was much easier for the respondent to prove the circumstances of the loss and consequently placed the burden of proof on this issue on the respondent.

Whether the parties' respective costs to access and present evidence will be relevant in international mass claims practice depends on the circumstances. The cost factor explains, for instance, why CRT-I has introduced a general duty for the respondent to make the relevant account files available to the claimant as soon as the latter has passed the screening phase. Although this burden-sharing mechanism does not amount to a reversal of the burden of proof,[112] it appears to be based on an appraisal of the respective difficulties for the parties to prove the facts. Similarly, with respect to the CRPC, it can be argued that the institution's own fact-finding role was strengthened because it was more costly for individual claimants to obtain extracts of the official property records than it was for the Commission to obtain the computerised property records.

In other situations, this rationale will offer little support for easing the claimant's burden of proof. In situations involving widespread harm affecting large parts of a population, it is quite possible that the respondent has no better access to information about individual cases

---

[110] Robinson, 'Multiple Causation', 733.

[111] See for instance the EU Directive 97/80/EC of 15 December 1997 on the burden of proof in cases of discrimination based on sex, O.J. 20.0198, L.14/6. This Directive shifts the burden of proof to the respondent as soon as the plaintiff has established a prima facie case of direct or indirect discrimination.

[112] It does not shift the risk of losing the case when the requisite information cannot be produced. On the technique of burden-sharing, see the part on the 'Rationales for strengthening the respondent's role' in Chapter 6.

than the individuals concerned, and the same can be true for the adjudicator.

In short, while the parties' respective costs to provide evidence are relevant in specific mass claims situations, it is rarely dispositive. The law 'does not routinely allocate burdens merely according to who is the best (cheapest) information-producer'.[113] It should only do so when the difference in the parties' respective costs is significant and risks skewing the outcome of the case, or when this rationale is combined with other justifications. Probability, as already indicated, is one such justification. The social cost of erroneous decisions is another.

Social cost of erroneous decisions

Since the community has a societal interest in the claims resolution, the third factor that affects the optimal allocation of the burden of proof is the social cost, i.e. the losses sustained by the society in the event of erroneous decisions.[114] When the claimant bears the burden of proof, as explained above, most errors will be false negatives, i.e. decisions that erroneously fail to award compensation. When the respondent has the burden of proof, most errors will be false positives, i.e. erroneous awards of compensation. Both types of errors may affect society differently.[115]

Accommodating such considerations in the allocation of the burden of proof is obviously a risky undertaking. The equality of the parties dictates that, as a general rule, both types of error should have the same weight and value. In very exceptional circumstances, however, a community values both types of errors differently. Two examples can be given.

False negatives are particularly undesirable, for instance, when the enforcement of a substantive rule is of fundamental importance to the society at large. If equality is considered a cardinal principle of society, the community may place a greater weight on a court's failure to enforce equality where discrimination actually took place, than on a court's erroneous recognition of discrimination when actually there was none. Given the importance of non-discrimination in such society, a careful employer should be able to demonstrate that they have not discriminated: if thy are unable to do so, they should bear the risk of losing the case.

---

[113] Robinson, 'Multiple Causation', 735.   [114] Hay, 'Allocating the Burden of Proof', 664.
[115] Hay, 'Allocating the Burden of Proof', 675: 'the optimal allocation depends in part on the court's assessment of these different possibilities'.

Likewise in cases where one of the parties – let us assume the respondent – has destroyed or removed the relevant evidence, the first reaction would be to infer that the evidence is likely to have been unfavourable to this party. This solution, sometimes referred to as the 'spoliation inference', assumes that the respondent would only destroy the evidence if it favoured the other party, because only in that situation would destruction be in the respondent's self-interest.[116] As such, the inference is partly based upon the probability factor. This probability, however, cannot always explain the spoliation inference. Sometimes, we simply do not know what the evidence contained, for instance, when a corporate respondent destroys documents as part of a policy under which non-active files are routinely shredded every five years, or where relevant evidence was accidentally destroyed by one of the parties. In these situations, the probable contents of the file cannot be inferred from the destruction and the adjudicator's decision to place the burden of proof with the respondent must be made on some ground other than probability or the desire to maximise accuracy in decision making.[117]

One possibility is that it is the concern for fairness that requires the adjudicator to assign the burden of proof to – and to place the risk that an erroneous decision will be made with – the party responsible for the loss of the evidence.[118] Any other burden allocation, it could be argued, would effectively reward the destruction of evidence, and increase the risk of erroneous decisions due to the lack of evidence. Furthermore, assigning the burden of proof to the party which is responsible for the destruction of evidence is an effective incentive to deter future acts of destruction.[119] Whatever precise motivation the adjudicator chooses, the decision to place the burden with the party responsible for the loss of evidence is based on the assessment that placing the burden of proof with the claimant will frustrate the societal objectives of the claims process, e.g. fairness, deterrence and compensation. It reflects the adjudicator's assessment that the community prefers, in this situation, false positives over false negatives.

---

[116] Lawrence B. Solum, 'You prove it! Why should I?', *Harvard Journal of Law and Public Policy* 17 (1994), 691, 699.

[117] Solum, 'You prove it! Why should I?', 700.

[118] On the fairness rationale in this situation, see Solum, 'You prove it! Why should I?', 701.

[119] Solum, 'You prove it! Why should I?', 701. For a similar analysis with respect to presumptions, see Robinson, 'Multiple Causation', 734. Robinson concludes, however, that 'the question remains whether the goal of encouraging future information-gathering justifies a present presumption [. . .]'.

Conclusion

The optimal allocation of the burden of proof is a function of the probable merits of the claims, the relative costs of presenting evidence to the parties and the social costs associated with different types of errors.[120] In ordinary situations, the weighing of these three factors will result in an allocation of the burden of proof to the claimant.

Giving the claimant the burden of proof, however, will not be an optimal allocation if:

- the probability that the claim is meritorious is substantially higher than the probability that the claim is meritless, and/or
- the claimant's costs of gathering and presenting evidence are substantially higher than the respondent's and the adjudicator's costs, and/or
- the social costs associated with a false negative are substantially higher than the social costs of a false positive.

Any one of these rationales, if sufficiently strong, justifies relaxing the claimant's burden of proof.[121]

Relaxing the claimant's burden of proof

In international mass claims processes, a relaxation of the claimant's burden of proof can be achieved by strengthening either the respondent's or the adjudicator's role with respect to the production of evidence. The following guidelines can be suggested to make the choice between these two options.[122]

Rationales for strengthening the adjudicator's fact-finding role

Whenever the adjudicator has better access to the relevant evidence – i.e. when the evidence is difficult or costly to obtain for both the claimant and the respondent, but less costly for the adjudicator to collect – strengthening the adjudicator's fact-finding role will minimise the total costs.[123]

---

[120] See Hay, 'Allocating the Burden of Proof', 679.

[121] Hay, 'Allocating the Burden of Proof', 677.

[122] Hay and Spier, 'Burdens of Proof in Civil Litigation', 429.

[123] Hay and Spier, 'Burdens of Proof in Civil Litigation', 430. It is assumed here that the tribunal's intervention in evidentiary matters takes place with full impartiality and that the tribunal collects evidence à charge et à décharge.

Arguably, this is often the case in mass claims practice, in particular when the outcome of the claims depends on evidentiary sources that are not within the control of one of the parties, e.g. official records kept by bodies not involved in the claims process. This was the case, for instance, for the cadastre records collected by the CRPC in Bosnia or the departure records gathered by the UNCC. Moreover, in mass claims processes, the adjudicator may be better placed to exploit economies of scale by accessing evidentiary sources that cover large groups of claims. This will allow the adjudicator to spread the initial costs of gathering the evidence over all claims and result in a substantially reduced per-claim cost. Finally, if the adjudicator is able to computerise the records, or when the relevant records already exist in electronic form, the costs of *processing* this evidence will be much lower than the cost of manually processing evidentiary documents submitted by the parties.

The adjudicator's superior access to the evidence is the only possible justification for strengthening the adjudicator's fact-finding powers. A high probability that the claim is meritorious and the high social costs associated with false negatives call for a strengthening of the respondent's role rather than a strengthening of the adjudicator's role. This becomes clear when one considers what happens when the adjudicator fails to find any evidence that supports or defeats the claim despite all efforts to locate and access such evidence. Two possibilities need to be distinguished.

First, the failure of the adjudicator to locate any evidence can lead to a negative decision, i.e. a rejection of the claim. Whenever this is the case, the effect is similar to leaving the burden of proof with the claimant. Indeed, the adjudicator assists the claimants in gathering evidence, but when their combined efforts fail, the claim will be rejected. Although the adjudicator's assistance will increase the chances that evidence is found and presented, the claimant will still lose the case if no evidence is found. Consequently, when there is a high probability that the claim is meritorious, this technique will reduce, but not minimise, the error costs.

Second, the adjudicator's failure to find evidence may lead to no result, i.e. the claim remains undecided until conclusive evidence is found. In this situation, the claimant no longer bears the risk of receiving a negative decision when there is no evidence confirming or defeating the claim. At least nominally, this approach succeeds in minimising the error costs when there is a high probability that the claim is meritorious: since no formal decision will be issued, no 'error' will be made. From a claimant's perspective, however, no decision is similar to a negative decision: the eligible claimant will not receive the compensation or restitution they are entitled to. In terms of the substantive goals of the mass claims process, therefore, the error cost in this system is identical to the one above: the error costs associated with issuing no decision on a meritorious claim equal the error costs caused by a negative decision on a meritorious claim.

In short, strengthening the adjudicator's fact-finding role is an appropriate technique when the parties' costs of gathering evidence are higher than the adjudicator's costs of gathering this evidence. It is a less appropriate technique, however, when the justification for relieving the claimants from this task lies in the high probability that the claim is meritorious or in the high social costs associated with false negatives.

Rationales for strengthening the respondent's role

If the respondent, rather than the adjudicator, has superior access to the evidence, on the other hand, assigning the burden of proof on the particular issue to the respondent will be a more efficient approach. In this respect, a distinction needs to be made between 'burden-shifting' and 'burden-sharing' techniques.

If the burden of proof is shifted to the respondent, this party will bear the risk of losing the case if they do not succeed in presenting evidence.[124] Such reversal of the burden of proof is called for in two situations:

- when the claimant's position on a particular issue is most probably correct, the total error cost can be minimised only by assigning to the respondent the risk of losing the case when no evidence is presented;
- when the social costs associated with false negatives are higher than the social costs of false positives, the total costs of the process will be minimised only if the respondent bears the risk of losing the case when no evidence is presented.

Burden-sharing techniques compel the respondent to share the evidence in their possession with the claimants or to disclose the evidence to the tribunal. Under the GFLCP, for instance, claimants could request information from German enterprises for which they performed forced labour. The CRT-I could order a Swiss Bank after the initial screening

---

[124] The use of presumptions and inferences, examined below, has such a burden-shifting effect.

procedure to disclose all available information on a claimed account. The use of such techniques is motivated by the parties' respective costs of gathering the evidence. Burden-sharing techniques, however, do not shift the risk of losing the case when no evidence is found. Consequently, they will not succeed in decreasing the error costs when there is a high probability that the claim is meritorious or when the social costs associated with false negatives are higher than the social costs of false positives. In these cases, a reversal of the burden of proof is required in order to minimise the total error costs.

7

Standards of evidence

This chapter explores whether the standards of evidence can be relaxed in the event the evidence is scarce.

Standards of evidence in international procedure

International tribunals and claims commissions enjoy considerable freedom in determining the weight of the evidence that the parties submit to them. In order to ensure equal treatment of claims, however, the tribunal should adopt 'standards of evidence', i.e. criteria against which it will weigh the value of evidence to determine whether or not the burden of proof has been met. While the burden of proof refers to the question, 'Who should bring the evidence for a particular fact or allegation?', it is the *standard* of evidence that aims to answer the question, 'How should the burden of proof be discharged?'. In international practice, four main standards can be distinguished: proof beyond reasonable doubt, clear and convincing proof, preponderance of evidence and prima facie evidence.[1]

---

[1] In Anglo-Saxon law, the usual standard of proof in civil cases is one of a 'balance of probabilities'. As Reiner explains, this standard implies 'something more likely true than not true', and requires 'a reasonable degree of probability, but not so high as is required in a criminal case' (Andreas Reiner, 'Burden and General Standards of Proof', *Arbitration International* 10(3) (1994), 328, 335). If the evidence is such that the tribunal concludes that a particular fact or allegation is more probable than not, the burden is discharged. If the probabilities are equal, it is not discharged. The standard used in continental law refers to the inner conviction of the judge (*la conviction intime du juge*). The judge considers the probative value of the evidence submitted by the parties and decides the case in accordance with their 'convictions' as to the existence of the facts or the correctness of the allegations. (See Devèze, 'La charge de la preuve en matière civile', p. 408). The practical result, however, appears to be virtually the same in both systems. (See Reiner, 'Burden and General Standards of Proof', 335.)

Proof beyond reasonable doubt

Proof beyond reasonable doubt is a particularly demanding standard. Defined as proof that 'precludes every reasonable hypothesis except that which it tends to support and which is wholly consistent with the defendant's guilt and inconsistent with any other rational conclusion',[2] it is the applicable standard in international criminal procedure. The ICTY Statute, for instance, accepts a prima facie standard for indictments but requires proof beyond reasonable doubt for a conviction.[3]

Although certainly not generally applicable, international tribunals have occasionally required proof beyond reasonable doubt in cases involving particularly serious charges of a quasi-criminal nature.[4] In the *Irish Case*, for instance, the European Commission and the Court of Human Rights applied the 'proof beyond reasonable doubt' standard.[5] The case involved allegations of practices contrary to Article 3 of the Convention, i.e. the prohibition of torture or inhumane or degrading treatment or punishment. Such explicit references to 'proof beyond reasonable doubt' are extremely rare. Moreover, even in the *Irish Case*, the Court appeared to have doubts about the feasibility of this standard of evidence when it added that 'such proof may follow from the coexistence of sufficiently strong, clear and concordant inferences or of similar unrebutted presumptions of fact'.[6] By referring to 'proof beyond reasonable doubt' as the applicable standard, the Court may have wanted to appear more stringent than it could realistically be. Likewise, in *Kurt* v. *Turkey*, a case involving an alleged forced disappearance, the Court referred to proof beyond reasonable doubt as the appropriate standard.[7]

---

[2] Garner, *Black's Law Dictionary*, p. 1215.

[3] Rules 47 and 87 of the ICTY Rules of Procedure and Evidence, 12 July 2007, IT/32/Rev. 40; Art. 19(1) of the Statute of the International Tribunal for the Prosecution of Persons Responsible for Serious Violations of International Humanitarian Law Committed in the Territory of the Former Yugoslavia since 1991; Art. 18(1) of the Statute of the International Criminal Tribunal for the Prosecution of Persons Responsible for Genocide and Other Serious Violations of International Humanitarian Law Committed in the Territory of Rwanda and Rwandan Citizens Responsible for Genocide and Other Such Violations Committed in the Territory of Neighbouring States, between 1 January 1994 and 31 December 1994.

[4] Sir Edward Eveleigh, 'General Standards of Proof in Litigation and Arbitration Generally', *Arbitration International* 10(3) (1994), 354, 354–5.

[5] ECHR, *Ireland* v. *United Kingdom (Irish Case)*, 18 January 1978, Eur. Ct. H.R. Rep., para. 161.

[6] ECHR, *Ireland* v. *United Kingdom (Irish Case)*, para. 161.

[7] ECHR, *Kurt* v. *Turkey*, 25 May 1998, Eur. Ct. H.R. Rep., para. 99.

In *Timurtas* v. *Turkey*, however, the ECHR appears to have altered its jurisprudence by permitting a lesser evidentiary standard in cases of forced disappearances.[8]

Clear and convincing proof

Clear and convincing proof, defined as 'proof which results in reasonable certainty of the truth of the ultimate fact in controversy',[9] is an intermediate standard, lying somewhere between 'proof beyond reasonable doubt' and 'preponderance of evidence'. This standard requires a belief by the fact-finder

> that it is highly probable that the facts are true or exist; while it is not necessary to believe to the point of almost certainty, or beyond a reasonable doubt that they are true or exist, or that they certainly are true or exist; yet it is not sufficient to believe that it is merely more probable that they are true or exist than it is that they are false or do not exist.[10]

In order to be considered clear and convincing, the evidence needs to be positive, precise and explicit. It necessarily implies a clear preponderance and it usually conveys the idea of certainty.

International courts have frequently applied this standard, though often without explicit references to it. In the *Corfu Channel* Case, for instance, the ICJ found in respect of the alleged Albanian connivance in the laying of a minefield, that a charge of such gravity against a sovereign State must be established by conclusive evidence involving 'a high degree of certainty'.[11] In the *Military and Paramilitary Activities Case*, the Court required 'convincing evidence' insofar as the nature of the case permits.[12] In the *Case concerning the Land and Maritime Boundary Between Cameroon and Nigeria*, the Court concluded 'that it was unable to form

---

[8] ECHR, *Timurtas* v. *Turkey*, 13 June 2000, Eur. Ct. H.R. Rep., para. 82. This attitude is more in line with the practice of the Inter-American Court of Human Rights although it is unclear to what degree the Court has lowered the standard. Gobind Singh Sethi, 'The European Court of Human Rights' Jurisprudence on Issues of Forced Disappearances', *Human Rights Brief* 8(3) (2000). On the practice of the Inter-American Court, see the *Velasquez Rodriguez* Case.

[9] Garner, *Black's Law Dictionary*, p. 251.

[10] Belton, 'Toward a Theory of Procedural Justice', 1221, footnote 62.

[11] ICJ, *Corfu Channel Case*, pp. 16–17.

[12] ICJ, Case concerning Military and Paramilitary Activities In and Against Nicaragua, *Nicaragua* v. *USA*, Merits, 27 June 1986, *ICJ Reports* 1986, para. 29, p. 24.

any 'clear and precise' picture of the events'.[13] In the *Velasquez Rodriguez Case*, the Inter-American Court of Human Rights required a higher level of cogency than usual because of the seriousness of the allegations:

> The Court cannot ignore the special seriousness of finding that a State Party to the Convention has carried out or has tolerated a practice of disappearances in its territory. This requires the Court to apply a standard of proof which considers the seriousness of the charge and which [. . .] is capable of establishing the truth of the allegations in a convincing manner.[14]

In other words, it was not sufficient that the evidence favoured one side, it had to be 'convincing'. As Buergenthal notes, this test was stricter than the test of preponderance of evidence but weaker than proof beyond reasonable doubt.[15]

Preponderance of evidence

In most cases, it is neither realistic nor practical for international tribunals to insist on receiving proof beyond reasonable doubt, or even clear and convincing evidence.[16] As stated by Lauterpacht, 'the degree of proof [. . .] to be adduced ought not to be so stringent as to render the proof unduly exacting'.[17] Both international arbitral tribunals and claims commissions have accepted the more flexible test of 'preponderance of evidence', i.e. evidence which 'is of greater weight or more convincing than the evidence which is offered in opposition to it; that is, evidence which as a whole shows that the fact sought to be proved is more probable than not'.[18]

This standard is close to the Anglo-Saxon standard of the 'balance of probabilities'. It is not based on an abstract degree of certainty or belief, but requires the international tribunal to weigh the evidence presented

---

[13] ICJ, *Case concerning the Land and Maritime Boundary Between Cameroon and Nigeria (Cameroon v. Nigeria)*; Equatorial Guinea Intervening, 10 October 2002, ICJ Reports 2002, para. 322, p. 145.

[14] The *Velasquez Rodriguez* Case, para. 138. See also the Court's remarks in para. 124.

[15] Buergenthal, 'Judicial Fact-Finding', 271. The reason why the Court did not choose the 'reasonable doubt' standard lies in the distinction between judicial protection of human rights and international criminal justice.

[16] Kazazi, *Burden of Proof*, pp. 347–8.

[17] ICJ, *Case of Certain Norwegian Loans (France v. Norway)*, 6 July 1957, Separate Opinion of Judge Lauterpacht, *ICJ Reports 1957*, 39.

[18] Garner, *Black's Law Dictionary*, p. 1182. See also Kevin M. Clermont and Emily Sherwin, 'A Comparative View of Standards of Proof', *American Journal of Comparative Law* 50 (2002), 243, 251.

by both parties in order to determine the party in whose favour the more weighty evidence is available.[19] As such, it is not necessarily a lower standard than that of 'clear and convincing proof.' In fact, the tribunal compares the evidence adduced by both parties to determine which of both sets of evidence it finds most conclusive or convincing.

Although few international decisions explicitly refer to the 'preponderance of evidence', it is generally accepted that this is the predominantly applicable standard in international procedure.[20]

Prima facie evidence

Prima facie evidence is usually defined as evidence 'which unexplained or uncontradicted is sufficient to maintain the proposition affirmed'.[21] Such general definition, however, hardly solves the problem. As Kazazi notes, the standard of prima facie evidence 'only emphasizes the importance of the subjective element inherent in the issues related to the standard of proof and at best replaces the question with another one, i.e. what is the evidence which, unexplained or uncontradicted, is sufficient to maintain a claim?'[22] There is no unequivocal definition of what evidence is required to reach the prima facie threshold, and it is left to the tribunal to decide what it considers the reasonable minimum required to sustain a judgment.

Prima facie evidence primarily affects the 'burden of proof':

> [w]herever provided, *prima facie* evidence shifts the burden of evidence from the proponent of the burden of proof to the other party. This is the effect in all instances. Before this stage the opposing party is not bound to respond to the case, and its silence may prove sufficient. But after one party has provided *prima facie* evidence it has in fact discharged its burden of evidence, and it is not required to carry its burden of proof any further before the other party rebuts the *prima facie* evidence already established by the proponent.[23]

---

[19] Jacomijn J. van Haersolte-van Hof, 'Innovations to Speed Mass Claims: New Standards of Proof', PCA/ICDR Forum, Brussels, 28 May 2003, at 1.

[20] See for instance Mojtaba Kazazi and Bette E. Shifman, 'Evidence before International Tribunals – Introduction', *International Law Forum* 1(4) (1999), 193, 195; Alan Redfern, 'The Practical Distinction Between the Burden of Proof and the Taking of Evidence – An English Perspective', *Arbitration International* 10(3) (1994), 317, 321. For references to case law, see Kazazi, *Burden of Proof*, pp. 348–9.

[21] Mexican–USA General Claims Commission, *Lillie S. Kling (USA)* v. *United Mexican States* (1931), 4 *UN Reports of International Arbitral Awards* 585.

[22] Kazazi, *Burden of Proof*, p. 329.   [23] Kazazi, *Burden of Proof*, p. 332.

If the opposing party succeeds in introducing doubt with respect to the claimant's prima facie case, the burden of proof shifts back to the claimant.[24] If the opposing party does not have strong enough evidence to rebut the prima facie evidence, however, the question arises as to whether the tribunal should consider the prima facie evidence as sufficient. Based mainly on the practice of the Iran–US Claims Tribunal, Kazazi takes a rather liberal position: '[. . .] *prima facie* evidence is not only enough to set the wheels in motion, and is the stage at which a mere silence or denial by the respondent may not necessarily be sufficient, but, if unrebutted, it is usually an acceptable standard of proof before international tribunals'.[25]

This view, however logical it is if one starts from the above definition, is not universally shared. Other authors are more reluctant to accept (unrebutted) prima facie evidence as sufficient in international procedure. Sandifer and Bin Cheng, for instance, restrict the prima facie standard to 'cases where proof of a fact presents extreme difficulty',[26] without defining or clarifying 'extreme difficulty'.

Traditional practice

Different standards of proof apply in international proceedings depending on the nature of the case and the context in which the tribunal operates. Bin Cheng wrote in 1953 that the required degree of cogency 'may vary with the nature of the allegation, its relative importance in the case, the strength of the legal and logical presumptions for or against such an allegation and the relative ease or difficulty for the parties to produce evidence in support or in rebuttal'.[27]

Arbitral tribunals rarely disclose in their decision the standard of proof required. Historical claims commissions and tribunals are no exception in this regard. Most claims tribunals, including the Iran–US Claims Tribunal, appear to have used the traditional yardstick of preponderance of evidence.[28] Others have set the standard of proof at a

---

[24] Kazazi, *Burden of Proof*, p. 333.   [25] Kazazi, *Burden of Proof*, pp. 336–7.

[26] Sandifer, *Evidence Before International Tribunals*, pp. 173–4.

[27] Bin Cheng, *General Principles of Law* (London: Stevens and Sons, 1953), p. 319.

[28] See for instance the Concurring Opinion of Richard Mosk in *William L. Pereira Associates* v. *Islamic Republic of Iran*, Award No. 116–1–3, 19 March 1984, 5 *Iran–US Claims Tribunal Reports* 230, at 231. See also *Combustion Engineering, Inc.* v. *Islamic Republic of Iran*, Award No. 506–308–2, 18 February 1991, 26 *Iran–US Claims Tribunal Reports* 60, 79–80 (para. 70); van Haersolte-van Hof, 'New Standards of Proof', 2.

higher level. In the already mentioned *Graniero Case*, for instance, the Italian-United States Conciliation Commission required 'clear and convincing proof' in support of the claimant's allegations.[29]

On a strictly ad hoc basis, however, historical claims commissions have occasionally been persuaded by *probatio diabolica* arguments and have agreed to lower the standard in specific cases or to take the war context into account when assessing the available evidence. The instances in which they did so are not numerous. Far from constituting a well-established practice, the doctrine of *probatio diabolica* appears to have been used sparingly and carefully.

The Mixed Arbitral Tribunals after the First World War

The Turkish–Greek Mixed Arbitral Tribunal, for instance, used unequivocal language in its decision in the already mentioned *Banque d'Orient Case:* 'le Tribunal, qui jouit d'une pleine liberté dans l'appréciation des preuves apportées, prendra sans doute en considération les difficultés que, pour l'administration de la preuve, les parties pourront éprouver à cause du bouleversement créé par la guerre et ses suites'.[30]

The Mixed Arbitral Tribunal between Hungary and the Serb-Croat-Slovenian State showed a similar willingness to take into account evidentiary difficulties. In *Compagnie pour la construction du chemin de fer d'Ogulin*, the Tribunal agreed for instance that the nature of the losses and the circumstances in which they took place make absolute proof of ownership impossible:

> Attendu que l'État S.C.S. s'est placé sur le point de vue que [. . .] lesdits objets doivent être restitués à leur propriétaire, mais que l'Etat exige que les personnes qui réclament les objets lui fournissent la preuve complète de leur droit de propriété; [. . .]
>
> Attendu que le Tribunal ne saurait admettre, d'une part, que l' État S.C.S. est fondé en droit d'exiger la preuve absolue de la propriété, étant donné que cette *probatio diabolica* est généralement impossible.[31]

Nonetheless, the Tribunal did not accept in this case the evidence submitted by the parties as sufficient to establish the losses.

---

[29] Italian–US Conciliation Commission, *Graniero Claim*, 453.

[30] Tribunal arbitral mixte turco–grec, *Banque d'Orient c. Gouvernement turc*, 974.

[31] Tribunal arbitral mixte hungaro-serbe-croate-slovène, *Compagnie pour la construction du chemin de fer d'Ogulin à la frontière, S.A. c. Etat serbe-croate-slovène*, 12 juillet 1926, *Recueil des décisions des tribunaux arbitraux mixtes*, Tome VI, at 509.

The British–Mexican Claims Commission

In the *Robert John Lynch Case*, the British–Mexican Claims Commission emphasised the impossibility of obtaining conclusive proof of nationality and lowered the standard:

> These considerations show clearly that it would be impossible for any international commission to obtain evidence of nationality amounting to certitude unless a man's life outside the State to which he belongs is to be traced from day to day. Such conclusive proof is impossible and would be nothing less than *probatio diabolica*. All that an international commission can reasonably require in the way of proof of nationality is *prima facie* evidence sufficient to satisfy the Commissioners and to raise the presumption of nationality, leaving it open to the respondent State to rebut the presumption by producing evidence to show that the claimant has lost his nationality through his own act or some other cause.[32]

In the *W. Allan Odell Case*, the same Commission formulated the following guideline:

> the weighing of outside evidence, if any such be produced, may be influenced by the degree to which it was possible to produce proof of a better quality. In cases where it is obvious that everything has been done to collect stronger evidence and where all efforts to do so have failed, a court can be more easily satisfied than in cases where no such endeavour seems to have been made.[33]

The claim was nevertheless dismissed in this case because the Commission could not believe 'that it would have been impracticable to produce at least some corroboration of the statements of the claimant'.[34]

The Iran–US Claims Tribunal

Conscious of the parties' difficulties in finding and producing evidence, the Iran–US Claims Tribunal was 'inclined to accept as adequate proof of claims and defenses evidence that fell far short of what one might normally consider the best evidence, particularly when the Tribunal was satisfied

---

[32] British–Mexican Claims Commission, *Robert John Lynch (Great Britain)* v. *United Mexican States*, 8 November 1929, 5 *UN Reports of International Arbitral Awards* 18, 18–19.

[33] British–Mexican Claims Commission, *W. Allan Odell*, 13 May 1931, 5 *UN Reports of International Arbitral Awards* 155.

[34] British–Mexican Claims Commission, *W. Allan Odell*, p. 155.

that it was the best evidence available to the party'.[35] In the *Rockwell Award*, for instance, the Tribunal agreed to lower the standard of evidence because of the claimant's difficulties to present better evidence: 'Prima facie evidence must be recognized as a satisfactory basis to grant a claim where proof of the facts underlying the claim presents extreme difficulty and an inference from the evidence can reasonably be drawn.'[36] The Tribunal adds that this is particularly true where the difficulty of proof follows from the respondent's failure to raise timely objections.

In the *Sola Tiles Case*, the Iran–US Claims Tribunal accepted that the claimant was unable to access records in Iran and that the chaotic conditions prevailing at the time of the loss hindered his efforts to submit proof. In these circumstances, the Tribunal 'must be prepared to take some account of the disadvantages suffered by the Claimant, namely its lack of access to detailed documentation, as an inevitable consequence of the circumstances in which the expropriation took place'.[37]

In other cases, however, the Tribunal refused to follow this path and did not relax the evidentiary standards. In the *Jalal Moin Case* for instance: 'The Tribunal is mindful of the difficulties faced by the Claimant in collecting evidence, although the Tribunal would expect that any taking of the properties in question would be indicated in some documentary evidence, for example, in contemporary correspondence. In any event, the Tribunal must base its awards on probative evidence.'[38] The Tribunal wondered, for instance, why the claimant's family, when they went to Iran in 1986, were not able to gather any such evidence.

Present-day mass claims practice

Present-day mass claims processes have generally taken a radically different approach with respect to the evidentiary threshold. Holocaust-related mass claims processes usually relied on 'relaxed' standards or 'plausibility',

---

[35] Aldrich, *The Jurisprudence of the Iran–US Claims Tribunal*, p. 333.

[36] Iran–US Claims Tribunal, *Rockwell International Systems* v. *Islamic Republic of Iran*, Award No. 438–430–1, 4 September 1989, para. 141, reprinted in 23 *Iran–US Claims Tribunal Reports* 150.

[37] Iran–US Claims Tribunal, *Sola Tiles, Inc.* v. *The Government of the Islamic Republic of Iran*, Award No. 298–317–1, 22 April 1987, para. 52, reprinted in 14 *Iran–US Claims Tribunal Reports* 223. See also Kazazi, *Burden of Proof*, p. 353.

[38] See Iran–US Claims Tribunal, *Jalal Moin* v. *Islamic Republic of Iran*, Award No. 557–950–2, 24 May 1994, para. 19, reprinted in 30 *Iran–US Claims Tribunal Reports* 70.

while the UNCC established a sophisticated set of evidentiary standards, varying according to the scope and nature of the claims.[39]

The United Nations Compensation Commission

Article 35 of the UNCC Rules establishes a complex system of evidentiary standards, which vary depending on the category of claims. This provision provides first that it is for each claimant to submit documents and other evidence, which 'demonstrate satisfactorily' that the claim is eligible for compensation.[40] As mentioned already, the phrase 'demonstrate satisfactorily' appears to require a lower level of cogency than is usually expected. The provision furthermore states that each Panel of Commissioners will determine 'the admissibility, relevance, materiality and weight of any documents and other evidence submitted' and then sets forth specific evidentiary standards for the different categories of claims.[41] Relaxed or lenient standards applied to smaller individual claims and more demanding standards to larger claims.

For small departure claims (Category "A"), claimants were required to provide 'simple documentation' of the fact and date of departure from Iraq or Kuwait.[42] Documentation of the actual amount of loss was not required, since the UNCC awarded fixed amounts of compensation to successful claimants in this category. The causal link between the departure and invasion or occupation of Iraq was presumed. Consequently, only the fact and date of departure needed to be established, and simple documentation was sufficient in this respect.

To receive fixed amounts for serious personal injury or death (Category "B" claims), claimants were likewise simply required documents on the fact and date of the injury or death (and, in the latter case, of the family relationship with the deceased).[43]

Claims for individual losses up to US $100,000 (Category "C" claims) had to be documented by appropriate evidence of the circumstances and

---

[39] There has been no similar relaxation of the standard of evidence in the CRPC and HPCC. Neither of these mass claims bodies has articulated the required degree of cogency in abstract terms. Instead, they list in their respective rules and regulations the types of evidence that are accepted as sufficient to prove property rights. See CRPC, Book of Regulations on Real Property, Arts 44–5. At least for the CRPC, it can be observed that the requisite documents, or combinations of documents, reflect a relatively high standard of evidence. These two mass claims facilities will not be included in the following discussion.

[40] UNCC, Provisional Rules, Art. 35.   [41] UNCC, Provisional Rules, Art. 35, para. 1.

[42] UNCC, Provisional Rules, Art. 35, para. 2(a).

[43] UNCC, Provisional Rules, Art. 35, para. 2(b).

the amount of the claimed loss. The required evidence was 'the reasonable minimum that is appropriate under the particular circumstances of the case'.[44] A lesser degree of documentary evidence was ordinarily sufficient for smaller claims such as those below US $20,000. To determine the 'reasonable minimum appropriate under the particular circumstances of the case' the panel was free to consider many elements, including the types of evidence routinely submitted, the circumstances in Iraq and Kuwait during the invasion and occupation, transactional practices in Iraq and Kuwait prior to the invasion (e.g. both were cash-only economies) and the socio-economic characteristics of claimants from different countries.[45]

Large claims had to be 'supported by documentary and other appropriate evidence sufficient to demonstrate the circumstances and amount of the claimed loss'.[46] For these claims, the standards of evidence were thus set at a somewhat higher level, requiring documentary proof of both the circumstances and the amount of the losses allegedly incurred. Nevertheless, even for larger individual claims, the Panels of Commissioners took into account the difficulties that individual claimants faced when collecting supporting evidence and took a balanced and pragmatic approach to the issue, as illustrated by a "D" Panel report:

> The Panel is aware that international tribunals [...] have recognised the principle that the law of evidence in international procedure is a flexible system shorn of any technical rules. The Panel is also conscious of the fact that the lack of standard international law rules of evidence and the fact that international tribunals are liberal in their approach to the admission and assessment of evidence does not waive the burden resting on claimants to demonstrate the circumstances and amount of the claimed loss. On the other hand, considering the difficult circumstances of the invasion and occupation of Kuwait by Iraq [...] many claimants cannot, and cannot be expected to, document all aspects of a claim. In many cases, relevant documents do not exist, have been destroyed, or were left behind by claimants who fled Kuwait or Iraq. Accordingly, the level of proof the Panel has considered appropriate is close to what has been called the 'balance of probability' as distinguished from the concept of 'beyond reasonable doubt' required in some jurisdictions to prove guilt in a criminal trial.[47]

---

[44] UNCC, Provisional Rules, Art. 35, para. 2(c).

[45] Christopher Gibson, 'Using Computers to Evaluate Claims at the United Nations Compensation Commission', *Arbitration International* 13 (1997), 167, 176, footnote 29.

[46] UNCC, Provisional Rules, Art. 35, para. 3.

[47] UNCC, Report and Recommendations Made by the Panel of Commissioners Concerning Part One of the First Instalment of Individual Claims for Damages Above US$ 100,000 (Category "D" Claims), 3 February 1998, UN Doc. S/AC.26/1998/1, para. 72.

Furthermore, the Panel added that 'the test of balance of probability has to be applied having regard to the circumstances existing at the time of the invasion and loss'.[48] This indicates that, even for large claims, the difficulties to submit evidence were taken into account.

The Claims Resolution Tribunal for Dormant Accounts

The CRT-I was the first to incorporate very relaxed standard of plausibility into the rules of an international mass claims process:[49] a claimant had to show that it was plausible in the light of all the circumstances that they were entitled to the claimed account.[50] The arbitrators had to assess all information submitted by the parties or otherwise available to them, bearing in mind the 'difficulties of proving a claim after the destruction of the Second World War and the Holocaust and the long time that has elapsed since the opening of these dormant accounts'.[51]

A finding of plausibility required, *inter alia*, that the claimant submitted all documents and other information 'that can reasonably be expected to be produced in view of the particular circumstances, including, without limitation, the history of the claimant's family and whether or not the published account holder was a victim of Nazi persecution'.[52] It also required that 'no reasonable basis exists to conclude that fraud or forgery affect the claim or evidence submitted; or that other persons may have an identical or better claim to the dormant account'.[53]

The plausibility standard was not used for all questions. According to Article 15 of the CRT Rules, the Sole Arbitrator or Claims Panel should 'reject a claim if, by *a preponderance of the evidence*, it is established that (i) the published account holder was acting as an intermediary for a victim of Nazi persecution; and (ii) the assets deposited in the account were looted from victims of Nazi persecution'.[54]

The plausibility standard has been maintained in the CRT-II. Article 17 (1) of the Rules provides that each claimant should demonstrate that

---

[48] UNCC, Report "D" claims, 1st inst., para. 72.
[49] Van Haersolte-van Hof, 'New Standards of Proof', 5.
[50] CRT I, Rules of Procedure, Art. 22. See also Beauchamp, 'The New Claims Resolution Tribunal', 1013.
[51] CRT-I, Rules of Procedure, Art. 22.   [52] CRT-I, Rules of Procedure, Art. 22.
[53] CRT-I, Rules of Procedure, Art. 22.
[54] CRT-I, Rules of Procedure, Art. 15 (emphasis added).

it is plausible in the light of all the circumstances that they are entitled, in whole or in part, to the claimed account.[55]

The German Forced Labour Compensation Programme

The German Foundation Act did not set forth a clear standard of evidence for the assessment of claims. Section 11 (2) of the Act simply provides that 'eligibility shall be demonstrated by the applicant by submission of documents', adding nevertheless that 'if no relevant evidence is available, the claimant's eligibility can be made *credible* in some other way'.[56] The Law did not specify what kind of evidentiary threshold was required for a claim to be 'credible'.[57]

The Foundation's Board of Directors gradually clarified the general evidentiary requirements for successful claims.[58] Not surprisingly, the Board's instructions to the partner organisations reflected a flexible approach and allowed virtually any kind of formal or informal evidence that could be used to demonstrate that the applicant's claim was true.[59] This included, for instance, copies of official and other documents, photographs, private letters from the period, privately obtained expert opinions, and written accounts by either the claimants or witnesses. The weight of these types of evidence had to be assessed according to the criterion of *überwiegender Wahrscheinlichkeit*, which largely corresponds to the standard of 'preponderance of evidence': based on the available information and documentation, it must be more probable that the claimants' statements are true than not.[60]

Likewise, the rules governing the property claims process took into account the difficulties for claimants to produce supporting evidence and integrated the *probatio diabolica* theory into the applicable evidentiary standards:

> The Commission's decisions on compensability shall be based on relaxed standards of proof taking into account the lapse of time between the date the loss occurred and the date the claim was made; the circumstances in which the specific loss or types of losses occurred; the information

---

[55] CRT-II, Rules of Procedure, Art. 17(1).
[56] German Foundation Act, Art. 11(2) (emphasis added).
[57] Van der Auweraert, 'The practicalities of Forced Labor Compensation', 311.
[58] Van der Auweraert, 'The practicalities of Forced Labor Compensation', 312.
[59] Van der Auweraert, 'The practicalities of Forced Labor Compensation', 313.
[60] Van der Auweraert, 'The practicalities of Forced Labor Compensation', 313.

available from other cases; and the background information available to the Commission regarding the circumstances prevailing during the National Socialist era and the Second World War and the participation of German enterprises in the commitment of National Socialist wrongs.[61]

However, a fact is 'considered established if it has been credibly demonstrated' and a claim 'cannot be rejected on the sole ground that it is not supported by official documentary evidence'.[62]

The International Commission on Holocaust Era Insurance Claims

The ICHEIC process also relies on a relaxed standard of evidence.[63] Integrating the *probatio diabolica* theory into the overall evidentiary framework, the rules oblige the insurance companies to consider at all times the difficulties of proving a claim after the destruction caused by the War and the Holocaust, and the lengthy period of time that has passed since the insurance policy under consideration was obtained.[64] Again, the required standard of proof is one of plausibility. A claimant shall show that

> it is plausible, in the light of all the special circumstances involved, including but not limited to the destruction caused by World War II, the Holocaust, and the lengthy period of time that has passed since the insurance policy in question was obtained, that the claimant is entitled, either in whole or in part, to the benefits of the insurance policy under consideration.[65]

The rules further add that the insurance companies have agreed not to demand unreasonably the production of any document or other evidence that, more likely than not, has been destroyed, lost or rendered inaccessible to the claimant.[66] In addition, the ICHEIC rules list a number of documents, ranging from an insurance policy to written correspondence, that are considered adequate to substantiate a claim. Other documents may be considered sufficient to establish the existence

---

[61] IOM Property Claims Commission, Supplemental Principles and Rules of Procedure, Section 22(1).
[62] IOM Property Claims Commission, Supplemental Principles and Rules of Procedure, Section 22(2).
[63] See also van Haersolte-van Hof, 'New Standards of Proof', 8.
[64] ICHEIC, Relaxed Standards of Proof Guide, rule B3.
[65] ICHEIC, Relaxed Standards of Proof Guide, rule A1.
[66] ICHEIC, Relaxed Standards of Proof Guide, rule B2.

of an insurance policy.[67] Information about personal circumstances may be gathered from a wide variety of evidentiary items, including photographs, maps, newspaper reports and notices, family trees, letters and any other evidence the claimant submits.[68]

Analysis: Towards a plausibility standard?

Introduction

Relaxing the standard of evidence is a second technique that can be used to ease the claimant's task of gathering and presenting evidence in support of their claim. Conceptually, this technique is to be distinguished from the techniques reviewed in Chapter 6. A relaxed standard of evidence reduces the degree of confidence required to award compensation or restitution rather than reversing the burden of proof or assisting claimants in discharging this burden. Under a relaxed standard of evidence, a claimant need not present the same quantum of evidence as would ordinarily be required.

The *probatio diabolica* has occasionally brought historical claims commissions and arbitral tribunals to either relax the evidentiary standard, or to take into account the claimant's difficulties when weighing the available evidence against the applicable standard. They have done so in specific cases only, thereby creating the appearance of ad hoc justice. Modern mass claims resolution facilities have been more consistent in their approach. Several processes have relaxed the standard of evidence either across the board or for certain categories of claims.

Relaxed standards of evidence obviously make it easier for claimants to reach the required evidentiary threshold. Unless their use is accompanied by other measures, however, relaxed standards of evidence also offer less protection against false or fraudulent claims. Lower standards of evidence appear to entail a certain loss of accuracy in claims outcomes. As such, the growing use of relaxed standards of evidence in some mass claims processes may simply indicate that outcome accuracy is not the predominant value or purpose, and that the adjudicator accepts to trade accuracy in fact-finding for other advantages.[69]

---

[67] See also van Haersolte-van Hof, 'New Standards of Proof', 8.
[68] ICHEIC, Relaxed Standards of Proof Guide, rule E.
[69] Compare with Saks' analysis of the pursuit of 'apparent inaccuracy' in Saks, 'Enhancing and Restraining Accuracy', 270.

Conceptual vagueness?

Although the terms 'relaxed standard of proof' and 'plausibility' – both of which are used interchangeably in recent mass claims practice – have been used in at least four mass claims processes, their precise meaning remains somewhat vague. No general definition has been provided as to what constitutes a plausibility finding.

The CRT-I Rules of Procedure, however, identify three concrete requirements for a finding of plausibility.[70] These three elements, it is submitted, are key to understanding the specificity of the plausibility standard.

First, a plausibility finding requires that the party with the burden of proof produces all documents and information that they can reasonably be expected to present in view of the particular circumstances. As demonstrated in the review of historical practice, adjudicators have always been free to take into account the party's difficulties when weighing the evidence and they have done so in specific cases. The plausibility standard, however, appears to impose a duty upon the adjudicator to determine the probative weight of the evidence and information submitted by the parties in accordance with the difficulties they faced and the efforts they have undertaken to obtain better evidence. It obliges the adjudicator to take into account the party's difficulties and to assess whether more could and should have been done. In this sense, the plausibility standard integrates the *probatio diabolica* theory in the adjudicative framework and ensures its consistent application throughout the caseload.

Plausibility appears to be based on an element of reasonableness, thereby underscoring the importance of the claimant's explanations for the lack of evidence. It is clear from the CRT's practice, for instance, that the adjudicators rely extensively upon the claimant's statements explaining why it was impossible to gather and present better evidence or more detailed information.

Second, if the claimant has presented all evidence and information that can reasonably be expected, the adjudicator needs to assess whether there exists a reasonable basis to believe that fraud or forgery affects the claim. The importance of this element should be seen in the light of the foregoing test. If the first element creates an obligation for the adjudicator to accept evidence that is of very little probative value, a shield against false or fraudulent claims is needed to allow the adjudicator to avoid manifest unfairness when there is reason to be suspicious.

---

[70] CRT-I, Rules of Procedure, Art. 22.

Third, the adjudicator needs to determine whether there exists a reasonable basis to conclude that other persons may have an identical or better claim. Otherwise, a finding based on plausibility may exclude other claimants with a better or identical claim.

Based on these three elements, one can try to distinguish the plausibility standard from the four general standards that are sometimes used in international adjudication.

The plausibility standard can easily be distinguished from 'proof beyond reasonable doubt' and 'clear and convincing proof'. Proof beyond reasonable doubt is proof that precludes every reasonable hypothesis except that which it tends to support. The intermediate standard of 'clear and convincing proof' requires a high probability that the facts are true or exist. Findings based on these two standards approach the level of certainty or 'near certainty'. Plausibility does not imply this sense of certainty. On the contrary, it accepts that the facts are not certain, as the following paragraph in a CRT-I decision makes clear:

> Comparing the information contained in the bank documents with the information provided by the Claimant, it is *far from certain* that the Claimant is entitled to the assets of the Account Holder. However, taking the requirements of Article 22 into account, the Claims Panel is satisfied that the Claimant has shown that *it is plausible* that she is the sole surviving relative of the Account Holder, and that she is entitled to the whole of the assets of the Account Holder.[71]

It is more delicate to distinguish the plausibility standard from the traditional yardstick of preponderance of evidence, which focuses on whether the evidence is of greater weight or more convincing than the evidence which is offered in opposition to it.[72] Such a comparative approach will in some cases result in findings based on a very high level of probability. It may even approach or exceed the level of clear and convincing proof. As a minimum, on the other hand, it requires that the fact sought to be proved is more probable than not. At least in common law, a preponderance of evidence is generally understood 'as implying a

---

[71] CRT-I, Partial Award, 29 June 1999, Docket No. 2334/0498/CP, available at www.crt-ii. org/_crt-i/frame.html (visited October 2007) (emphasis added).

[72] See Kevin M. Clermont and Emily Sherwin ('A Comparative View of Standards of Proof', *American Journal of Comparative Law* 50 (2002), 243, 251), who argue that the 'standard of preponderance of the evidence translates into more-likely-than-not'.

threshold degree of certainty just above 50 per cent for a ruling in favour of the party with the burden of proof':[73]

> The slightest preponderance of the evidence in his favour entitle[s] the plaintiff to a verdict. All that is required in a civil case of one who has the burden of proof is that he establish his claim by a preponderance of the evidence. When the equilibrium of proof is destroyed, and the beam inclines toward him who has the burden, however slightly, he has satisfied the requirement of the law, and is entitled to a verdict. A bare preponderance is sufficient, though the scales drop but a feather's weight.[74]

This suggests that the real difference between preponderance of evidence and plausibility lies in the nature of the two tests rather than in the degree of probability they require. The former is based on an almost mathematical weighing of the evidence with a view to determining the overall probability of a party's position. The latter implies a more qualitative examination of the documentation and information submitted by the claimant with a view to determining the coherence and reasonableness of his position.

Similarly, it is difficult to distinguish the plausibility standard from the concept of prima facie evidence, i.e. the minimum required to maintain the proposition affirmed. Again, plausibility could hardly be said to imply less than this minimum of evidence. Nor can it be maintained that a finding based on plausibility necessarily requires more than this minimum of evidence. This is not to say that these standards can be equated. The distinction between the prima facie standard and plausibility lies in the special emphasis that the latter places on reasonableness and coherence. If the information and the evidence submitted by the claimant are coherent and if the absence of better evidence is reasonably explained, the claimant's position can be said to be believable and likely to be true. Plausibility depends on inferential coherence and reasonableness rather than on probability.

In conclusion, plausibility can easily be distinguished from 'proof beyond reasonable doubt' and 'clear and convincing evidence'. It does

---

[73] Dominique Demougin and Claude Fluet, 'Preponderance of Evidence', CIRANO Scientific Series, No. 2002s–61 (2002), at 1 (available at www.cirano.qc.ca/pdf/publication/2002s-61.pdf (visited October 2007)). See also Steve Gold, 'Causation in Toxic Torts: Burdens of Proof, Standards of Persuasion, and Statistical Evidence', *Yale Law Journal* 96 (1986) 376, 382–3 (arguing that 'the jury must be more than 50% confident in its conclusion').

[74] Quoted in Demougin and Fluet, 'Preponderance of Evidence', 1.

not imply a sense of certainty and, moreover, accepts that the facts are not certain. Distinguishing plausibility from the preponderance of evidence and the prima facie standard is more difficult. The distinction should be made based on the nature of the test to be applied rather than the abstract degree of probability required. The plausibility standard requires reasonableness and coherence rather than a particular level of probability.

In sum, the notion of plausibility remains somewhat vague and ambiguous compared to more traditional standards of evidence. It is important to be aware of the conceptual quicksand that one risks stepping into when introducing new standards of evidence. While a certain degree of subjectivity is inherent in all evidentiary standards, the difficulty in defining plausibility should caution against too liberal a usage of this particular standard.

Impact upon outcome accuracy

Relaxed standards of evidence clearly have an impact upon the overall accuracy of the decision making. By requiring less certainty or confidence than strict evidentiary standards, relaxed standards appear to accept a certain loss of accuracy.

However, the loss of accuracy associated with a relaxed standard is not necessarily higher than the inaccuracies generated by high standards of evidence. Indeed, both types of evidentiary standards – high and relaxed – generate certain error costs when the relevant evidence is difficult to obtain. When the burden of proof is assigned to the claimants in a situation of evidentiary scarcity, a high standard of evidence increases the risk of rejecting meritorious claims for failure to meet the evidentiary threshold. High standards may therefore generate false negatives. The introduction of a relaxed standard of evidence, on the other hand, reduces the risk of issuing false negatives but increases the chances that meritless claims will be erroneously compensated. Relaxed standards generate predominantly false positives.

Both types of errors would have to be measured and compared to evaluate the impact of evidentiary standards upon outcome accuracy. However, the error cost of a particular standard cannot be measured easily, nor can the respective error costs of different standards be compared in a satisfactory manner. The only conclusion that can be drawn is that under a high standard of evidence (and assuming that the claimant bears the burden of proof) the error cost will be borne predominantly by the claimants. With a relaxed standard of evidence, the error cost will be borne mostly by the respondent or – exceptionally – by competing claimants.

Placing the error cost with the respondent

In most situations, the error costs of relaxed standards of evidence will be borne predominantly by the respondent party. This technique therefore reflects a clear policy choice: knowing that absolute certainty is not a realistic goal, it may be preferable in some situations to award restitution or compensation in case of doubt, rather than to exclude potentially deserving claimants from the process. Outcome accuracy is not seen as the predominant value in these situations and the adjudicator is prepared to run the risk of issuing some false positives for the benefit of the overall fairness of the claims process.

The appropriateness of this approach depends entirely on the specific circumstances giving rise to the claims process. In the case of the UNCC, for instance, the scope of the damage caused by Iraq's invasion and occupation of Kuwait had been extensively documented. Moreover, Iraq's liability for mass losses had been established by the Security Council Resolution 687 (1991) and accepted by the Government of Iraq.[75] Furthermore, the claimants' evidentiary difficulties stemmed directly from the respondent's actions. It is precisely this overall responsibility for mass losses and, either directly or indirectly, for the lack of evidence that justified placing the error cost with the respondent, i.e. the party responsible for the loss of evidence. Any other solution would frustrate the societal objectives of the claims process, in particular in terms of fairness, compensation and deterrence.

A similar contextual analysis explains why relaxed standards of evidence were deemed appropriate in the case of the CRT-I. The Volcker Report had established that several thousand Swiss bank accounts had a 'probable' or 'possible' connection to a Holocaust victim and that there was confirmed evidence of 'questionable and deceitful actions by some individual banks in the handling of accounts of victims, including withholding of information from Holocaust victims or their heirs about their accounts, inappropriate closing of accounts, failure to keep adequate

---

[75] See UN Security Council Resolution 687 (1991), para. 16; Identical letters from the Permanent Representative of Iraq to the United Nations, addressed respectively to the Secretary-General and the President of the Security Council, 6 April 1991, UN Doc. S/22456.

records, [...] and a general lack of diligence'.[76] Knowing that the respondents' behaviour had resulted in mass losses and had made it difficult for the claimants to establish their losses with a reasonable degree of certainty, the error costs were placed with the respondents rather than with the claimants.[77]

However, the CRPC in Bosnia and the HPD/HPCC in Kosovo did not introduce relaxed standards of evidence. The two property commissions are different from the other mass claims processes in the sense that they do not have to deal with an institutional respondent, considered responsible for mass losses. The claims they received were in essence private disputes between individuals, i.e. the pre-war owner or occupant and the post-war owner or occupant of the claimed property. If restitution of property were ordered on the basis of a relaxed standard of evidence, the error cost would be borne by the individual respondents, who may or may not have acted in good faith. They surely were neither responsible for mass losses, nor for the absence of evidence, and therefore cannot be expected to bear the costs associated with inaccuracies in the decision making.

A final rationale for placing the error costs with the respondent may lie in the effect on future perpetrators or wrongdoers. A stringent standard of evidence has the perverse effect of encouraging future wrongdoers to destroy the evidence of the wrongs committed.[78] By eliminating the direct evidence, they can shield themselves from liability. Relaxed standards of evidence place the risk associated with the destruction of evidence where it belongs, i.e. with the party that caused or contributed to the lack of evidence.

Error cost to the claimants

In specific cases, relaxed standards of evidence will generate error costs for the claimants rather than the respondent. This will be the case when there are competing claims to the same asset, as the following example from CRT-I illustrates.[79]

---

[76] Volcker Report, p. 13.

[77] A different analysis would apply to the other Holocaust-related mass claims processes that were born out of a settlement agreement. It could be argued that the respondents in these cases agreed to bear the error costs.

[78] For a similar reasoning, see Sethi, 'The European Court of Human Rights'.

[79] The example is also reported by Roger P. Alford, 'The Claims Resolution Tribunal', 267–8.

Two individuals came forward to claim the assets in a bank account that had been held by a Hungarian national who died in Auschwitz in 1945.[80] One submitted significant documentary evidence establishing that he was the nephew of the account holder. The other claimant alleged that he was the son of the account holder and had been separated from his family during the war due to a serious head injury. To support his story, he relied on circumstantial evidence only, including a statement by two witnesses who recalled a small Jewish boy in a foster home with a head injury who was from the town where the account holder had lived. Another witness testified that the account holder's smallest child suffered a head injury in July 1944. The claimant provided physical evidence indicating that he had suffered a head injury in the past and established that he was circumcised and therefore allegedly Jewish. Despite requests from the Sole Arbitrator, the claimant did not provide any official documentation, such as a birth certificate, to establish his relationship to the account holder. To explain the absence of such official documentation, the claimant stated that significant parts of his hometown were rased to the ground during the war, making it impossible to locate his birth certificate. Based on the relaxed standard of evidence, the Tribunal concluded that it was at least plausible that this claimant was indeed the son of the account holder. It further found that because a son has a better claim of entitlement to the assets in the account, the nephew should not receive any of the assets.

Had the standard of evidence not been relaxed, the outcome might have been entirely different. The alleged son's claim would in all likelihood be rejected for lack of sufficient evidence and the nephew's claim, supported by much stronger evidence, would be upheld.

Cost to the overall claims process

One final cost should be mentioned. By requiring a lower level of confidence in the accuracy of the facts underlying the claims, the use of relaxed standards of evidence may also negatively affect the integrity and the credibility of the claims process. The same can of course be said of high standards of evidence when applied in a situation of evidentiary scarcity: if they result in a large number of false negatives, large parts of the victim population may reject the process as unnecessarily strict, formalist and largely unhelpful.

[80] CRT-I, Partial Award, 14 October 1999, Consolidated Docket No. 5427/0798/SR/KD/RO.

The use of relaxed standards nonetheless requires a careful weighing of various factors. If outcome accuracy is a key value in the claims process, relaxed standards of evidence are clearly not appropriate. On the other hand, if the primary aim is to provide some justice to the victims in an efficient and timely manner, relaxed standards of evidence may be the most practical way to achieve this objective.

Conclusion

Some mass claims processes have refused to use a demanding standard of proof that many claimants might fail to meet and that might add only marginally to the adjudicator's understanding of the merits of the case. As Saks argues, '[a]ny dispute resolution process has to be satisfying to the disputants, including the losing parties, and to the larger society. At various stages of our society's development, that may mean preferring one set of procedures rather than another, even if the favored rule reduces rather than increases the system's factfinding capability'.[81]

The standard of plausibility requires that the party with the burden of proof presents all documents and information that can reasonably be expected in view of the particular circumstances. This relaxed evidentiary standard incorporates the *probatio diabolica* theory into the evidentiary framework of a mass claims process and therefore ensures consistency in the treatment of similarly situated claimants. The plausibility standard requires less certainty than 'proof beyond reasonable doubt' and 'clear and convincing proof'. Contrary to the 'preponderance of evidence' and 'prima facie' standards, it requires the adjudicator to place special emphasis on the coherence and reasonableness of the position asserted by the claimant.

While it is impossible to measure with precision the impact of different standards of evidence upon outcome accuracy, it is clear that relaxed standards reduce the risk of issuing false negatives. Since they generate false positives rather than false negatives, they place the costs of error predominantly with the respondent. While caution is obviously needed, this effect may be desirable in the specific situations in which certain mass claims processes operate.

---

[81] Saks, 'Enhancing and Restraining Accuracy', 244.

8

Presumptions and inferences

Presumptions and inferences alleviate the claimants' burden of proof. They are particularly effective and valuable tools in mass claims programmes when evidence is scarce or difficult to gather.

Concept and general rules

Terminology

Presumptions are a recognition in law of the relationship between two facts, whereas conclusions are 'drawn from known facts about unknown facts'.[1] Presumptions can be either legal or judicial. The former are prescribed by law and can be relied upon in virtually all claims. The latter, also called 'inferences', are presumptions drawn by courts and depend on the specific circumstances of the case at issue. Presumptions are either *juris tantum* (i.e. rebuttable) or *juris et de jure* (i.e. irrebuttable).

Legal presumptions

The existence of legal presumptions in international procedure has been disputed in the past. Because of the absence of a supreme law-making power in international law, some authors argued that *legal* presumptions were unknown to international procedure.[2] Today, it is generally recognised that international tribunals rely on legal presumptions whenever necessary.[3] In international procedure, the adjective 'legal' does not refer to the laws of States nor does it imply the existence of a supreme law over and above States. It simply refers to the sources of international law as enumerated in Article 38 of the Statute of the ICJ, namely conventions, custom and general principles of law.[4]

[1] See e.g. article 1349 of the French and Belgian *Code Civil*.
[2] See for instance Witenberg, 'Onus Probandi', 329–30.
[3] Sandifer, *Evidence Before International Tribunals*, p. 141.
[4] Kazazi, *Burden of Proof*, p. 244.

There are plenty of legal presumptions based on, for instance, the general principles of good faith and sovereignty of States.[5] An example of a treaty-based presumption is found in paragraph 6 of Article 75 of the Treaty of Peace between the Allied and Associated Powers and Italy, which provides that '[c]laims for the restitution of property shall be presented [. . .] by the Government of the country from whose territory the property was removed, it being understood that rolling stock shall be regarded as having been removed from the territory to which it originally belonged'.[6]

Similar to the effect of presumptions in national courts, presumptions affect the allocation of the burden of evidence, i.e. the burden of producing evidence, in international tribunals.[7] When one of the parties relies upon a presumption, the other party will have the opportunity to rebut this presumption by providing proof of the contrary. The effects are similar to the effects of prima facie evidence. If the opposing party is not able to rebut the prima facie evidence created by a presumption, the Tribunal decides in favour of the proponent. If there is some evidence against a presumption, the Tribunal will weigh this evidence to decide whether it is sufficient to rebut the presumption. Obviously, it is always incumbent upon the adjudicators to decide on the admissibility and relevance of the presumptions relied upon by the parties.

A practical problem arises when tribunals or claims commissions apply a legal presumption on their own initiative: they usually disclose their decisions only at the end of the proceedings, i.e. when the party against whom the existence of a fact has been presumed no longer has an opportunity to prove the contrary.[8] Kazazi therefore concludes that 'presumptions affect the burden of proof in the sense that, in the process of evaluating the evidence, the tribunal takes into account any presumption applicable in favour of the proponent of the burden of proof and not refuted by the adversary'.[9]

Occasionally, international judicial and arbitral decisions make use of irrebuttable presumptions.[10] They are particularly delicate for two reasons.

---

[5] For examples, see Kazazi, *Burden of Proof*, pp. 246–7.
[6] Treaty of Peace with Italy, Paris, 10 February 1947.
[7] Bin Cheng, *General Principles of Law*, p. 304.   [8] Kazazi, *Burden of Proof*, p. 251.
[9] Kazazi, *Burden of Proof*, p. 251.
[10] For an example, see ICJ, *Legal Consequences for States of the Continued Presence of South Africa in Namibia (South West Africa) notwithstanding Security Council Resolution 276 (1970)*, Advisory Opinion of 21 June 1971, Dissenting Opinion of Judge Sir Gerald Fitzmaurice, *ICJ Reports* 1971, at 274–5.

First, presumptions against which no rebuttal is allowed are particularly radical. Second, irrebuttable presumptions are difficult to reconcile with the freedom that international tribunals enjoy in weighing evidence and the ensuing rule that no evidence with prefixed probative value can be imposed upon an international tribunal.[11] According to Kazazi, irrebuttable presumptions should therefore not be considered as true presumptions based on the reoccurrence of certain facts, but rather as 'conclusions necessitated by the rules of law, prescribed for purpose of policy and disguised in the form of irrebuttable presumptions'.[12] Kazazi explains it as follows: '[. . .] when reasons for prescribing a rule of law in the form of a presumption are other than and more important than a mere repetition of a reoccurring fact, then it is necessary that such a legal presumption and its effect could not be avoided even by contrary proof'.[13]

Inferences

International tribunals and claims commissions may also draw themselves reasonable inferences from facts. The admissibility of reasonable inferences in international procedure was recognised early on by the International Court of Justice in the *Corfu Channel Case*. In respect of the difficulties that a victim of a breach of international law faces in finding direct proof of facts in the territory of another State, the Court observed that:

> [s]uch a State should be allowed a more liberal recourse to inferences of fact and circumstantial evidence. This indirect evidence is admitted in all systems of law, and its use is recognized by international decisions. It must be regarded as of special weight when it is based on a series of facts linked together and leading logically to a single conclusion.[14]

Inferences can be based on actions as well as non-actions (e.g. the non-denial of a particular fact or state of affairs). They should 'leave no room for reasonable doubt'[15] and should not be 'inconsistent with facts incontrovertibly established by the evidence'.[16] They should be sufficiently

---

[11] See Kazazi, *Burden of Proof*, p. 256. [12] Kazazi, *Burden of Proof*, p. 257.

[13] Kazazi, *Burden of Proof*, p. 257.

[14] ICJ, *Corfu Channel Case*, p. 18. Not all judges agreed. See the Dissenting Opinions of Judge Krylov and Judge Azevedo, *ICJ Reports* 1949, p. 69 and 90–1.

[15] ICJ, *Corfu Channel Case*, p. 18.

[16] Dissenting Opinion of Sir Percy Spender, ICJ, *Case Concerning the Temple of Preah Vihear (Cambodia v. Thailand)*, Merits, *ICJ Reports* 1962, p. 109. See also the *Velasquez Rodriguez* Case, para. 130: 'Circumstantial evidence, indicia, and presumptions may be considered, so long as they lead to conclusions consistent with the facts.'

strong, clear and concordant.[17] It is for the tribunal or claims commission to decide whether a particular inference is reasonable and appropriate under the circumstances of a given case.

While inferences do not provide immediate proof of the facts, they 'make the charge probable with the assistance of reasoning'.[18] Since they are always rebuttable, the other party can contradict an inference by presenting direct evidence or relying on another inference. It is up to the tribunal to weigh the counterevidence and decide whether it is sufficient to rebut the inference. Again, tribunals enjoy a wide margin of discretion in this respect. They may draw from the facts a different conclusion than a party or make reasonable assumptions in the absence of any specific evidence from the parties.[19]

Traditional practice

Claims commissions and tribunals have traditionally been reluctant to rely on inferences and presumptions.

The Italian Conciliation Commissions

Of course, the legal presumptions created by the peace treaties were readily applied by the Conciliation Commissions. In the *French State Railways Claim* – a property restitution claim brought under Article 75 of the Treaty of Peace – the Franco–Italian Conciliation Commission reversed the burden of proof on the basis of a legal presumption.[20] Article 75(7) of the Treaty of Peace between the Allied and Associated Powers and Italy of 1947 provided that:

> The burden of identifying the property and of proving ownership shall rest on the claimant Government, and the burden of proving that the property was not removed by force or duress shall rest on the Italian Government.[21]

The latter part of the sentence creates a presumption of duress, thereby relieving the claimant Government from the otherwise heavy burden of

---

[17] Kazazi, *Burden of Proof*, pp. 265–6.
[18] Dissenting Opinion of Judge Badawi Pasha in the ICJ *Corfu Channel* Case, p. 59.
[19] Kazazi, *Burden of Proof*, p. 269.
[20] Franco–Italian Conciliation Commission, *French State Railways Claim*, 10 March 1953, *International Law Reports* 20 (1953), 481, 488–90.
[21] Treaty of Peace with Italy, Paris, 10 February 1947.

proving duress or force. For the purposes of Article 75 procedures, it was presumed that all removals during the war took place under duress or force, and it was incumbent on the respondent to prove that a particular item was *not* removed by force or duress.

The Conciliation Commissions were more reluctant with respect to presumptions or inferences proposed by the parties, as the decision of the Italian–United States Conciliation Commission in the *Greiner Claim* illustrates.[22] This case concerned the loss of four lots of paper, containing 344 reels and 20 bales, which were on board a ship that took refuge in the port of Naples. There was evidence that the Prefect of Naples seized at least 222 reels and all the bales of paper. In 1949, a claim for compensation was submitted to the Italian authorities. The Italian Government accepted responsibility as to the bales and 222 reels and made an offer of settlement in this respect. The claim for the remaining 122 reels was rejected because there was no evidence 'that the property was either requisitioned by the Italian authorities or that it was otherwise lost, since further inquiries [. . .] resulted in no trace of these goods'.[23] The claimant accepted the offer and reserved his rights to compensation for the unsettled portion of his claim.

The remaining part of the claim became the subject of proceedings before the Conciliation Commission. The US Government argued that, although there was no concrete proof, it could easily be presumed that the remaining part of the paper was either requisitioned by the Italian authorities or otherwise lost. This presumption would arise from a number of established facts, including the presence of the goods aboard the ship, the fact that they were discharged at Naples, the fact that it was Italy's entry into the war which finally frustrated efforts to obtain release of these goods and the fact that many such cargoes discharged and warehoused in Naples were afterwards bombed.[24]

The Conciliation Commission applied the *actori incumbit probatio* rule vigorously and declined to show any flexibility: '[t]he burden of proof lies with the claimant not only to establish the existence and ownership of property but also to prove that the property was lost or damaged as a result of the war'.[25]

---

[22] Italian–United States Conciliation Commission, *Greiner Claim*, 12 February 1959, 30 *International Law Reports* 454–6.
[23] Italian–United States Conciliation Commission, *Greiner Claim*, p. 454.
[24] Italian–United States Conciliation Commission, *Greiner Claim*, p. 455.
[25] Italian–United States Conciliation Commission, *Greiner Claim*, p. 455.

The Commission rejected the presumption invoked by the US agent on the following grounds:

> A presumption is an inference that an act has been committed or that a fact exists and it is based on circumstances that usually attend such an act or fact. In the case at bar there is no logical basis which would allow the Commission to infer that the remaining lots of paper in question were requisitioned or destroyed as a result of the war. Any number of things, including the possibilities suggested by the claimant, might have happened to the paper. However, the Commission is not in possession of any evidence which would justify the acceptance of the claimant's presumption or explanation *to the exclusion of any other possibility.* The fact that the Italian Government requisitioned a portion of the paper does not necessarily lead one to presume that it also requisitioned the remainder.[26]

The Arbitral Commission on Property, Rights and Interests in Germany

Similarly, presumptions and inferences played a limited role in the Arbitral Commission on Property, Rights and Interests in Germany, which was established after the Second World War pursuant to the Convention on the Settlement of Matters Arising out of the War and the Occupation.[27] For instance, in the *Levis and Levis Case*, the claimants, US nationals, filed a claim with the *Landgericht* for compensation in respect of household effects, which were confiscated during the war by German authorities while they were in transit in Trieste. In accordance with Article 4 of Chapter 5 of the Settlement Convention, Germany was obliged to pay compensation if the property to be restituted had, after 'identification in Germany' been destroyed or otherwise disposed of.

The claimants successfully established that the property was confiscated by the German authorities, but they were unable to prove that the property was shipped back to Germany and subsequently lost. The claimants argued that, because of the difficulty for them to furnish evidence to this effect, the burden of proof should shift and it should be incumbent upon the respondent to prove that the confiscated property

---

[26] Italian–United States Conciliation Commission, *Greiner Claim*, pp. 455–6 (emphasis added).

[27] For general information on the Arbitral Commission, see Karl Arndt, 'Arbitral Commission on Property, Rights and Interests in Germany', in Rudolf Bernhard (ed.), *Encyclopedia of Public International Law* (Amsterdam: North-Holland, 1981), Vol. I, pp. 9–13.

did not reach Germany.[28] The claimants supported their submissions *inter alia* by an official certificate showing that their property had already been declared forfeit to the German *Reich* by publication in the German Official Gazette in 1941. Consequently, they argued, it can be 'assumed with almost complete certainty that the *Reich* had taken over for itself the confiscated property, that is to say, that the property had actually been shipped to the present federal territory or to Berlin'.[29] Moreover, Germany, in its negotiations with Belgian and Dutch authorities, had admitted that 80 per cent of the Jewish furniture confiscated in those countries had been shipped to the territory of the present Federal Republic. The claimants further argued that

> since [they] had proved these typical occurrences by the submission of documents, the burden of proof in the individual cases now rested on the defendant, which had itself caused the difficulties concerning evidence. The complainants themselves were not in a position to prove that the furniture had been discovered in Karlsruhe, Dortmund, Cologne or elsewhere, but it could be assumed almost with certainty that the property removed from the complainants had reached Germany.[30]

The Commission, however, took a rigorous stance and dismissed the appeal, because the claimants had failed to prove that the confiscated property had been in Germany at a certain time and at a certain place. The Commission stated that although it is 'well aware of the difficulties of supplying proof encountered by victims of former National-Socialist persecution',[31] this awareness

> must not lead to a state of affairs where mere allegations submitted by a complainant [. . .] may be accepted as *prima facie* evidence. A reversal of the burden of proof – as suggested by the complainants – could be considered only if it had been sufficiently shown that the defendant held documents of evidential value which it refused to submit.[32]

---

[28] Arbitral Commission on Property, Rights and Interests in Germany (Third Chamber), *Levis and Levis* v. *Federal Republic of Germany (Merits)*, 9 June 1959, 28 *International Law Reports* 518–9.

[29] Arbitral Commission on Property, Rights and Interests in Germany (Third Chamber), *Levis and Levis* v. *Federal Republic of Germany (Merits)*, p. 521.

[30] Arbitral Commission on Property, Rights and Interests in Germany (Third Chamber), *Levis and Levis* v. *Federal Republic of Germany (Merits)*, p. 521.

[31] Arbitral Commission on Property, Rights and Interests in Germany (Third Chamber), *Levis and Levis* v. *Federal Republic of Germany (Merits)*, p. 523.

[32] Arbitral Commission on Property, Rights and Interests in Germany (Third Chamber), *Levis and Levis* v. *Federal Republic of Germany (Merits)*, p. 523.

The Iran–US Claims Tribunal

A last – and perhaps the most regrettable – example of reluctance to draw reasonable inferences is found in the practice of the Iran–US Claims Tribunal.[33] Some 45,000 American expatriates working in Iran had left the country over a period of four months. The record was replete with evidence of threats, attacks, bombings and virtually every form of overt assault on the persons and property of Americans in Iran during that period. Some 1,500 American expatriates filed a claim with the Tribunal based on wrongful expulsion.[34] The Iran–US Claims Tribunal declined to rely on inferences and imposed stringent requirements of individual proof of causation and attribution that in practice left very few of these claimants with an effective remedy.

In *Alfred L. W. Short* v. *The Islamic Republic of Iran*, the claimant sought compensation for loss of employment income, benefits and personal property allegedly resulting from Iran's wrongful acts, which compelled him to leave the country.[35] The Tribunal recognised that there was a strong anti-American sentiment, which gave to Americans present in Iran reason to believe that their lives were in danger, and accepted the notion of constructive expulsion.[36] It nevertheless refused 'to assume that all the departures of all aliens of a certain nationality from a country, during a certain period of political turmoil, would be attributable to the State, unless the State is able to demonstrate the contrary, would contradict the principles and rules of the international responsibility of States'.[37] Consequently, the Tribunal dismissed the claim for failure to prove that the acts, which motivated the claimant's departure from Iran, were attributable to the Iranian Government.

Judge Charles Brower dissented. He considered it reasonable to conclude that there was a cause and effect relationship between the successive statements by the leadership of the Revolution and the events that befell Americans in that country from the beginning of

---

[33] For an additional example in which the Iran–US Claims Tribunal declined to rely on an inference, see Iran–US Claims Tribunal, *George Edwards* v. *The Government of the Islamic Republic of Iran, et al.*, Award No. 451–251–2, 5 December 1989, para. 12, reprinted in 23 *Iran–US Claims Tribunal Reports* 290, 294.

[34] Brower, 'Lessons from the Iran–US Claims Tribunal', 55.

[35] Iran–US Claims Tribunal, *Alfred L. W. Short* v. *The Islamic Republic of Iran*, Award 312–11135–3, 14 July 1987, para. 1, reprinted in 16 *Iran–US Claims Tribunal Reports* 76.

[36] Iran–US Claims Tribunal, *Alfred L. W. Short* v. *The Islamic Republic of Iran*, para. 31

[37] Iran–US Claims Tribunal, *Alfred L. W. Short* v. *The Islamic Republic of Iran*, para. 30.

November 1978.[38] Having accepted the legal validity of the concept of constructive expulsion, in his view, the Tribunal should 'treat this Case on those terms and cannot properly fault Claimant for failing to prove an allegation he never made. It is inherent in a constructive mass expulsion that the acts effectuating it will be, in a high degree, general, unspecific, unfocused and indirect'.[39] Judge Brower concluded that:

> all of the evidence before us suggests that, at least from 1 February 1979, the day the Ayatollah returned triumphantly to Iran and announced his intention to 'appoint a government' and the imperative to see 'all foreigners [. . .] out of the country', the departure of any American then still in Iran was very likely due to the applied anti-Americanism of the Ayatollah and his followers. [. . .] The appropriate way for the Tribunal to approach this Case (and others like it) would be to presume that any American claimant here alleging that he was wrongfully expelled by Iran who departed Iran after 1 February 1979 did so because of the aforementioned acts and omissions of Ayatollah Khomeini, his supporters and followers. In order to leave it open to the Tribunal to find in a given case that the departure in question was due to other factors, and thus rule in favor of the Respondent, such presumption should be rebuttable.[40]

The Tribunal did not follow this view and, as Caron notes, instead adopted 'requirements of proof that denied the realities outlined by Brower and ultimately denied relief to virtually all claimants'.[41] After ten years of the Tribunal's existence, only one claimant was ever reimbursed for wrongful expulsion.[42]

---

[38] Iran–US Claims Tribunal, *Alfred L. W. Short v. The Islamic Republic of Iran*, Dissenting Opinion of Judge Brower, para. 13, reprinted in 16 *Iran–US Claims Tribunal Reports* 86.

[39] Iran–US Claims Tribunal, *Alfred L. W. Short v. The Islamic Republic of Iran*, Dissenting Opinion of Judge Brower, para. 15.

[40] Iran–US Claims Tribunal, *Alfred L. W. Short v. The Islamic Republic of Iran*, Dissenting Opinion of Judge Brower, para. 31–32. See also Brower, 'Lessons from the Iran–US Claims Tribunal', 54–5.

[41] David D. Caron, 'The UNCC and the Search for Practical Justice', in Richard B. Lillich, *The United Nations Compensation Commission – Thirteenth Sokol Colloquium* (Irvington, NY: Transnational, 1995), 374.

[42] According to Brower, this was a case 'where someone actually was fetched by an identifiable revolution guard and with force of arms was marched to a certain location and then taken out the country'. See Brower, 'Lessons from the Iran–US Claims Tribunal', 55; Carmel Whelton, 'The United Nations Compensation Commission and International Claims Law: A Fresh Approach', *Ottawa Law Review* 25 (1993) 607, 619. Eventually, the two governments settled all of these claims by a lump-sum settlement. The claims have been processed by the US Foreign Claims Settlement Commission.

This attitude marks a sharp contrast with the flexible approach taken by the Iran–US Claims Tribunal in other cases. A good example thereof is the *Daley Case*. The claimants, Mr and Mrs Daley, were seeking compensation for several items of jewellery, gold coins, bank notes and a Rolex watch. The Tribunal rightly started by stating that the claimants 'must bear the burden of proving possession, expropriation and value of the items for which they now seek compensation'.[43] Since the claimants were unable to establish possession of the cash, gold coins and jewellery, the Tribunal rejected the claims for all these items.

As to the Rolex watch, however, the Tribunal made an exception and took a radically different approach. Although this part of the claim was not supported by evidence either, the Tribunal accepted it on the basis of a number of inferences:

> The Tribunal is satisfied that there is sufficient evidence to make a judgment on the possession of Mr. Daley's watch. A specific brand, Rolex, is mentioned and the Tribunal finds that it is probable that Mr. Daley, like the majority of business people, would possess and wear a watch in the normal course of events, as he stated in evidence that he was in the habit of doing. In addition, the description is sufficient to determine that the value he places on the watch, US $800, appears entirely reasonable.[44]

This reasoning is remarkable, particularly since the claimants had only proven one tenth of their claim, casting doubts on the veracity of the claimants.[45] Based on a vague and general presumption – business people are presumed to wear watches – the Tribunal found it probable that Mr Daley was no exception. It accepted the uncorroborated statements of the claimant that he owned a watch and that this watch was seized. Moreover, the Tribunal accepted that the watch was a Rolex and agreed to the value suggested by Mr. Daley. The contrast with the Tribunal's attitude in the above-mentioned expulsion cases could hardly be more marked. Kazazi explains that 'perhaps humanitarian concerns led the arbitrators, before whom Mr Daley appeared at the Hearing of the case, and who were accustomed to issuing multi-million dollar awards in corporate claims before the Tribunal, to award to the claimants compensation for a small portion of their claims'.[46]

---

[43] Iran–US Claims Tribunal, *Leonard and Mavis Daley*, Award No. 360–10514–1, 20 April 1988, para. 30, reprinted in 18 *Iran–US Claims Tribunal Reports* 232.
[44] Iran–US Claims Tribunal, *Leonard and Mavis Daley*, para. 32
[45] Kazazi, *Burden of Proof*, p. 272.   [46] Kazazi, *Burden of Proof*, p. 272.

Present-day mass claims practice

The United Nations Compensation Commission

Because of the enormous number of claims and the difficulties that claimants faced to produce complete evidence, presumptions and inferences played an important role in the UNCC. Numerous presumptions and inferences can be found in the Commissioners' Reports.

Losses could only be compensated by the UNCC when they resulted from invasion and occupation of Kuwait.[47] In an effort to simplify the evaluation of the causality element, the Governing Council defined five types of situations, which, if present in a particular claim, establish the required causal link:[48] (1) military operations or threat of military action by either side during the period from 2 August 1990 (the date of the invasion) to 2 March 1991 (the date of resolution 686, which marked the end of hostilities); (2) departure from or inability to leave Iraq or Kuwait, or a decision not to return, during that period; (3) actions by officials, employees or agents of the Government of Iraq or its controlled entities during that period in connection with the invasion or occupation; (4) the breakdown of civil order in Kuwait or Iraq during that period; or (5) hostage taking or illegal detention. If a causal link is shown between the claimed loss and one or more of these activities or events, the loss is considered to be a result of Iraq's invasion and occupation of Kuwait.[49]

The inclusion of departures from Iraq or Kuwait in this list is especially noteworthy. In sharp contrast with the attitude of the Iran–US Claims Tribunal, for instance, the UNCC Rules presume that any departures from Iraq or Kuwait during the relevant time period were caused by the Iraqi aggression and/or occupation of Kuwait.[50] Consequently, Article 35 of the UNCC Rules provides that simple documentation of the fact and date of departure is sufficient to be eligible for compensation.[51] Once it is

---

[47] See Norbert Wühler, 'Causation and Directness of Loss as Elements of Compensability Before the United Nations Compensation Commission', in Richard B. Lillich, *The United Nations Compensation Commission – Thirteenth Sokol Colloquium* (Irvington, NY: Transnational, 1995), 213.

[48] UNCC Governing Council, Decision No. 1, para. 18. See also Wühler, 'Causation and Directness', 212.

[49] Wühler, 'Causation and Directness', 212–3.

[50] John R. Crook, 'The United Nations Compensation Commission – A New Structure to Enforce State Responsibility', *American Journal of International Law* 87 (1993), 144, 148.

[51] UNCC, Provisional Rules, Art. 35 (2)(a).

established that the claimant departed from Kuwait or Iraq during the relevant time period, Iraq is presumed to be liable for any departure-related losses the claimant incurred.

Taking the reasoning one step further, the UNCC Commissioners sometimes relied on presumptions and inferences to determine whether a claimed loss could be attributed to any of the five above-mentioned liability categories. In personal injury or death claims, for instance, the causal link could be inferred from the nature of the injury.[52] For claims involving gunshots or explosion wounds, the Commissioners required no explicit evidence of a causal link and simply presumed that the gunshot or explosion was related to military operations and therefore fell under the first liability category. Likewise, for some claims, the causal link could be inferred from the cause of death, e.g. torture or execution.

In other cases, the Commissioners concluded that a statement by the claimant mentioning or implying a causal link created 'a presumption that the injury may be attributed to Iraq'.[53] In a slightly bizarre twist, the Commissioners added that 'this presumption is rebuttable by information in the file'.[54] In other words, the Commissioners created a presumption in favour of claimants, which could be rebutted by these same claimants. In fact, it makes more sense to think of this rule as a presumption based upon the presence of certain indicia in the claim file. The presumption arises whenever a number of elements are present in the claim file. If these indicia are not present or if they are contradicted by other information, the presumption does not arise.

For instance, for claims for personal injury or death caused by road traffic accidents, all accidents were presumed to fall under causality categories (1), (3) or (5) when the claim mentioned that it involved an Iraqi military vehicle.[55] Likewise, a car accident was presumed to be a consequence of the 'breakdown of civil order' (causality category 4)[56] when the claim mentioned that it occurred on the first day of or on the days immediately following the invasion of Kuwait. On the other hand, the farther the place of the accident from the claimant's point of departure from Iraq or Kuwait, the more unlikely it was that the accident could be linked to the invasion and occupation under the causality category (2).[57] If a particular traffic accident presents none of these indicia, no presumption

---

[52] UNCC, Report "B" claims, p. 24; UNCC, Report "C" claims, 1st inst., p. 110.
[53] UNCC, Report "C" claims, 1st inst., p. 110.
[54] UNCC, Report "C" claims, 1st inst., p. 110.   [55] UNCC, Report "B" claims, p. 24–5.
[56] UNCC, Report "B" claims, p. 25.   [57] UNCC, Report "B" claims, p. 25.

arises and the accident is not considered directly linked to the invasion and occupation of Kuwait.

The Second Claims Resolution Process for Dormant Accounts (CRT-II)

While the first Claims Resolution Process for Dormant Accounts received nearly 10,000 claims, the second CRT received over 32,000 claims. Because of the significantly larger number of claims, Special Masters Volcker and Bradfield, appointed by New York judge Korman to oversee the distribution of the settlement fund, wanted to accelerate the resolution of claims while maintaining the full benefits of due process of law.[58]

Under its new approach, the burden of proof remained (at least in principle) upon the claimant and the applicable standard of evidence remained one of plausibility.[59] New in CRT-II, however, is the introduction of a number of presumptions, designed to further simplify the burden of proof in specific categories of claims. This includes, for instance, a presumption that owners of a joint account have equal shares.[60] When the specific value of an account was unknown, Article 35 presumed that its value was the average value of that type of account.

A more controversial presumption concerns a specific category of bank accounts, so-called 'accounts closed unknown by whom'. These are accounts that have been closed, but for which it cannot be ascertained who closed them and who received the proceeds. Obviously, a claimant would not be entitled to an award if the account was paid to the original account holder or to their heirs. However, if the Swiss bank in question destroyed or failed to maintain the account records, it is particularly difficult for the claimant to prove that they have *not* received the proceeds.

The CRT-II rules deal with this problem by defining a number of situations in which it is presumed that the original account holder or their heirs did not receive the proceeds of the account. Some of these presumptions are hardly controversial. For instance, if the only surviving account owner was a child, it is reasonable to presume the child did not know of the account and has not received the proceeds. Others have given rise to controversy. Some have argued that by presuming that the proceeds went to the Nazis or to the Swiss banks in all of these

---

[58] See generally CRT-II, Introduction to the Claims Resolution Process, available at www.crt-ii.org/introduction.phtm (visited October 2007).
[59] CRT-II Rules of Procedure, Art. 17(1).   [60] CRT-II Rules of Procedure, Art. 25(1).

situations, CRT-II calls into question the findings of the Volcker report and effectively assumes 'that it was usual practice of the banks to transfer assets belonging to Jewish account owners to the Nazis or to pocket them themselves', a position apparently rejected by the Volcker Report.[61]

To justify the presumption, CRT-II relies on the same historical evidence developed by the Independent Committee of Eminent Persons. According to CRT-II, the ICEP investigation demonstrated that the funds of Nazi victims in Swiss banks were disposed of in various ways:

> In some cases, the account owners and/or their families withdrew and received the funds. In other cases, Nazi authorities coerced account owners to withdraw the balances in their Swiss accounts and transfer the proceeds to banks designated by the Nazi authorities, and the funds fell into Nazi hands. For other accounts, no transfers occurred, but account values were consumed by regular and special bank fees and charges, which resulted ultimately in closure without any payment to the account owners. In still other cases, particularly after a period of inactivity or dormancy, the proceeds were paid to bank profits.[62]

Since the Swiss banks went to considerable lengths to conceal information or destroy the relevant bank records, the CRT-II recognised that it could not determine with certainty who received the proceeds of the account. Under these circumstances, it drew 'an adverse inference against the banks where documentary evidence was destroyed or is not provided to assist the claims administrators'.[63] Such adverse inference is a well-known legal technique: unless the party can show a convincing reason for not producing essential evidence in their possession or control, they risk an adverse decision.[64]

[61] Hans Peter Born, 'Awarding the millions, eyes closed' (on file with the author). Similar criticism is found in Luzi Stamm, 'Amerika wo bleibt dein Rechtsstaat? Skandalöse Vorgänge beim Verteilen der Holocaust-Gelder', Schweizer Zeit Nr. 16, 28 June 2002, available at www.schweizerzeit.ch/1602/rechtsstaat.htm (visited October 2007). The Volcker Report established that: 'the auditors have reported no evidence of systematic destruction of records of victim accounts, organized discrimination against the accounts of victims of Nazi persecution, or concerted efforts to divert the funds of victims of Nazi persecution to improper purposes'. The report continues, however, that there is 'confirmed evidence of questionable and deceitful actions by some individual banks' (Volcker Report, p. 13).
[62] See for instance CRT-II, *Certified Award in re Account of Helene Rudnicki*, Claim Number 213215/JS, p. 3, available at www.crt-ii.org/_awards/index.phtm. (visited October 2007)
[63] CRT-II Rules of Procedure, Art. 28 (footnote 5).
[64] Sandifer, *Evidence Before International Tribunals*, p. 153. The use of this adverse inference in this case is nonetheless controversial. According to some, the banks were not legally required to keep account records for over five decades. For an overview of the problem, see the Volcker Report, Annex 7.

Moreover, according to CRT-II, the use of these presumptions is justified because of the extremely low likelihood that the account owner received the proceeds of the account. In the case of account holders who fled Germany, for instance, CRT-II is relying in part on research cataloguing more than forty different laws, acts and decrees used by the Nazi regime to confiscate Jewish assets abroad:

> These laws included, for example, increasingly stringent registration and repatriation requirements for assets held outside Germany and special confiscatory taxes for emigrants who wished to flee Germany. Until 1937, the laws generally did not explicitly target Jews, although in practice the laws were enforced more stringently against Jews. After 1937, however, the spoliation process became increasingly wholesale and systematic and Nazi expropriations of Jewish assets held in Swiss banks and elsewhere became widespread. A decree dated 26 April 1938 required Jews to register their assets, and subsequent to that date the Nazi regime began to enact legislation and orders to repatriate and confiscate foreign assets both for Jews who sought permission to flee the Reich and for those unable to flee.[65]

As a result of these laws, Jewish account holders who fled Germany in the relevant time period would have been unlikely to escape without their assets being confiscated. The Tribunal consequently considers it reasonable to presume in such cases that the proceeds were not paid to the account holder.

Some questions nevertheless remain. Article 28 (a), for instance, which presumed that the account owner did not receive the proceeds if the account was closed after the imposition of Swiss visa requirements, on 20 January 1939, and before the end of the War, may have been too broadly formulated. Indeed, its rationale was the '*low likelihood* that a non-Swiss Jew trying to enter Switzerland during this period would have succeeded'.[66] In fact, the historical research conducted by the Bergier Commission indicates that this rule on Swiss visa requirements was not applied if the applicant had a valid visa for another country, such as France or Italy.[67] Individuals in possession of such valid visas were granted transit via Switzerland. The possession of a visa for France or Italy would therefore 'clearly rebut the presumption'.[68] However, it would have been very unlikely that a claimant would present such

---

[65] See for instance CRT-II, *Certified Award in re Account of Helene Rudnicki*, p. 3, footnote 2.
[66] Beauchamp, 'The New Claims Resolution Tribunal', 1021, footnote 118 (emphasis added).
[67] Beauchamp, 'The New Claims Resolution Tribunal', 1021.
[68] Beauchamp, 'The New Claims Resolution Tribunal', 1021.

evidence and the CRT-II was not required to verify *proprio motu* whether the account holder had such a visa.

The Commission for Real Property Claims

The CRPC introduced a series of jurisdictional presumptions to facilitate the administration of evidence. It was presumed that claimants were refugees or displaced persons.[69] Only when there were clear indications to the contrary was the status of the claimant examined. It was also presumed that CRPC claimants were not in possession of the real property they claimed.[70]

Moreover, the CRPC used presumptions to deal with a complex and sensitive issue, i.e. the validity of wartime property transactions. Under the Dayton Agreements, 'the Commission shall not recognize as valid any illegal property transaction, including any transfer that was made under duress, in exchange for exit permission or similar documents, or that was otherwise in connection with ethnic cleansing'.[71] There was ample evidence that forced property transfers (often at gunpoint) had taken place throughout the country during the entire period of the war. The CRPC therefore confirmed property rights as of 1 April 1992, i.e. the commencement of hostilities, and obliged the competent administrative bodies to return decision holders into possession of these properties.[72] By doing so, the CRPC effectively presumed that there was no valid transfer of property rights during the entire war period.[73] Taking into account that the Commission was not set up to conduct oral hearings and that it would be impossible to establish duress only on the basis of written evidence, this presumption was the only effective way to deal with the reality of excessive war-time duress in property transactions.[74]

---

[69] CRPC, Book of Regulations on Real Property, Art. 12.

[70] CRPC, Book of Regulations on Real Property, Art. 11.

[71] Dayton Peace Agreement, Annex 7, Art. 7(3).

[72] CRPC, Book of Regulations on Real Property, Art. 62.

[73] The presumption could be rebutted only in specific circumstances through a special procedure before the national courts.

[74] Similar presumptions of duress were used in other contexts. The 1990 German Claims Law or *Vermögensgesetz*, for instance, which permits claims to be filed for property lost in the former territory of East Germany, presumes that sales by Jewish sellers from 1933 to 1945 are affected by duress unless the buyer proves that a fair market price was paid for the property. See also the Inter-Allied Declaration against Acts of Dispossession committed in Territories under Enemy Occupation of Control, London, 5 January 1943.

The IOM claims processes

The German Forced Labour Compensation Programme operated under the presumption that a category of claimants, i.e. former forced labourers from West European countries, were excluded from the compensation process. They were presumed not to meet the requirement of 'extremely harsh living conditions' and not to have been accommodated under 'conditions resembling imprisonment'. This presumption could be rebutted only by official documents proving that the accommodation in a camp effectively resembled imprisonment.[75]

The IOM Property Claims Commission also relied on presumptions to establish the 'essential, direct and harm-causing participation' of a German enterprise. Historical research had shown that some German enterprises had been significantly, pervasively and recurrently involved in the targeting, confiscation, use and retention of 'productive assets' – i.e. assets of a commercial or income-generating nature. According to the Commission, this research justified 'a presumption that in such areas and at such times, considering the nature of the property that was lost, the [claimed] loss occurred in connection with the essential, direct and harm-causing participation of a German enterprise'.[76] Even if the claimant did not document the participation of a German enterprise or was unable to identify a specific enterprise, the Commission recognised that German enterprises were active in the area where the property was lost and that there was a high probability that the German enterprises were involved.

Under the Holocaust Victim Assets Programme, members of Slave Labor Class I must have laboured for companies or entities that actually or allegedly deposited the revenues of proceeds of that labour with, or transacted such revenues or proceeds through, the Releasees.[77] Each of these elements was difficult to prove, since the economic history of the Holocaust remains incomplete. Nevertheless, historical research demonstrated the pervasiveness of slave labour across all of conquered Europe and the close financial relation between German slave-labour using entities and Swiss financial entities.[78] This information, together

---

[75] See Van der Auweraert, 'The Practicalities of Forced Labor Compensation', 305.

[76] Quoted from the standard text of the individual decisions of the IOM Property Claims Commission.

[77] Settlement Agreement, Section 8.2(c).

[78] See CRT-II, Plan of Allocation and Distribution, p. 143. See also at 147: 'This is not to suggest that the Swiss banks or other entities with which German entities transacted had knowledge that some of these funds may have been derived from the exploitation of slave labor, or that the Swiss entities necessarily were aware that their German depositors

with the difficulties for individual claimants to prove the financial relationship between the company for which they performed slave labour and the Swiss banks, permitted the Court to adopt a legal presumption that 'all former slaves for German entities should be presumed to be members' of Slave Labour Class I.[79]

Analysis: Justifying the use of presumptions and inferences

Presumptions and inferences are useful to reach a fair outcome when the production of other types of evidence is impossible or excessively difficult. Through a process of logic and reasoning, presumptions and inferences can make a claim sufficiently probable to arrive at a sound and fair legal conclusion.

The effect of presumptions and inferences, as explained above, is primarily on the allocation of the burden of evidence. By making the facts probable with the assistance of reasoning and logic, the party benefiting from the presumption is exonerated from proving the presumed fact and it is incumbent upon the other party to present counter-evidence rebutting the presumption. The justifications for the use of the presumptions and inferences should therefore be found within the framework developed in Chapter 6 with respect to the allocation of the burden of proof.

The three conventional criteria for the use of presumptions are probability, judicial convenience and public policy.[80] As the following review will demonstrate, these criteria correspond to the three rationales identified in Chapter 6 to justify departures from the general rule that the claimant should prove their entitlement to compensation or restitution.

Probability

Probability, as defined above,[81] is both the strongest and most common basis for presumptions and inferences.[82] Most presumptions are based

---

made use of slave labor. The available data [. . .] indicate simply that known slave labor-using companies or entities deposited the revenues or proceeds of that labor with, or transacted such revenues or proceeds through, Releasees [. . .]'.

[79] CRT-II, Plan of Allocation and Distribution, p. 147.

[80] Abraham and Robinson, 'Aggregative Valuation of Mass Tort Claims', 147. A more extensive review is found in Robinson, 'Multiple Causation', 731–2.

[81] It includes both 'unconditional' and 'conditional' probability. See the part on 'Justifying the exceptions to the general rule' in Chapter 6.

[82] Robinson, 'Multiple Causation', 732.

on the likely relation between the 'proved' and the 'presumed' fact. In the absence of evidence to the contrary, this likelihood is sufficient for the law to recognise the relationship. Probability-based presumptions and inferences are of singular importance if evidence is scarce or non-existent. They are therefore of critical importance in most mass claims situations.

The role of probability is most clearly illustrated by the different attitude taken by the UNCC and the Iran–US Claims Tribunal with respect to departure-related losses. Although the situation in Iran and in Kuwait was very different,[83] there was in both cases reliable statistical information showing that the overwhelming majority of expatriates left their respective countries of residence within a well-defined time frame. This time frame coincided, in the case of Iran, with the campaign of violence against and harassment of Americans and, in the case of Iraq, with the invasion and occupation of Kuwait. The fact that most expatriates left their country of residence at the time that these events took place made a causal relationship between both facts probable. The UNCC recognised this relationship, the Iran–US Claims Tribunal did not. By failing to recognise the probability factor, the latter was incapable of guaranteeing timely and adequate remedies to most individual departees. By introducing a simple – though entirely reasonable – presumption based on the probability of a causal relationship, the UNCC, on the other hand, succeeded in offering a measure of justice to over 900,000 individuals.

If presumptions and inferences are motivated by the probability of the presumed fact, they have to be based upon clear and objectively verifiable indicia that usually attend the occurrence of this fact. Put differently, the adjudicator must be able to infer a conclusion from elements present in the claim. These indicia must be sufficiently strong, clear and concordant, leading to a single unequivocal conclusion. If this is the case, using a presumption or inference will maximise accuracy in decision making. Failing to use a presumption might result in increased error costs. Indeed, if evidence is scarce or inexistent and if claimants are refused the benefit of a probability-based presumption, false negatives will be generated.

---

[83] Moreover, the circumstances under which both institutions arose were radically different. This may explain to some extent why they took radically different approaches to similar issues. See Brower, 'Lessons from the Iran–US Claims Tribunal', 51–2.

Probability-based presumptions and inferences should be formulated in precise and narrow terms. The level of precision will determine their impact upon the overall accuracy of the decisions. If presumptions are too vaguely or too broadly construed, the result might be an increase in false positives.

This conclusion, finally, underscores the importance of research – both historical and statistical data – in a mass claims context. If unbiased and undisputed research succeeds in establishing a clear and precise picture of the events that generated the claims process, it will provide a valuable tool, based upon which the probability of certain facts in individual claims can be assessed. It will create an evidentiary platform that enables the designers of the mass claims process to elaborate and formulate precise and detailed legal presumptions and will allow the adjudicator to develop sound and legitimate inferences.

Practical convenience

A second common justification for presumptions and inferences is practical convenience.[84] The convenience rationale supports 'placing the burden on the cheapest information-provider'.[85] It largely corresponds to the second rationale, that justifies shifting the burden of proof, i.e. the parties' relative cost of presenting evidence.

This rationale will be sufficient to shift the burden of proof only in specific mass claims situations, in particular when the respondent has superior access to the relevant information and evidence. The legal presumption created by Article 75(7) of the Treaty of Peace between the Allied and Associated Powers and Italy of 1947 could be considered as partly relying on this rationale. There are, however, no clear examples of presumptions and inferences based on this rationale in modern mass claims practice.

Public policy

Presumptions and inferences, finally, are often motivated by public policy considerations.[86] In present day mass claims practice, presumptions are often inspired by the socio-political objectives of the claims process. As explained in Chapter 6, the social costs associated with erroneous decisions justify in very specific cases a shift in the burden of proof.

---

[84] Robinson, 'Multiple Causation', 733.   [85] Robinson, 'Multiple Causation', 733.
[86] Robinson, 'Multiple Causation', 735.

The CRPC's presumption that all wartime property transactions were affected by duress, for instance, is arguably based on social policy considerations. Forced property transactions had been part and parcel of the various ethnic-cleansing campaigns that ravaged Bosnia from 1992 to 1995. Entire communities had been forced to abandon their homes and, in exchange for an exit permit or a safe departure, to sign contracts giving up their property rights. The property records had been removed, destroyed or falsified in an effort to prevent these owners from ever returning or reclaiming their homes. The international community's post-war policy, as laid down in the Dayton Peace Agreement, was aimed at reversing the consequences of ethnic cleansing and at restoring a multi-ethnic Bosnia. In order to do so, it was imperative for the CRPC to unravel the chain of transactions that took place during the war. Knowing how difficult it would be for individuals to prove the presence of duress or force in individual transactions, the CRPC had to relieve victims of ethnic cleansing from this heavy evidentiary burden in order to meet the mandate it had been entrusted with by the international community and the parties to the Dayton Peace Agreement. Consequently, all wartime transactions were considered to have been concluded under duress or force.

Another example is the UNCC's presumption that all departures in the relevant time period were triggered by the invasion and occupation of Kuwait. This presumption is partly explained by the probability that there was such causal link in individual cases. Partly, however, it is also based on public policy considerations. Because of the general scarcity of evidence and the chaotic circumstances in which the expatriate community left Iraq and Kuwait, the presumption was considered a 'reasonable answer to problems of proof that would otherwise stand in the way of innocent victims of the war' and was 'reasonably calculated to do at least partial rough justice in an unprecedented number of claims in a relatively quick way'.[87] It reflected the international community's determination to grant relief to the hundreds of thousands of individuals who left the country under threatening and dangerous circumstances *despite* the lack of evidence in individual cases. Since Iraq's unlawful invasion and occupation of Kuwait had generated the evidentiary problems, placing the burden of proof on this point with the individual claimants would have frustrated the societal objectives of the claims process.

---

[87] Markham Ball, 'The Iraq Claims Process – A Progress Report', *Journal of International Arbitration* 9(1) (1992) 37, 44.

Many presumptions and inferences are at least partly motivated by social policy considerations. Such presumptions are not explained by the desire to maximise outcome accuracy; rather, they are aimed at coping with uncertainty in the way that the community finds most desirable. If the truth is unknown and probability does not allow to 'infer the unknown from the known', policy considerations – fairness, deterrence or compensation – may affect the burden of proof.

However, presumptions and inferences motivated by policy considerations should be formulated in sufficiently precise and detailed terms. The level of precision will determine their acceptance by the community and their aptness to reach the policy objectives.

PART III

Mass claims resolution techniques

A mass claims process, as defined in the introductory part, must be capable of resolving a large number of claims in an expeditious and fair manner, and at a minimal transaction cost. Recently established mass claims processes have experimented with new decision-making techniques to further these goals. The most important of these techniques are: common issue determination and precedent-setting procedures, computerised data matching, statistical sampling and regression analysis. This part examines how these techniques have been used in mass claims practice and discusses their impact upon the fundamental values of efficiency, accuracy, consistency and, to a lesser extent, party participation.

9

Precedent setting and common issue determination

Introduction

The notion of mass claims, as defined in the introductory part, requires common legal and factual issues, which allow for rationalising the decision making: because the issues are common to a large number of claims, it is efficient to resolve them on a 'wholesale' basis rather than on a 'retail' basis.[1] A strict claim-by-claim approach would involve examining these issues time and again, in each individual claim, thereby increasing the risk of inconsistencies and inequalities and, quite simply, wasting efforts and resources.

Mass claims bodies therefore sometimes resolve common issues by reviewing a limited number of test cases that are considered representative of the claims population. On the basis of these test claims, the adjudicator may establish 'precedents': actual decisions on which he will rely and to which he will refer when deciding the remainder of the claims. Alternatively, the adjudicator may review the test cases to develop written guidelines, criteria or standards capable of resolving the entire category of similar claims. The first type of process is hereinafter referred to as 'precedent setting' or 'precedent based'; the second technique concerns 'the advance determination of common issues' or simply 'common issue determination'.

In both cases, the basic idea is to first resolve the issues that are common to a particular category of claims and that are decisive for the outcomes of the claims. Once these issues are resolved, all claims belonging to the specific category are adjudicated by applying the principles that emerge from the review of the test claims. This is an important difference with the statistical methodologies – sampling and regression analysis – analysed in later chapters: in a procedure relying on precedent and advance determination of common issues, claims are still processed on an individual basis. Only the common issues are resolved on a wholesale basis.

---

[1] See also Veijo Heiskanen, 'Speeding the Resolution of Mass Claims', 80.

Concepts

A 'precedent' has been defined as 'an adjudged case or decision of a court, considered as furnishing an example or authority for an identical or similar case afterwards arising or a similar question of law'.[2] The term also refers to a rule of law established for the first time by a court for a particular type of case and thereafter referred to in deciding similar cases. As such, the term refers to the policy of '*stare decisis et non quieta movere*' that courts in common law countries use in order not to unsettle what already has been established. Once a court has laid down a principle of law as applicable to a certain state of facts, it will apply this principle to all future cases in which the facts are substantially the same, whether the parties are the same or not. Outside the common law world, precedents merely have the value of an example, the authority of which largely depends on the hierarchical status of the court in which the precedent was adopted.[3]

The process of common issue determination has the same intent and the same practical benefits as the reliance on precedents. Its mechanics are however different and consist of three steps.[4] Firstly, the adjudicator specifies the issues that are generic or common to a large number of cases. He then examines those issues in a representative sample (so-called 'test claims'). Finally, the results of the review are captured in the form of written criteria or guidelines and subsequently applied to all cases.

Both techniques are based on a review of test cases. In a system of precedent, the test cases are immediately and fully adjudicated and the results of the sample review are extrapolated by reference to the actual decisions made on the test claims. In the case of common issue determination, the test claims are not immediately decided. The extrapolation is achieved by issuing written rules for the processing of all similar claims. In brief, common issue determination is a rules-based approach, while a system of precedent is based on actual decisions.[5] While common issue determination enables the decision-making body to issue decisions

[2] Garner, *Black's Law Dictionary*, p. 1176. See also the definition of 'précédent jurisprudentiel' in Jean Salmon (ed.), *Dictionnaire de droit international public* (Bruxelles: Bruylant, 2001), p. 866.

[3] Salmon, *Dictionnaire de droit international public*, p. 1051.

[4] See the description of common issue extrapolation by McGovern, 'The Intellectual Heritage', 194.

[5] See the comparison between adherence to precedent and conformity to rules in Bayles, *Procedural Justice*, p. 104.

on all similar claims simultaneously, precedent-setting necessarily requires two subsequent stages.[6]

National mass claims practice

National legal systems have made use of both precedent-setting techniques and common issue determination when confronted with mass claims.

Canada's early experience with class actions provides an example of precedent-setting techniques. In the early eighties, the Superior Court of Québec and the Federal Court of Canada received some 6,000 individual lawsuits for material and health damages caused by ureaformaldehyde foam insulation (MIUF), the use of which had been subsidised for house insulation. To process this caseload, plaintiffs and defendants selected six representative cases. The Superior Court delivered precedent-setting judgements in these test cases. These judicial precedents resolved the main legal and factual issues arising from the claims and could be applied thereafter to the remaining cases.[7]

In the United States, the asbestos class action litigation used also common issue determination, when the Texas District Court isolated a number of issues, such as product defect and punitive damages, which were common to all pending cases. These issues were submitted to a jury, decided in favour of the plaintiffs and the results were subsequently applied to the remaining claims.[8]

International litigation

The notion of precedent that the international judicial order embraced is less technical and less forceful than the *stare decisis* rule of the common law system. The binding force of precedent is not part of the international legal order.[9] This does not imply that an argument based on precedent is devoid of all value in the international judicial order; rather, it means that the force of a precedent is persuasive rather than binding.

---

[6] Bayles, *Procedural Justice*, p. 88.
[7] Claude Masse, 'La compensation des victimes de désastres collectifs au Québec', *Windsor Yearbook of Access to Justice* 9 (1989), 3, 10.
[8] *Cimino* v. *Raymark Industries, Inc.*, 751 F.Supp. 649, at 653 (E.D.Tex., 1990). See also McGovern, 'The Intellectual Heritage', 194. In a subsequent phase, the court applied statistical methodologies. See the part on 'asbestos litigation' in Chapter 11.
[9] See for instance ICTY, *Kupreskic et al.*, Case No. IT-95–16-T, 14 January 2000, para. 540.

The International Court of Justice, for instance, like its predecessor the Permanent Court of International Justice, is not bound by judicial precedents, at least not in the formal legal sense. The Statute of the ICJ reveals a certain tension in this regard. On the one hand, Article 38(1)(d) of the Statute refers to judicial decisions as a subsidiary means to determine rules of law. On the other, Article 59 of the Statute provides that a decision of the Court has no binding force except between the parties and in respect of that particular case and leaves no scope for a *stare decisis* policy in the international judicial order. It prevents the Court from deciding 'a case in a certain way *solely because* a previous case has been decided in that way'.[10]

Nevertheless, in practice, the ICJ has occasionally relied upon or cited judicial precedents. It most often refers to its own jurisprudence, rarely to decisions of arbitral tribunals or other courts.[11] Even though the Court does not consider itself bound by previous decisions (at least not in the formal sense), the judges try to take them fully into account in arriving at subsequent decisions. As Sir Gerald Fitzmaurice concludes, it is 'mandatory for [the Court] to apply judicial decisions in the sense of employing them as part of the process whereby it arrives at its legal conclusions in the case'.[12] In short, although there is no theory of binding precedent in international law, only in very exceptional circumstances will the Court depart from principles laid down in its jurisprudence.[13]

The practice of other permanent international courts has been diverse. The European Court of Human Rights, for instance, refers only occasionally to judicial precedents.[14] International arbitral tribunals frequently refer to ICJ decisions, less so to the decisions of other courts.[15]

---

[10] Sir Gerald Fitzmaurice, *The Law and Procedure of the International Court of Justice* (Cambridge: Grotius, 1986), Vol. II, p. 584.

[11] In the *Nottebohm case*, the ICJ referred for instance to the *Alabama* case (Preliminary Objection, Judgment of 18 November 1953, *ICJ Reports* 1953, 111, 119). In the *Land, Island and Maritime Frontier Dispute (El Salvador/Honduras: Nicaragua intervening)*, the Court referred to a 1917 judgment of the Central American Court of Justice (Judgment of 11 September 1992, *ICJ Reports* 1992, 351, 604). In the *Case Concerning Maritime Delimitation in the Area between Greenland and Jan Mayen (Denmark v. Norway)*, finally, the Court made reference to a 1977 Anglo-French Arbitral Award (Judgment of 14 June 1993, *ICJ Reports* 1993, 38, 58).

[12] Fitzmaurice, *The Law and Procedure of the ICJ*, p. 584.

[13] See also the Arbitral Tribunal's Award in the *Larsen – Hawaiian Kingdom Arbitration*, 5 February 2001, *International Law Reports* 119 (2001), 566, para. 11.21.

[14] For a list, see Nathan Miller, 'An International Jurisprudence? The Operation of 'Precedent' Across International Tribunals', *Leiden Journal of International Law* 15 (2002), 3, 503.

[15] For an example, see the *Larsen–Hawaiian Kingdom Arbitration*.

The International Criminal Tribunal for the former Yugoslavia, though it regularly cites previous decisions, has explicitly rejected the doctrine of binding precedent in international criminal courts.[16]

Common issue determination is not practiced in classic international litigation. Few international courts have had to deal with a substantial docket filled with similar cases, all raising common issues and all arising simultaneously. On the contrary, most international courts tend to have a small and diverse docket. Consequently, they have had little or no incentive to develop a system of common issue determination.

International mass claims processes

Precedent-based procedures and common issue determination have played a prominent role in past and present-day mass claims commissions. This section selects a few examples and provides a short overview of how these techniques were employed.

The United States–German Mixed Claims Commission

An early example of common issue determination is given by the US–German Mixed Claims Commission[17] that disposed after the First World War of 20,433 claims and rendered 7,025 decisions, awarding a total amount of over US $181 million.[18] From the outset, the Commission sought efficient ways to process its considerable caseload. One of these methodologies was the adoption of so-called 'administrative decisions', in which the Commission announced principles and rules applicable to a group of cases.[19] The administrative decisions were based on an analysis of the various claims and covered a number of generic issues common to all claims in a certain group, including for instance the definition of the terms used in the claims settlement instrument, the applicable law and questions of nationality and causation, the quantum of damages and awarding of interest and the principles for handling estate claims.[20]

---

[16] See ICTY, *Kupreskic et al.*, para. 540.

[17] The US-German Mixed Claims Commission was established pursuant to an Agreement concluded on 10 August 1922 and extended by the Agreement of 31 December 1928.

[18] For an introduction to the Commission, see the historical note at 7 *UN Reports of International Arbitral Awards* 5.

[19] Mixed Claims Commission, United States and Germany, Rules of Procedure, Art. VIII (c) reprinted in 8 *UN Reports of International Arbitral Awards* 469, 473.

[20] See for instance Mixed Claims Commission, United States and Germany, Administrative Dec. No. 1, 1 November 1923 (7 *UN Reports of International Arbitral Awards* 21),

This procedural technique is said to have contributed significantly to the efficiency of the Commission.[21] Subsequent claims commissions followed its practice. For instance, the Tripartite Claims Commission between the United States, Austria and Hungary[22] also used administrative decisions to resolve issues common to many claims.[23]

The United Nations Compensation Commission

The UNCC relied extensively upon common issue determination, precedent-based procedures or a combination of both techniques.[24] The legal basis for this approach was apparently Art. 38 (a) of the UNCC Provisional Rules, which provided that, in so far as possible, claims with significant common legal and factual issues had to be processed together.[25]

Many general issues arising from particular groups of claims were resolved through decisions issued by the UNCC Governing Council.[26] Based upon an initial review of a group of claims conducted by the secretariat, the Governing Council laid out substantive criteria and principles for the resolution of issues common to large groups of claims,

---

Administrative Dec. No. 2, 1 November 1923 (7 *UN Reports of International Arbitral Awards* 23), and Administrative Dec. No. 3, 11 December 1923 (7 *UN Reports of International Arbitral Awards* 64).

[21] David J. Bederman, 'Historic Analogues of the UN Compensation Commission', in Richard B. Lillich, *The United Nations Compensation Commission – Thirteenth Sokol Colloquium* (Irvington, NY: Transnational, 1995), 257, 273.

[22] Agreement between the United States and Austria and Hungary for the determination of the amounts to be paid by Austria and by Hungary in satisfaction of their obligations under the Treaties concluded by the United States with Austria on 24 August 1921, and With Hungary on 29 August 1921, signed 26 November, 1924, reprinted in 6 *UN Reports of International Arbitral Awards* 199. The Commission issued only a small amount of decisions (see 6 *UN Reports of International Arbitral Awards* 195).

[23] See for instance Claims Commissioner (Parker) appointed under Special Agreement of 26 November 1924 between the United States, Austria, Hungary, Administrative Dec. No. 1, 25 May 1927, 6 *UN Reports of International Arbitral Awards* 203, and Administrative Dec. No. 2, 25 May 1927, 6 *UN Reports of International Arbitral Awards* 212.

[24] Norbert Wühler, 'A New Contribution', 264.

[25] See also Section 19.5 of UNMIK Regulation No. 2000/60.

[26] Examples are the UNCC Governing Council Decision No. 3 on Personal Injury and Mental Pain and Anguish, 23 October 1991, UN Doc. S/AC.26/1991/3, *International Legal Materials* 31 (1992), 1028; Decision No. 4 on Business Losses of Individuals and Decision, 23 October 1991, UN Doc. S/AC.26/1991/4, *International Legal Materials* 31 (1992), 1030; Decision No. 11 on the Eligibility for Compensation of Members of the Allied Coalition Armed Forces, 26 June 1992, UN Doc. S/AC.26/1992/11, *International Legal Materials* 31 (1992), 1067. On the authority of the Governing Council to decide common issues, see Report of the Secretary-General of 2 May 1991, para. 10.

with a view to ensuring consistency and efficiency in the Commissioners' review of the claims.

The Commissioners themselves also determined common issues while processing claims for mental pain and anguish resulting from hostage-taking, illegal detention or forced hiding (so-called "C1-MPA claims").[27] The Panel examined sample claims from each of the three "C1-MPA" loss categories. On the basis of the review of these sample claims, the Panel adopted criteria and guidelines, which were then applied to the remaining claims by the Secretariat. The results were verified and approved by the Panel.

The UNCC also relied on precedent setting. For claims in a certain category that raised similar legal and factual issues, the Commissioners set relevant precedents during the review of the first instalment. When reviewing subsequent instalments, the Panels simply applied these precedents, thereby 'limiting their work to the verification and valuation of the claims and the calculation of any allowable compensation'.[28]

Precedent-setting procedures were of particular importance in claims Category "C", which covered a wide range of diverse loss types and included a total of approximately 420,000 individual claims. In addition, the Central Bank of the Government of Egypt submitted a consolidated Category "C" claim comprising 1,240,000 individual claims. In a first 'precedent' phase, the evaluation and compensation criteria for each of the loss elements claimed in Category "C" were developed.[29] In the first instalment, each claim was to be analysed as a 'sample' of the many other claims that presented similar factual and legal issues. Or, as one commentator wrote, each of the claims included in the first instalments 'must, first and foremost, be regarded as a tool to help draw general "brightline" criteria, whether they be related to issues of causation, evidence, or otherwise'.[30] Because of the vast number of claims in this category, the criteria had to be simple and capable of easy application. The size of the instalments in this phase was relatively small so as to facilitate the review and processing of the claims.[31] At the same time, the number of claims included in the precedent instalments had to be large enough to ensure that the sample was sufficiently representative of the total population of

---

[27] UNCC, Report "C" claims, 1st inst., p. 85.   [28] Wühler, 'A New Contribution', 264.
[29] UNCC, Report "C" claims, 1st inst., p. 45.
[30] Gibson, 'Mass Claims Processing', 169, footnote 42.
[31] UNCC, Report "C" claims, 1st inst., p. 45. See Christopher S. Gibson, 'Using Computers to Evaluate Claims at the United Nations Compensation Commission', *Arbitration International* 13 (1997), 167, 172.

"C" claims. Moreover, the first instalments had to include claims from all countries that submitted "C" claims and a sufficient number of claims from countries that submitted the largest numbers of claims, to identify important country-specific issues or patterns. The first instalment submitted to the Commissioners, for instance, contained less than 3,000 individual claims.[32]

During the second phase, the criteria developed by the Commissioners were applied to all remaining cases. The UNCC secretariat played a prominent role in this phase. The secretariat developed a comprehensive set of internal guidelines for reviewing claims, thereby shifting from 'precedents' to 'common issue determination'. The role of the Commissioners evolved in this phase: while they continued to consider any new legal or factual issues that arose during the processing of the claims, their primary focus moved to ensuring that the criteria adopted during the precedent phase were properly implemented by the secretariat.[33]

The Commission for Real Property Claims

The CRPC received an enormous number of claims that were all very similar. This type of caseload, neatly divided into a few categories, simply calls for common issue determination and adherence to precedent.

In an initial preparatory period, the CRPC Commissioners reviewed a number of test claims, some of which were decided immediately. These early decisions had strong precedential value. They guided the CRPC lawyers in the subsequent resolution of similar claims and enabled the legal department to gradually submit larger and larger batches of claims to the Commission for approval.

From the Commissioners' deliberations on these early claims, criteria and guidelines emerged for the resolution of these common issues, which were gradually incorporated in the CRPC Book of Regulations, thus shifting from a precedent-based process to a rule-based system.[34]

The Iran–United States Claims Tribunal

The Iran–US Claims Tribunal's recourse to precedent setting and common issue determination was far less overt. Nevertheless, the Tribunal's practice

---

[32] UNCC, Report "C" claims, 1st inst., p. 2.   [33] Gibson, 'Mass Claims Processing', 173.
[34] The Dayton Peace Agreement authorised the Commission to 'promulgate such rules and regulations [. . .] as may be necessary to carry out its functions' (Annex 7, Art. XV).

with regard to forum selection clauses provides another example of a precedent-setting technique.

The 1981 Claims Settlement Declaration excluded from the jurisdiction of the Tribunal claims that arose from contracts that included forum selection clauses conferring exclusive jurisdiction to the Iranian courts in the event of a dispute.[35] In order to determine at an early stage which forum selection clauses fell outside its jurisdiction, the Tribunal selected nine test cases out of over a thousand such cases. Since in a number of cases more than one contract was involved, the nine cases contained nineteen forum selection clauses that were deemed representative of all the forum selection clauses found in the cases before the Tribunal.[36] The decisions on these test cases were used as guidance for the adjudication of the remaining cases.[37]

Analysis

Common issue determination and precedent-based procedures have become part and parcel of mass claims procedure.[38] The reasons for the success of these techniques in the mass claims context are not substantially different from the justifications for precedent-setting procedures or *stare decisis* policies in other contexts. However, the specificity of mass claims makes certain justifications more relevant than others. The analysis therefore focuses on the values of equality, consistency and efficiency.

Equality and consistency

The most commonly offered justifications for precedent are equality and consistency.[39] Dworkin notes, for instance, that 'the gravitational force of a

---

[35] Iran–US Claims Tribunal Settlement Declaration, Art. II.

[36] For an analysis, see R. Haklan Berglin, 'Treaty Interpretation and the Impact of Contractual Choice of Forum Clauses on the Jurisdiction of International Tribunals: The Iranian Forum Clause Decisions of the Iran–United States Claims Tribunal', *Texas International Law Journal* 21 (1985), 39; Ted L. Stein, 'Jurisprudence and Jurists' Prudence: The Iranian-Forum Clause Decisions of the Iran–US Claims Tribunal', *American Journal of International Law* 78 (1984), 1, 3. See also Abumohammad Asgarkhani, 'Compromise and Cooperation at the Iran–United States Claims Tribunal', *Arbitration International* 19(2) (2003), 149, 158.

[37] See in the *Yearbook Commercial Arbitration* 8 (1983), 282. For a short overview, see Aldrich, *The Jurisprudence of the Iran–US Claims Tribunal*, pp. 102–4; Brower and Brueschke, *The Iran–United States Claims Tribunal*, pp. 60–72.

[38] See R. Cross and J. W. Harris, *Precedent in English Law* (Oxford: Clarendon, 1991); Schauer, 'Precedent', 571.

[39] Schauer, 'Precedent', 595. See the part on the 'Social choices at stake' in Chapter 4.

precedent may be explained by appeal, not to the wisdom of enforcing enactments, but to the fairness of treating like cases alike'.[40] A rule of precedent tells a current decision maker to follow the decision issued in a previous case. It constrains the decisional options available to the adjudicator and ensures consistency between the first and the latter decision.[41]

A written rule flowing from the determination of a common issue likewise compels the decision maker to decide a claim in a way that is consistent with the rule.

Strong versus weak precedential constraint

The extent to which precedents and common issue determination promote equality and consistency depends on whether one opts for a system with strong precedential constraint or one with weak or little constraint. The strength of 'precedential constraint' – the term is used here to refer to the degree to which the choices of an adjudicator are constrained by either precedent or common issue determination – is a function of two elements.

First, it depends on the precise effect that is given to a precedent or to a rule resulting from the determination of a common issue (hereinafter: 'a rule'). A precedent can have binding force, leaving the adjudicator no choice other than to follow the precedent, or it can have a merely persuasive effect, leaving it to up to a conscientious adjudicator to decide whether following the precedent ensures a just and acceptable outcome in the particular case being considered. Likewise, a system of common issue determination can lead to rules that are binding upon the adjudicator, or it can result in mere guidelines and recommendations, under which the adjudicator has some discretion in determining whether the application of the rule might be unjust or otherwise inappropriate.

The second element is the scope of the precedent or rule and the level of detail and precision used in its formulation. What should be understood by 'alike cases'? When are two claims sufficiently similar to be treated in an identical manner? Should categories of likeness be large or small? If the precedent is defined in very narrow terms, allowing the adjudicator to take into account virtually every variation between claims, then the norm of precedent hardly constrains the adjudicator's options.[42] A system of precisely or narrowly defined precedents or rules

---

[40] Ronald Dworkin, *Taking Rights Seriously* (Cambridge, MA: Harvard University Press, 1977), p. 113.
[41] Schauer, 'Precedent', 588.   [42] Schauer, 'Precedent', 596.

which leave the adjudicator 'more or less at liberty to consider any possible way in which [a] particular array of facts might be unique'[43] will only affect a limited number of very similar claims and have very weak constraint. On the other hand, 'if relatively large categories act to group many slightly different particular cases under general headings of likeness, then the stricture of deciding like cases alike makes reliance on precedent a substantial constraint'.[44] In short, generally formulated precedents or rules affect many cases that are more or less similar and thus lead to strong precedential constraint, while narrowly defined precedents affect fewer claims, which are all very similar.

In mass claims procedure, two considerations plead for strong precedential constraint.

First, a system of strong precedential constraint that standardises claim outcomes enhances credibility. Mass claims processes deal, as mentioned above, with similar legal and factual issues. This similarity implies that any difference in claim outcomes will be immediately noticeable and requires a particularly high level of consistency within decisions.

Second, a system with a strong precedential constraint offers claimants more predictability and legal certainty.[45] As Schauer argues, 'when a decisionmaker must decide this case in the same way as the last, parties will be better able to anticipate the future. The ability to predict what a decisionmaker will do helps us plan our lives, have some degree of repose, and avoid the paralysis of foreseeing only the unknown.'[46] Especially in a mass claims context resulting from war or other extreme conditions, claimants arguably have a strong craving for legal certainty. Precedential constraint offers claimants certainty and enables them to anticipate their future.

Reconciling consistency and accuracy in mass claims procedures

The above considerations indicate that mass claims procedures benefit from the use of a system of strong precedential constraint. Does this mean, as Schauer's analysis suggested, that precedents and rules should

---

[43] Schauer, 'Precedent', 596.   [44] Schauer, 'Precedent', 596.

[45] The principle of predictability is another commonly offered justification for precedent-based systems. See for instance Richard A. Wasserstrom, *The Judicial Decision: Toward a Theory of Legal Justification*, (Stanford, CA: Stanford University Press, 1961), pp. 60–1.

[46] Schauer, 'Precedent', 597. Or, as Wasserstrom argues, '[m]en ought to be able to predict the consequences of their actions since it is by this means that they are able to exercise a greater degree of control over their environment and to alter and shape the course of future events' (Wasserstrom, *The Judicial Decision*, p. 61).

be defined in very general and broad terms? Should precision and detail be abandoned in favour of broadly defined precedents and rules affecting large groups of more or less similar claims? If this path is followed, a system of strong precedential constraint may very well end up sacrificing outcome accuracy of the individual claim in favour of overall equality and consistency.[47]

Claimants certainly prefer consistent and predictable decisions to less consistent and less predictable outcomes, but it is doubtful whether they do so at the cost of accuracy.[48] Ideally, precedent or common issue determination should reconcile and balance both values.

In a traditional adjudication where courts rarely face identical claims, a precedent has little or no constraining power unless it is formulated in relatively general terms, broadening the scope of claims for which it will be relevant.

In a mass claims context, on the other hand, the claims are often very similar. Even if the precedent is formulated in very narrow, detailed and precise terms, the class of claims affected by the precedent is still likely to be substantial in size and affect the consistency of many claims. Precedents and rules can therefore be formulated with a great level of precision and still maintain outcome accuracy.

Efficiency

In mass claims process, precedent-based procedures and the advance determination of common issues increase efficiency by reducing direct costs and not increasing error costs.

Minimising direct costs

Precedents make decisions less costly because the adjudicator does not have to rethink each decision and can rely on earlier experience and analysis.[49] Less scrutiny is required, which substantially reduces the decision process.[50]

This is especially significant in a mass claims context where otherwise the merits of each case would need to be determined *de novo* even

---

[47] Schauer, 'Precedent', 602.   [48] See the discussion by Schauer, 'Precedent', 601–2.

[49] Ronald A. Heiner, 'Imperfect Decisions and the Law: On the Evolution of Legal Precedent and Rules', *Journal of Legal Studies* XV (1986), 227, 229. For a similar view, see Max Radin, 'Case Law and Stare Decisis: Concerning Präjudizienrecht in Amerika', *Columbia Law Review* 33(2) (1993), 199, 204.

[50] Schauer, 'Precedent', 599.

though the major legal and factual issues are common to every claim and have been previously determined.[51] As the adjudicator would need to look at each case in its entirety, the parties would have to present the case in its entirety. Such repetition would make the price of individual justice rather high.

A process relying on precedents or the advance determination of common issues avoids these unnecessary costs and reduces the decision-making effort and its direct costs.[52] The more common the issues, the more substantial the gain.

Effect on error costs

Moreover, precedent and common issue determination have no negative effect on the accuracy of the claims outcomes, at least not if two conditions are met.

First, the issues, which are resolved by precedent or common issue determination, need to be truly common to all the claims concerned. Otherwise, i.e. if there are legally relevant differences between the affected claims, the precedent or rule may lead to inaccurate decisions in some cases. Second, the accuracy of the claim outcomes depends on how precisely the precedent or rule has been formulated. Very vaguely defined precedents or rules, affecting a large class of relatively diverse claims, might produce inaccurate decisions for claims that are situated in the border-zone of the class. Precisely and narrowly defined precedents or rules, targeting a smaller class of virtually identical claims, result on the other hand in accurate decisions for all claims within the class. Because of the similarity of the claims, precedents or rules can be formulated for mass claims in narrow terms and still preserve strong constraining force, thereby reconciling consistency and accuracy.

If those two conditions – true commonality and precise formulation of the precedent or rule – are met, the use of precedent and the advance determination of common issues will have no negative impact upon the accuracy of the decisions.

Moreover, precedent and common issue determination may also increase accuracy and effectively reduce error costs. In fact, a case-by-case approach without precedent or common issue determination forces

---

[51] For a similar reasoning with respect to aggregative techniques used in mass torts, see David Rosenberg, 'Class Actions for Mass Torts: Doing Individual Justice By Collective Means', *Indiana Law Journal* 62 (1987), 561, 563–4.

[52] See also Schauer, 'Precedent', 599.

the adjudicator to investigate each individual claim in isolation from all other similar claims and offers little protection against occasional or random errors. By constraining the options, precedents and rules place a curb on arbitrariness, bias, weakness, inexperience, etc.

Practical implications and recommendations

Choosing between precedent and common issue determination

This paragraph focuses on the comparative advantages of precedent and common issue determination in a mass claims process.

First, as already mentioned, rules make it possible to incorporate the results of the review of the test claims in a more abstract and authoritative formulation.[53] They allow for the elaboration of different hypotheses and sub-hypotheses, thus ensuring a more comprehensive and coherent approach; precedents are by definition limited to the factual and legal issues arising from the particular claim to which they refer.

Moreover, the formulation of a rule is fixed and cannot be altered by individual decision makers. Each of them has to rely on the original wording of the rule. In a system of precedent, subsequent decision makers can still extend, qualify or simply re-formulate the precedent in their decision.[54]

Since the resolution of mass claims inevitably involves many decision makers, it is important that the substantive rules resulting from the review of test cases can be applied consistently by all reviewers over an extended period of time.[55] Although preferences depend on individual taste and familiarity with one or the other system, a rules-based system appears to offer more guarantees for consistent application of this kind:

> Because of their authoritative wording, it is usually easier to determine the implications of a rule than a precedent. Rules are often adopted as a group with an eye to their consistency and coherence. Being determined on a case by case basis, precedents frequently lack the systematic coherence of many sets of rules. Indeed, rules are often adopted precisely when it is thought to be important to provide a systematic framework to achieve some purposes rather than rely on case by case determinations.[56]

---

[53] Bayles, *Procedural Justice*, p. 104.   [54] Radin, 'Case Law and Stare Decisis', 203.
[55] In the same vein, see Wühler, 'A New Contribution', 257: 'In a system that has to handle hundreds of thousands of claims, clear criteria and guidelines that are to be followed by all decision makers are essential for the fairness and efficiency of the process.'
[56] Bayles, *Procedural Justice*, p. 105.

Common issue determination and rules have the additional advantage that the review of the test claims does not immediately lead to an actual decision on these particular claims, thus allowing the simultaneous release of all decisions or at least of a substantial number on similarly situated claims. This may be preferable in mass claims context. However, experience has taught that the rules may need to be corrected or modified in the course of the claims review process.[57]

Working with test cases

In a precedent-based system, the selection of the test case is to some extent a matter of coincidence, determined primarily by the chronological order in which cases are filed. The first case presenting a particular legal question or problem already established the precedent. However, test cases are often selected according to certain criteria, such as the fact that the case is representative of a class of similar claims, the clarity of the issues, the comprehensiveness of the case etc. The advance determination of common issues and the formulation of rules always involve such a functional selection of test claims.

A functional selection of test cases requires an analysis of the potential claims to accurately identify the factual patterns arising from the claims, the legal issues they share and also the minor variations among them. An adequate selection among tens of thousands of claims can only be made through an adequate and comprehensive claims database capturing all legally relevant (or potentially relevant) data. Consequently, information technologies are important for mass claims processing.

Sufficient lead time should be given to analyse the claims, design and develop a claims database, and select and review test cases. For instance, a year elapsed between the commencement of CRPC claims registration activities in 1996 and the issuance of the first decisions in late 1997. This time was needed in order to set up the necessary computer systems, to conduct analyses of the claims population and to identify legal and factual issues that were common to all claims in a particular category. The CRPC claims resolution started at a very slow pace, with initially no more than a handful of individual decisions per monthly Commission

---

[57] The CRPC, for instance, repeatedly revised and amended its Books of Regulations. Each time, the revisions concerned a further relaxation of the evidentiary requirements or a broadening of the eligibility criteria. Since the CRPC had delayed the release of all negative decisions, the Commission was still in a position to review these claims in accordance with the new rules.

session. At the peak of its activities, however, the CRPC easily produced 10,000 individual decisions per plenary session. This increase is explained – at least in part – by the increasing reliance on already established precedents and rules, gradually making the preparation of decisions a standardised operation.

Rules and precedents have to be established in terms of the entire class of claims raising the same issue.[58] Precedent and common issue determination thus have a forward-looking dimension entailing that the adjudicators and decision makers have 'to commit the future before we get there'.[59] Moreover, rules and precedents need to be simple and clear in order to be capable of easy application to the remaining claims.[60] Furthermore, they must lead to a just outcome, not just for the test cases, but for all claims belonging to the same group.

Lastly, common issue determination and precedent-based systems enable a settlement programme to maximise the expertise of legal personnel working on specific categories of claims. The division of claims into categories and the development of precise and clear guidelines or criteria allow the claims handlers to specialise in specific parts of the claims verification process and to maximise relevant expertise.

---

[58] Gibson, 'Mass Claims Processing', 169, footnote 42: 'When using a system that relies on sample claims to examine and to highlight proposed criteria, one must avoid a common pitfall: thinking only in terms of what is necessary to resolve the particular claim. Each claim must be approached as a "sample" of the numerous other claims that are similarly situated with respect to the factual and legal issues contained therein [. . .]'.

[59] Schauer, 'Precedent', 572–3.   [60] See also UNCC, Report "C" claims, 1st inst., p. 46.

10

Computerised data matching

Information technology can expedite and strengthen decision making. As in other areas of modern society, current computer technology promises enormous efficiency gains in the fair and expeditious resolution of mass claims.

Computer technology can assist mass claims adjudicators in many ways,[1] such as analysing the claims, producing reports and overviews, controlling the quality of the decisions and tracking the claims in the decision process. These computer applications, however critical they are to the efficient running of the claims process, are not examined in this chapter. Instead, the focus will be on the assistance that information technology can offer in the verification of the validity and value of claims.

A first section discusses the general concept of data matching techniques and illustrates how they have been used on the domestic level. This is followed by an overview of how these techniques function in international mass claims practice. A third section briefly evaluates the use of data matching and suggests a proper role for computerised verification methodologies in mass claims processing.

General introduction

Different types of matching

In various mass claims programmes computers provided assistance by 'performing elaborate matching routines between evidence independently procured by the [mass claims facility] and the information contained in the claim database'.[2] Such 'data matching' involves a computerised process that brings together data from different sources and compares them.

[1] For examples, see B. Thomas Florence and Judith Gurney, 'The Computerization of Mass Tort Settlement Facilities', *Law and Contemporary Problems* 53 (1990), 189, 192.
[2] Gibson, 'Using computers', 175–6.

In its most simple form, a data matching software programme compares, for each claimant, information contained in the claims database with the equivalent data in a second database, which is used for verification or evidentiary purposes. To the extent that the verification database provides reliable and sufficient evidence of eligibility or compensability, a match with the information contained in the claim form is sufficient to generate a positive decision, without any further examination of the claim.

In addition to this basic type of computerised data matching, current computer technology offers a range of more advanced systems that can be used to evaluate claims.[3] So-called 'case matching' involves a computerised comparison of the key variables in previously resolved cases with the same variables in pending cases. Generally, this technique 'contemplates isolating the key variables that drive the outcomes of claims and systematically collecting the information in these variables in a computerized format. [...] These same variables in a pending case then can be collected and the case compared with similar previously resolved cases to insure that its value, updated to present value, is not inconsistent with similar cases'.[4]

Particularly sophisticated management information systems (MIS) approximate the human decision-making process. If the reasoning for decisions on a particular type of claims can be identified and precisely captured in 'if ... then' statements, and if the relevant data can be gathered in electronic format, then it is in principle possible to construct a computer programme that applies these rules to the claims data and that provides an 'expert opinion' on the claims.[5]

With the exception of the UNCC, international mass claims processes appear not to have made use of such sophisticated types of computerised claim verification. This chapter therefore focuses on simple data-matching techniques, which are more prevalent in international mass claims processes.

Data matching in national mass claims practice

A striking example of computerised data matching is found in the payment programme created for the 1985 settlement in the Agent Orange Product Liability litigation in the US. Although this programme

---

[3] In the United States, some mass tort settlement facilities have made use of very sophisticated computer systems. For examples see Florence and Gurney, 'Computerization', 194.

[4] McGovern, 'The Intellectual Heritage', 191–2. A specific type of case matching will be examined in the part on the 'Abraham-Robinson proposal' in Chapter 12.

[5] For an illustration, see McGovern, 'The Intellectual Heritage', 194.

did not cover restitution of property, it is relevant for its elaborated and pioneering data matching.

Background

During the Vietnam War, the US military is said to have sprayed 77 million litres of Agent Orange, the codename for a herbicide, to make it more difficult for communist troops to take advantage of the jungle terrain. The defoliant Agent Orange was afterwards blamed for causing a variety of mental disorders, bodily deformities, cancer and other diseases.

In 1979, Vietnam veterans and their family members filed a class action suit against seven chemical companies for injuries the veterans believed were caused by exposure to Agent Orange and other herbicides in Vietnam. On 7 May, 1984, a settlement was reached in which the manufacturers of Agent Orange agreed to pay US $180 million to veterans who claimed serious illnesses from Agent Orange exposure. In May 1985, the court issued an order directing distribution of approximately US $130 million (subsequently increased to US $170 million) to a payment programme which would compensate individual veterans and their family members.[6] Some 245,000 claims were filed with the Agent Orange Computer Centre, the entity that processed the compensation claims under court supervision.[7]

Computerised data matching

The design of a practicable and fair payments programme posed many challenges. The available evidence of causation was deemed far too speculative to serve as a primary basis for a distribution plan. However, as exposure was a jurisdictional requirement for class membership, some substantial showing of exposure was required.[8] Given the difficulties inherent for numerous claimants to establish exposure some twenty years after the fact, a practical solution was designed.

Applications were processed under a computerised exposure evaluation system, which compared information regarding a veteran's service location with data on spraying operations obtained from the so-called 'HERBS' tape, a computerised record of individual herbicide dissemination missions in Vietnam prepared from log books maintained at US military

---

[6] See *In re Agent Orange Product Liability Litigation*, 689 F.Supp. 1250 (E.D.N.Y., 1988), 1257.
[7] *In re Agent Orange Product Liability Litigation* (1985), 1401.
[8] A presumption that all claimants were exposed was deemed unfair to a truly exposed class member whose award otherwise would be higher. See *In re Agent Orange Product Liability Litigation* (1985), 1415.

headquarters in Saigon. The HERBS tape contained precise information on the location of the majority of spray missions conducted and the type and quantity of herbicide used.[9]

Under the computerised data matching system, the veteran's locations and times of service in Vietnam were compared to the spray dates and locations on the HERBS tapes to determine whether the veteran was located within a certain distance of a spray site either during or shortly after spraying. The matching process involved two basic steps. A questionnaire was sent to all claimants. In addition to providing information concerning death or disability, each claimant was asked to indicate the dates and locations of service in Vietnam. Subsequently, the claims were entered into a computerised process that compared the veteran's location data with the HERBS tape data to determine the correlation, if any, between the veteran's whereabouts in Vietnam and the location of spraying missions. A veteran who was present in a sprayed area at the time when the spraying occurred was considered exposed.[10] A veteran who was in a location near a sprayed area during or shortly after spraying was also considered exposed, subject to certain temporal and geographic conditions.

Because the HERBS tape did not account for all possible exposures, an appeal process supplemented the HERBS tape determinations. Veterans who claimed exposure despite a contrary finding based upon the HERBS data could request further consideration of their claim through an appeal to an independent board of review.

Evaluation

In 1985, Judge Weinstein had formulated the requirements of fairness and practicability that the payment programme had to meet: 'To be both practicable and fair, a program of individual benefits must minimise transaction costs, be relatively easy to administer and involve relatively simple, understandable and objective eligibility criteria, while maximising protection of those said to have suffered as a result of exposure to dioxin-contaminated Agent Orange.'[11]

In light of these requirements, the Court found the matching process to be 'the most comprehensive mechanism for judging exposure at moderate cost'.[12] Since the HERBS tape had some shortcomings, however,

---

[9] *In re Agent Orange Product Liability Litigation* (1985), 1416.
[10] *In re Agent Orange Product Liability Litigation* (1985), 1417.
[11] *In re Agent Orange Product Liability Litigation* (1985), 1410.
[12] *In re Agent Orange Product Liability Litigation* (1988), 1264.

the Court was careful to consider the computerised evaluation system as a 'probability analysis' only: the system was not intended to prove, by a preponderance of the evidence, that certain individuals were or were not exposed. Rather, it was aimed at making informed distinctions between those who might have been exposed and those who could not have been exposed.

This cautious attitude was explained in particular by the fact that the HERBS computer tapes did not cover all spray areas and the fear that the claimants' declarations about service in Vietnam might be inaccurate or the relevant information might be lost or otherwise unavailable. Moreover, there were contradictory scientific findings as to the causal relationship between the absorption of significant amounts of dioxin and the veterans' death or disability. Finally, the matching process extrapolated exposure from location and timing without further consideration of the actual intensity of contact with Agent Orange.[13]

While noting these inadequacies, the court remained of the view that the scientific evidence regarding causality and linkages between intensity of exposure and severity of injury was too weak and imprecise to warrant a more refined evaluation process. In the Court's view, any alternative system would lead to substantially greater expense in the administration of the payment programme and cause substantial costs to claimants in attempting to prove intense contact. These costs would be borne at little benefit to most claimants because only showings of intense exposure could support larger awards.

Data matching in international mass claims processes

International mass claims programmes have quickly realised the potential benefits of computerisation and have invested heavily in the design and development of software and database packages. Various types of data-matching techniques have been used in contemporary mass claims practice.

The United Nations Compensation Commission

The UNCC made extensive use of data-matching techniques to resolve the enormous number of claims in Category "A", i.e. claims for departure from Iraq or Kuwait during the period from 2 August 1990 to 2 March

---

[13] *In re Agent Orange Product Liability Litigation* (1988), 1265.

1991.[14] Iraq's invasion and occupation of Kuwait generated a mass exodus of expatriates out of Kuwait and Iraq. Before the invasion, in mid-1990, there were more than 2.6 million foreign nationals living in Kuwait and Iraq.[15] All together, around 2 million people are estimated to have left Kuwait and Iraq between the date of the invasion and the end of the occupation.

As explained above, the Governing Council established relaxed standards of evidence and fixed amounts of compensation for the claimants in this category. Under this system, the UNCC only required evidence of the fact and the date of departure. The matching of claims data with other sources of information enabled the Panel to accomplish the verification of around 350,000 claims in a period of roughly one year.[16]

For the claims of category "A", a computerised verification process determined whether a given claimant appeared in one or more of the records that constituted the Arrival/Departure Database and which the Panel found to establish departure from Iraq or Kuwait during the relevant jurisdictional period.[17] For those claims that matched the records, the Panel was not required to review the evidence attached to the claim forms.

Moreover, in anticipation of the high number of Category "A" claims, the UNCC secretariat developed computer software (the "A" Claim Form Data Capture System or 'DCS'), which it distributed to the submitting Governments and organisations. The DCS replicated in computer format all the fields contained in the paper claim form, with the exception of the documentary evidence that the claimants submitted. In accordance with Article 7 (1) of the Rules, the submitting entities arranged for the information provided by the claimants on the paper claim form to be entered into the DCS and submitted the claims on diskettes to the Secretariat.[18]

---

[14] UNCC, Provisional Rules, Art. 37 (1): 'The secretariat will proceed to check individual claims by matching them, insofar as is possible, against information in its computerized database. The results of the database analysis may be cross checked by the panel.'

[15] Statistics from the UNCC, Report "A" claims, 1st inst., p. 10. For a detailed description of the departure and relocation patterns, see also UNCC, Report "C" claims, 1st inst., pp. 60–6.

[16] UNCC, Report and Recommendations Made by the Panel of Commissioners Concerning the Fourth Instalment of Claims for Departure from Iraq or Kuwait (Category "A" Claims), 12 October 1995, UN Doc. S/AC.26/1995/4, para. 34.

[17] UNCC, Report and Recommendations Made by the Panel of Commissioners Concerning the Second Instalment of Claims for Departure from Iraq or Kuwait (Category "A" Claims), 22 March 1995, UN Doc. S/AC.26/1995/2, p. 12.

[18] See UNCC, Report "A" claims, 1st inst., pp. 7–8. By September 1994, the Commission had received over 900,000 Category "A" claims. See also Gibson ('Using Computers', 179), arguing that 'the Category "A" requirement of submitting claims in computer

Many Governments and international organisations had kept records on individuals that had travelled from the conflict region to their home country.[19] Thirty Governments and two international organisations (IOM and UNHCR) made records available to the UNCC. All the records that met the technical and legal criteria were downloaded into the Arrival/Departure Database.

The Database included three main components: information in computerised format provided by the Government of Iraq, computerised information provided by Kuwait and manual records provided by Governments and international organisations.[20] This reflected a wide range of different types of records, including travel records, immigration and customs records, diplomatic records and refugee camp rosters. The relevant data were captured in electronic format by an outside company using software developed by the secretariat. The departure data retained in the software included numeric information such as passport and other identification numbers and dates, and non-numeric information such as name, gender and nationality, as well as details of the journey in which the individuals were included.[21]

In order to ascertain the evidentiary value of these records, the Panel checked each set of data to determine whether it provided what is required for Category "A" claims to be compensable, i.e. 'simple documentation of the fact and date of departure from Kuwait or Iraq'.[22] The evidentiary value was determined by examining the data contained in the records themselves together with external information, such as departure reports, claims statistics and other available departure information.[23] Several records, including for instance those provided by the Governments of Iran and Jordan, were found to show departure from Iraq or Kuwait during the jurisdictional period. A claimant who matched against one or more of these records was therefore considered to meet the applicable evidentiary requirements and was entitled to compensation. On the other hand, a number of records were excluded

format should have been extended to all of the claims categories. In retrospect this would have avoided significant costs (to the UNCC), delays and duplicated work'.

[19] Most departees were evacuated from the Gulf region through Government-sponsored evacuation programmes and/or with the assistance of international organisations. See UNCC, Report "A" claims, 1st inst., p. 12 and p. 25.
[20] UNCC, Report "A" claims, 1st inst., pp. 33–4.
[21] See also Gibson, 'Using Computers', 183.
[22] UNCC, Provisional Rules, Art. 35 (a).
[23] UNCC, Report "A" claims, 1st inst., pp. 35–8.

from the database since they showed neither departure from Kuwait and Iraq, nor arrival in neighbouring countries.

The computerised matching process checked the presence of a claimant in the Arrival/Departure Database on the basis of the data that each claimant provided in the Category "A" claim form. The computer relied on a number of 'matching tools' such as the claimant's passport number or national identity card number, name, civil identification number issued by Kuwait, number of residency permit issued by Iraq, nationality, year of birth and gender. The basic operation performed by the computer was to compare, for each claimant, one or more of the matching tools contained in the claims database with the equivalent data in the Arrival/Departure Database.[24]

Comparing these data was only possible to the extent that the format of the matching tools was the same in the Claims Database and in the Arrival/Departure Database. In order to enhance the match rate, claims were subjected to several preliminary processes intended to standardise as far as possible the format of the matching tools.[25]

The computer reproduced the results of the matching process in a table with the UNCC's identifying number of each claim for which a match was achieved, as well as the identifying number of the corresponding entry in the Arrival/Departure Database. In this way, the claims eligible for compensation, and the evidence relevant to these claims, could always be identified.

The Commission for Real Property Claims

The CRPC designed similar, though less sophisticated, data-matching techniques. Early on, it developed a standard claim form to submit a property claim.[26] The electronic claims database recorded all information given by the claimant, including the information needed to identify the exact location of the property.[27] The CRPC also recovered and reconstructed most of the computerised pre-war cadastral data,

---

[24] UNCC, Report "A" claims, 1st inst., p. 39. See also Gibson, 'Using Computers', 183, footnote 16.

[25] UNCC, 'Report "A" claims, 1st inst.

[26] CRPC, Book of Regulations on Real Property, Art. 9.

[27] The precise identification of claimed real properties was complex. In many rural areas, there were no street names. In many cities, the street names changed frequently, making it difficult to rely on addresses to identify claimed properties. Wherever possible, CRPC therefore identified the claimed properties on the basis of the relevant cadastral data.

which it used as a verification database. To verify the accuracy of these data, they were *inter alia* checked against other property records and compared with manual records from cadastral field offices. The cadastral data covering approximately 70 per cent of the territory of Bosnia and Herzegovina were then put into an easily manageable and searchable database. In addition, the CRPC had a copy of the 1991 census database that indicated the main residence of all citizens.

The computerised claims data were checked against the CRPC cadastral and census records.[28] Where the data matched, the CRPC lawyers prepared a decision without further examination of the evidence submitted by the claimant. Where there was no match, the claims and the supporting evidence were verified against other property records.

The Second Claims Resolution Process for Dormant Accounts (CRT-II)

In CRT-II, all admissible claims of victims or their heirs were 'matched with the Account History Databases and Accounts published in 1997'.[29] The Account History Databases, developed by the auditors of the Independent Committee of Eminent Persons (ICEP) contained account names and related information for 36,000 accounts 'probably or possibly belonging to victims'. The databases had been consolidated into a single database to facilitate the use of the information in the claims process.[30] Claims for which no match to a 'probable or possible account' was achieved, were checked against all the accounts in the so-called 'Total Accounts Databases of the Participating Banks'.[31]

If the names matched, a list of the accounts deemed relevant by the CRT-II was automatically generated and sent to both the Data Librarian and the CRT-II.[32] Copies of the complete computer records for each account in the list were extracted by the computer programmes,

---

[28] Software was designed to fully computerise the matching process. Due to technical problems, however, the matching process was in many cases undertaken manually and at the level of individual claims, i.e. by comparing the computerised information for a particular claim to the corresponding information in the cadastral data.

[29] CRT-II, Rules of Procedure, Art. 19 (1).

[30] See Data Librarian Rules, Appendix A to the CRT-II Rules of Procedure, Art. 4 (b).

[31] CRT-II, Rules of Procedure, Art. 21. These databases remain located at each bank. The CRT has access to these databases through a secure encrypted limited-access network.

[32] CRT-II, Rules of Procedure, Art. 20.

downloaded to the CRT's system and queued to the appropriate CRT staff members designated to work on the adjudication of the claims.[33]

The International Commission on Holocaust Era Insurance Claims

The ICHEIC also developed procedures for matching claims against computerised verification data, in particular a database of Holocaust Era policyholders (composed on the basis of lists submitted by various companies) and a database from archives.[34] In the German Foundation Agreement, moreover, it was agreed that named and unnamed company claims relating to policies that are likely to have been issued by German companies would be matched against the comprehensive electronic list of insurance policies compiled by the German federal agency for the supervision of financial services.

The first step in the matching process was to electronically compare the data from the claims database and the data from the list of policyholders. Subsequently, the matches were divided into different categories depending on how well the two sets of information matched. 'High probability' or 'exact matches' were distributed to the companies for review. Unless the insurer could provide evidence showing that the match was invalid, the 'exact matches' would be considered to meet the relaxed standards of proof in so far as the existence of a policy was concerned.[35] 'High probability matches' would be considered as providing 'strong evidence that the policyholder named by the claimant owned the policy'.[36] If the company rejected the match, it needed to disclose the reasons for the rejection.

The IOM-administered claims programmes

Section 11 (2) of the German Foundation Law tasked the partner organisations, responsible for the processing of claims, to adduce relevant evidence in support of the claims. For forced labour claims, both the IOM and the other partner organisations systematically checked claims data against the archives in the Red Cross International Tracing

---

[33] CRT-II, Data Librarian Rules, Art. 6.   [34] ICHEIC, Processing Guide, p. 37.
[35] Principles of the ICHEIC-AWZ Matching Process, Annex F to the AWZ-Settlement Agreement, 11 July 2003, para. 7.
[36] Principles of the ICHEIC-AWZ Matching Process, paras 8–9.

Service ('ITS') in Bad Arolsen.[37] The ITS archive was created soon after the the Second World War by the Red Cross and contained over 40 million records of individuals and their whereabouts during the war. Its primary purpose was to assist in tracing persons who went missing during the war.

The matching process was largely electronic. The partner organisation submitted an electronic query to ITS. A search was conducted and the information resulting from the query was sent electronically to the partner organisation. If more detailed information was needed, manual searches were conducted. A positive ITS search result confirming incarceration in an officially recognised slave labour camp was accepted as sufficient evidence for payment of compensation.

If no evidence was found, the IOM checked the claims with the Foundation-funded '*Archivverbund*', which provided centralised access to some 400 local archives all over Germany.[38] This was an on-line type of data matching: queries were sent to a website, where the results were later posted and picked up by the partner organisation. This system was an important innovation, allowing the claims resolution facility to check claims against a multitude of relevant archives through one single coordination point. Obviously, the Internet created new possibilities in this respect and offered the prospect of making decisions based on archives located across the globe without significant cost or effort.

Analysis

Computerised data-matching techniques entail clear benefits for the overall claims resolution process, the individuals who depend upon it and the adjudicators. This chapter briefly outlines these benefits in terms of efficiency and outcome accuracy and suggests a few guidelines for their use.

Efficiency

Computerised data-matching techniques reduce the need for personnel, one of the largest items in a mass claims budget.[39] Moreover, once

---

[37] See also Van der Auweraert, 'The Practicalities of Forced Labor Compensation', 312.

[38] Van der Auweraert, 'The Practicalities of Forced Labor Compensation', 312.

[39] Florence and Gurney, 'Computerization', 194.

the proper computer processes are set up, masses of claims can be processed quickly, which significantly reduces delays in decision making. For instance, the UNCC used computer technology to become more efficient:

> With a conventional, individualized approach, claimants would have to endure unreasonable delays as they awaited hearing, while respondents would be forced to bear the heavy costs of defending separately at each hearing. The UNCC recognized these twin injustices – unreasonable delay for claimants and unreasonable costs for both claimants and respondents – which would inevitably result from application of a traditional case-by-case system. These concerns necessitated the development of new methodologies and techniques relying on computer support to facilitate more expeditious and cost-efficient 'justice' for the parties involved.[40]

However, computerised data-matching techniques might require significant initial investments. Moreover, the design, programming and testing involves initial delays.[41] The option to invest in computerised claim verification systems should therefore be made on the basis of the specific needs of the adjudication process:

> The fit between the needs of the organization in each of its functional areas and the capabilities of the computer system to meet these needs is especially important [. . .]. [One] should avoid, at all costs, a poor fit in either direction: (1) a system that cannot perform the analyses necessary in the time required or (2) an unnecessarily complex system for handling a simple task. To avoid these outcomes, decisions regarding computerization must begin with the identification of the organizational functions that the computer systems will support and conclude with the identification of the appropriate computer technology.[42]

Outcome accuracy and consistency

Data matching ensures consistency among outcomes while retaining an individualised examination of each claim. Each claim is still decided on the basis of its own merits: the claim outcomes are based upon the specific information submitted by the claimant and reliable external data.

---

[40] Gibson, 'Using Computers', 171.
[41] With respect to the UNCC, see Gibson, 'Using Computers', 181–2: 'the investment in the computer system [was] substantial and developing it [created] delays as programmers continued to design and implement the software'.
[42] Florence and Gurney, 'Computerization', 189.

In this sense, it is not radically different from traditional case-by-case adjudication.

Furthermore, data matching, if properly done, enhances outcome accuracy. It excludes human error, bias or fraud and guarantees a higher level of consistency than a traditional adjudication could possibly offer, especially when the claims are numerous.

To achieve accuracy and consistency, however, three conditions need to be met. A first prerequisite for successful data matching is that the claim forms 'must be carefully tailored to request the most useful information'.[43] All relevant variables must be captured in electronic format. Ideally, the precise matching process and the identification or matching tools upon which it is based would be known in advance, so that one could then work backwards to determine the type of data that is required from claimants to match the claim against the verification database. Professional experts in designing surveys could then formulate unambiguous questions, taking into account the different cultural and socio-economic backgrounds of the claimants. Moreover, successful data matching requires a high level of accuracy in claims registration. As one author concluded, if all of this is done 'with the proper legal standards and processing methodologies in mind, the information obtained would ultimately yield claims determinations that [are] more fair and more accurate'.[44]

Second, the outcome accuracy depends on the quality of the computerised verification sources that are used. Inaccuracies in these records will be replicated automatically in the decisions. A critical assessment of the evidentiary records is indispensable.

Third, outcome accuracy also depends on the matching process itself. Glitches or systemic errors in the data matching systematically affect all decisions.

Toward a proper role for computerised verification techniques in mass claims processes

The growing use of computerised data matching techniques in mass litigation is irreversible. The Internet moves claims submissions from traditional paper claims or diskettes to on-line filings and, furthermore, allows for an instantaneous access to archives, records and other types of evidentiary documentation across the globe. The claims adjudicator no

---

[43] Gibson, 'Using Computers', 180.   [44] Gibson, 'Using Computers', 180–1.

longer needs to be physically present where the evidence is kept or where the claimants reside.

Investments in such computer techniques should nonetheless be made with caution. As Florence and Gurney have cautioned, the risk of designing a 747 jetliner where a bicycle would do the job is a realistic one.[45] Given the initial costs involved in setting up sophisticated computer systems, computer applications in this area are 'high-risk, high-payoff endeavors'.[46] The decision whether to rely on computer support to verify claims – and, if so, which type of computer support – should be made on the basis of a careful analysis of the precise needs of the process. Three elements, in particular, have to be taken into account.

First, the volume of the data and the complexity of the eligibility rules will have a significant impact upon the cost of the design and the development of databases and software. A relatively simple and inexpensive computer programme can handle small volumes of information and make straightforward comparisons. A more sophisticated and thus more expensive computer system will be required to handle larger volumes of data and to carry out complex comparisons. Consequently, if the verification process itself is complex and the number of claims relatively low, data matching may not be an economically worthwhile option. If the data and rules are simple, however, and the number of claims is huge, then computerised data matching will result in enormous savings of money and time.

Second, the ease of collecting the verification data in a computerised format is also relevant. If the evidentiary data already exist and are accessible in computerised format, not making use of them would be a waste of resources. On the other hand, if these data exist in manual form only, substantial preliminary investments will be needed to capture the data in an easily accessible format.

Third, the accuracy of computerised awards essentially depends on the reliability and accuracy of the evidentiary records against which the claims are checked. Investments in computerised data matching only make sense if the verification data are a reliable source of evidence.

---

[45] Florence and Gurney, 'Computerization', 194.
[46] See Florence and Gurney, 'Computerization', 194.

11

Adjudication by sampling

Introduction

The two previous chapters discussed techniques to rationalise or expedite individualised claims adjudication. This chapter takes the discussion a step further and focuses on the relatively new world of aggregative or statistical claims adjudication.

The general objective of statistics is to gain understanding from data and to obtain information about a larger group just by looking at a small part of that group.[1] Sampling is a statistical technique, the goal of which is 'to examine a section of a population, i.e. a sample, in order to draw conclusions about the entire population as accurately as possible'.[2] A sample is generally selected because the population is too large to study in its entirety. Therefore, a principal factor in designing a sample is to maximise the likelihood that, with respect to the characteristics being considered, the sample is representative of the non-sampled population.

Sampling methodologies can be used to adjudicate a large population of similar claims. Rather than examining each individual claim separately, all claims are aggregated and a representative sample is selected for individual review. The sample outcomes are analysed and extrapolated to all other claims in the population, without subjecting the latter to an individual review.

Domestic law has only recently started discovering the potential benefits of this type of statistical adjudication. While statistical evidence is more and more used in the courtroom, utilising statistical samples to actually adjudicate claims is a 'bridge too far' for many judges, lawyers and scholars. Statistical adjudication has been used only a few times in

---

[1] On the use of statistics generally, see also *Cimino* v. *Raymark Industries, Inc.* (1990), 660.
[2] UNCC, Report and Recommendations Made by the Panel of Commissioners Concerning the Second Instalment of Individual Claims for Damages up to US $100,000 (Category "C" claims), 30 May 1996, UN Doc. S/AC.26/1996/1, para. 26.

the domestic legal sphere, in particular in the context of mass claims procedures in the United States, where it has sparked vigorous debates.

In international claims practice, statistical adjudication has been used twice. Not surprisingly, it was in the United Nations Compensation Commission that the technique was tested for the first time. The UNCC faced the daunting task of resolving 2.6 million claims, most of which were relatively small – but urgent – individual claims. Necessity is the mother of invention and, for the first time, statistical sampling found its way into international legal practice.

The example set by the UNCC was recently followed by the IOM, which also developed statistical techniques to resolve large groups of Forced Labour Compensation claims. These efforts were triggered by a sense that using routine ways to resolve these claims would be so expensive and time-consuming as to deny meaningful compensation to many claimants. In particular, it was felt that the traditional adjudicatory system, designed to achieve corrective justice in a simple two-party setting, could not guarantee timely remedies for the many elderly victims of forced labour.

Statistical modes of adjudication are understandably attractive for mass claims resolution. Time savings, speed and efficiency are unquestionable merits of statistical adjudication and, as argued before, these are key values in a mass claims context. When applied properly, moreover, sampling methodologies may provide reliable projections of the characteristics of the claims under consideration and produce 'accurate' decisions. Some even argue that sampling leads to more accurate results than case-by-case adjudication.[3]

However, statistical adjudication also raises serious concerns, in particular from a due process perspective. It inevitably challenges the popular and deep-rooted belief that individualised, case-by-case adjudication is the only way to maintain and ensure the integrity and fairness of adjudication.

This chapter discusses at some length the use of sampling in a mass claims context. A first section analyses how statistical sampling was used in mass litigation in the US and verifies whether there have been precedents in international practice. A second section reviews the use of sampling techniques by the UNCC for the processing of claims in Categories "A" and "C". Since there is little information available with

---

[3] See for instance, in the context of mass torts in the US, Saks and Blanck, 'Justice Improved', 815.

respect to the IOM's use of statistical methodologies, the review focuses exclusively on the UNCC. A third section will then evaluate the relevance of sampling for efficiency, outcome accuracy and procedural due process. A final section suggests guidelines to determine whether sampling is appropriate and formulates minimum requirements to combine efficiency and fairness.

In search of precedents: Sampling in international and domestic practice

The legal profession does not take innovation and change lightly. When the first UNCC Panels of Commissioners decided to venture into the uncharted territory of statistical adjudication, they must have felt a strong sense of renewal and responsibility. This is apparent from their lengthy justification and motivation for using a sampling methodology to process claims.[4] The justification relied partly on substantive arguments, ranging from judicial economy to increased accuracy,[5] which will be fully analysed in a later section. It also referred to the 'evolving principles and practice both under international and national jurisdictions'[6]:

> Faced with situations of mass claims and other situations where a large number of cases involving common issues of law and fact arise, courts, tribunals and commissions have adopted methodologies, including that of sampling [. . .] The legal principle involved may be stated as follows: in situations involving mass claims or analogous situations raising common factual and legal issues, it is permissible in the interest of effective justice to apply methodologies and procedures which provide for an examination and determination of a representative sample of these claims. Statistical methods may be used to determine the size and composition of the sample claims and to apply the results of the review of the sample to the remaining claims. [. . .] The use of statistics and sampling in adjudicatory processes has been evolving over a considerable period. While there are direct precedents for the use of such methods in the national legal systems of Canada and of the United States where the use of statistics in the adjudicatory process is becoming quite common, the legal principle, as formulated above, has formed the basis of numerous determinations under international and national jurisdictions.[7]

---

[4] See especially the following report: UNCC, Report "A" claims, 4th inst., paras 9–34.

[5] UNCC, Report "C" claims, 1st inst., p. 41 and UNCC, Report "A" claims, 4th inst., paras 2 and 9.

[6] UNCC, Report "A" claims, 4th inst., para. 9.

[7] UNCC, Report "A" claims, 4th inst., paras 9–10.

International legal practice

According to the UNCC Commissioners, the sampling methodology that they developed was not without precedent in international legal practice. The UNCC Report referred to the following three examples.

The Iran–United States Claims Tribunal

As a first precedent for its sampling techniques, the UNCC Report referred to the methodology applied by the Iran–US Claims Tribunal to resolve claims containing forum selection clauses. As explained above, in order to determine at an early stage which forum selection clauses were within the scope of Article II, and consequently fell outside its jurisdiction, the Full Tribunal selected nine test cases out of over a thousand such cases. On the basis of these test cases, the Full Tribunal issued on 5 November 1982 a series of Interlocutory Awards, which served as guidance for the Chambers on this particular jurisdictional issue.[8]

Whether this methodology can serve as a proper precedent for statistical sampling is questionable. While it is correct that the Tribunal reviewed representative test cases to resolve these jurisdictional issues at an early stage, this was not done in order to extrapolate the results to all remaining claims, without further individual examination, and to make probability predictions as to the outcomes of the remaining claims. The Tribunal's approach involved no statistics. The purpose of the sample review was simply to identify issues common to a group of claims and to arrive at a comprehensive and prompt resolution of these common issues, to be consistently applied by the Tribunal's three Chambers.[9] In this sense, the Tribunal's approach is closer to 'precedent setting' – i.e. the establishment of a rule of law by an adjudicator for a particular type of cases, to which it can be referred when deciding subsequent similar cases – than to statistical sampling. Contrary to the way in which sampling operates, the results of the sample review were applied to the remaining claims on a case-by-case basis, requiring the adjudicator to verify in each case whether the facts of the case before him are sufficiently similar to the facts of the case on which the precedent was established.[10]

---

[8] See in the *Yearbook Commercial Arbitration* 8 (1983), 282. For a short overview, see Aldrich, *The Jurisprudence of the Iran–US Claims Tribunal*, pp. 102–4; Brower and Brueschke, *The Iran–United States Claims Tribunal*, pp. 60–72.

[9] Aldrich, *The Jurisprudence of the Iran–US Claims Tribunal*, pp. 102–4.

[10] This is illustrated by the wording used by the Tribunal in its Award in Case No. 7 (141–7–2), 29 June 1984, *Yearbook Commercial Arbitration* 10 (1985), 219, 221 and in

Sampling is different. It examines a section of a population in order to draw conclusions about the entire population, without further individual examination. Because the sample is considered sufficiently representative of the overall population to allow predictions at a certain confidence level, the sample results are valid for all claims in the larger population. Sampling is thus far more radical than precedent setting.

The European Commission and the Court of Human Rights

Second, the UNCC Report referred to the European Commission and Court of Human Rights, which also drew conclusions on the basis of representative cases.[11]

In *Ireland* v. *United Kingdom*, the Irish Government claimed that the use of special powers in Northern Ireland by the United Kingdom had contravened the European Convention on Human Rights, in particular its Article 3 (prohibition of torture) and Article 5 (right to liberty and security of person). With respect to the allegations under Article 3, Ireland submitted written evidence relating to 228 incidents. The Commission examined only 16 so-called 'illustrative' cases, which had been selected by Ireland at the Commission's request, and a further 41 cases on which it had received medical reports and written comments (so-called 'remaining' cases).[12] On the basis of these cases, the Commission came to the conclusion that five types of practices constituted inhuman and degrading treatment in breach of Article 3 of the Convention.[13] The Court followed the same methodology and endorsed the conclusion the Commission had arrived at.[14]

The Court, however, was not expected to pronounce on individual cases of Convention violations. Through the sample, the Court merely aimed to verify whether the alleged incidents were sufficiently numerous and related, as to amount to a practice in breach of the Convention. There are no indications that the Court would have adopted the same approach, had it been requested to pronounce on 228 individual applications.

Case No. 388 (ITM 13–388-FT), 4 February 1983, *Yearbook Commercial Arbitration* 9 (1984), 216, 218.

[11] UNCC, Report "A" claims, 4th inst., paras 13–14.

[12] ECHR, *Ireland* v. *the United Kingdom*, 18 January 1978, paras 93 and 16.

[13] ECHR, *Ireland* v. *the United Kingdom*, para. 184.

[14] ECHR, *Ireland* v. *the United Kingdom*, para. 168. See also Jochen A. Frowein, 'Fact-Finding by the European Commission on Human Rights', in Richard B. Lillich (edn), *Fact-Finding Before International Tribunals – Eleventh Sokol Colloquium* (Ardsley-on-Hudson, NY: Transnational, 1992), p. 247.

A similar approach was taken by the European Commission on Human Rights in respect of Turkey's breach of the Convention in Cyprus.[15] With regard to evidence on alleged killings in violation of Article 2, the Commission heard a number of representative witnesses on the situation and heard eye-witnesses on only one incident. On this basis, the Commission was able to conclude that breaches of the Convention had taken place on a larger scale and were not confined only to this particular incident.[16]

A similar approach was taken by the Commission in its report of 4 October 1983 on a claim by Cyprus against Turkey. Cyprus asserted *inter alia* that about 2,000 Greek Cypriots, allegedly in Turkish custody, were still missing. Given the lack of cooperation from Turkey and the perceived need to protect both the missing persons and Cyprus's informants, a special procedure was devised. Cyprus was invited to select and document fifty illustrative cases of missing persons and to submit the names and other details of all missing persons.[17] Furthermore, the Commission decided to obtain oral evidence in five cases it considered representative.[18] A Commission delegation examined the five cases and found that in three of these cases the missing persons concerned were in Turkish custody in 1974. In the other two cases, the witness evidence was not entirely consistent. On the basis of this sample, the written evidence submitted by Cyprus for the fifty illustrative cases and the names and particulars of 1,619 persons, the Commission found sufficient indications that 'of the remaining 1,614 missing persons, an indefinite number have been in Turkish custody in 1974 after the cessation of hostilities'.[19] Here again, there was no need for the Commission to arrive at a binding finding on a particular case of a missing person; a mere conclusion that an 'indefinite' number of missing persons were in Turkish custody was sufficient to conclude that Turkey had violated the Convention.

In conclusion, none of these three instances involves statistical sampling techniques to determine claims. While the Commission and Court

---

[15] European Commission of Human Rights, *Report concerning Applications No. 6780/74 and 6950/75*, 10 July 1976, special publication of the Council of Europe, para. 110–14 and 117–19.

[16] Frowein, 'Fact-Finding', 247–8.

[17] European Commission of Human Rights, *Report on Application No 8007/77*, 4 October 1983, in Decisions and Reports, Vol. 72 (1992), para. 90.

[18] European Commission of Human Rights, *Report on Application No 8007/77*, para. 91. These cases were suggested by the Applicant Government.

[19] European Commission of Human Rights, *Report on Application No 8007/77*, para. 115.

relied on illustrative cases, they did not extrapolate the results of these cases to other individual cases. The review of the sample claims simply constituted evidence of a certain practice and did not result in individual findings of fact or of law for other cases. Consequently, what the European Court and the European Commission of Human Rights did, cannot be considered a direct precedent for the sampling techniques of the UNCC.

The United States–German Mixed Claims Commission

The third example referred to in the UNCC Report is the practice of the United States–German Mixed Claims Commission. As mentioned above, this Commission made use of 'administrative decisions' for issues that were common to a large number of claims.

The UNCC Report claims that the Mixed Claims Commission 'issued its awards through the adjudication of representative claims within each of the consolidated case groups'.[20] It is certainly correct that the Commission grouped claims, reviewed a number of 'typical' cases in each group and rendered collective decisions covering the whole group of claims.[21] The conclusions with respect to the cases reviewed were, however, not directly extrapolated to the remaining claims in the group. Rather, the review led to general rules or criteria to be applied to each of the individual claims. The representative claims thus made 'bi-national disposition of the remainder easier'.[22]

In *Garland Steamship Corporation and Others (US)* v. *Germany*, for instance, the Commission examined a group of thirteen typical cases in which the United States sought compensation for the destruction of ships by Germany or her allies. It examined the relevant facts of each of the test cases as well as the applicable law and distilled a number of general rules to be applied to each individual case. However, the facts in each case were 'carefully examined and weighed', and the Commission

---

[20] UNCC, Report "A" claims, 4th inst., paras 15–17.
[21] For instance, all cases arising out of the sinking of the steamship *Lusitania* were treated together. See the Opinion in the *Lusitania* cases, 1 November 1923, 7 *UN Reports of International Arbitral Awards* 32. For other examples, see *United States Steel Products Company, Costa Rica Union Mining Company and South Porto Rico Sugar Company*, 1 November 1923, 7 *UN Reports of International Arbitral Awards* 44; *Garland Steamship Corporation and Others*, 25 March 1924, 7 *UN Reports of International Arbitral Awards* 73; and *Provident Mutual Life Insurance Company and Others* v. *Germany*, 18 September 1924, 7 *UN Reports of International Arbitral Awards* 91.
[22] Bederman, 'Historic Analogues', 273.

had to determine whether or not each particular case met the test.[23] The Commission's procedure therefore remained wholly within the ambit of individualised claims adjudication and did not resemble the statistical claims processing developed by the UNCC.

Conclusion

The UNCC's reference to the above 'precedents' is correct only to the extent that they provided for an examination and determination of a representative sample of claims. However, no statistical methods were used to apply the results of the review of the sample to the remaining claims.

Practice in national jurisdictions

The UNCC was on firmer grounds when it referred to national judicial practice. Indeed, the increase in mass tort litigation since the nineties has prompted considerable innovation in the way mass claims were handled by national courts. Faced with a deluge of claims and concerned at the unacceptable delays and enormous costs that a traditional case-by-case approach would entail, some national courts, in particular in the United States, have relied on statistical sampling to adjudicate mass claims.

Nonetheless, the picture presented by national practice is not unequivocal either. The courts' experimentation with statistical methodologies has not been received with general approval and enthusiasm. The defendants, mostly large industries, have consistently challenged the appropriateness of sampling techniques because of *inter alia* their effect on due process. On more than one occasion – including in some of the litigation cited in the UNCC Report[24] – appellate courts have been persuaded by these arguments and have rejected the statistical procedures devised by the trial courts. A short review of national mass claims litigation and the use of statistical sampling is thus called for.

The following overview includes only cases before US courts. This choice is motivated by the fact that American judges have applied statistical adjudication techniques more readily than courts in other countries. This does not imply, however, that national practice involving

---

[23] *Garland Steamship Corporation, and Others*, 90–1.

[24] The sampling methodology initially devised in the *Cimino* v. *Raymark Industries* litigation was cited in a UNCC Report in 1995, but overturned by the Court of Appeals in 1998. See also the part on the 'asbestos litigation' in Chapter 11. UNCC, Report "A" claims, 4th inst., paras 25–6.

the use of sampling to adjudicate mass claims is limited to the US.[25] In Canada, for instance, the class proceedings legislation of several provinces explicitly approves of the use of sampling techniques to determine the amount or distribution of an aggregate monetary award.[26]

Moreover, the following overview is not exhaustive. In fact, sampling techniques have been crucial in a wide variety of situations to determine particular elements of liability. For instance, sampled information is often employed in trademark litigations to assess damage.[27] In toxic tort cases, causation is sometimes determined on the basis of sampled information.[28] These cases have not been included in the overview.[29] Only the few cases in which sampling was clearly used as a decision-making technique, i.e. a means to adjudicate individual claims, have been selected.

Asbestos litigation

The odyssey of asbestos litigation spanned several decades and involved a myriad of changing players, rules and fora.[30] According to the RAND Institute for Civil Justice, over 600,000 people filed claims and over 6,000 companies were named as defendants.[31] The litigation spread far beyond the asbestos and building products industries and caused dozens of bankruptcies. Cases migrated to different states and venues in the late nineties. A total of US $54 billion was spent on asbestos litigation, with transaction costs consuming more than half of total spending.[32] Some commentators refer to the asbestos litigation as 'the mass tort that dwarfs all others'.[33] The following review focuses on the two main instances in which US courts experimented with sampling to cope with the great number of parties in asbestos litigation.

[25] For references, see UNCC, Report "A" claims, 4th inst., paras 29–31.
[26] Uniform Class Proceedings Act, 1997, Art. 30 (1), available at www.ulcc.ca/en/us (visited October 2007).
[27] The leading case in this respect is *Zippo Manufacturing Co.* v. *Roger Imports*, 216 F. Supp. 670 (D.C.N.Y. 1963), 680–1. See also *Exxon Corp.* v. *Texas Motor Exchange*, 628 F.2d 500 (5th Cir. 1980), 507.
[28] See for instance *Brock* v. *Merrell Dow Pharmaceuticals*, 874 F.2d 307 (5th Cir. 1989), 311.
[29] It can be argued that in these cases the use of statistics follows logically from the nature of the substantive right. See Bone, 'Statistical Adjudication', 576 footnote 44.
[30] See RAND Institute for Civil Justice, Asbestos Litigation Costs and Compensation – An Interim Report, 2002.
[31] RAND Institute for Civil Justice, Interim Report, 2002, p. 40. Annual claim filings rose sharply in the late nineties (p. 42).
[32] RAND Institute for Civil Justice, Interim Report, 2002, pp. 53–5.
[33] Hensler and Peterson, 'Mass Personal Injury Litigation', 1004.

In re Fibreboard Corp.   The use of sampling in the Fireboard litigation stemmed from the Texas Eastern District Court's attempts to come to grips with 3,031 asbestos exposure claims brought by insulation and construction workers, their survivors and household members. The District Court, which had consolidated the cases for certain purposes and certified a class for the issue of actual damages, developed a trial plan consisting of two phases: a Phase I trial on liability and punitive damages, and subsequently a Phase II trial on actual damages. In the Phase II trial the jury was, amongst other things, to determine actual damages in a lump sum for each of 5 disease categories for all plaintiffs in the class.[34] This was to be done on the basis of a full trial of liability and damages for 41 sample claimants. These included the 11 class representatives and 30 'illustrative plaintiffs'. The defendants and plaintiffs were each to choose 15 illustrative cases.

The defendants objected to the proposed procedure and petitioned to the Court of Appeals. Comparing the contemplated aggregate methodology with a traditional one-on-one trial, the Court of Appeals first noted that:

> [. . .] under Phase II there will inevitably be individual class members whose recovery will be greater or lesser than it would have been if tried alone. Indeed, with the focus in Phase II upon the 'total picture', with arrays of data that will attend the statistical presentation, persons who would have had their claims rejected may recover. Plaintiffs say that 'such discontinuities' would be reflected in the overall omnibus figure. Stated another way, plaintiffs say that so long as their mode of proof enables the jury to decide the total liability of defendants with reasonable accuracy, the loss of one-to-one engagement infringes no right of defendants. Such unevenness, plaintiffs say, will be visited upon them, not the defendants.[35]

The Court of Appeals further observed that the class was a diverse group and that there existed many disparities among class members.[36] Texas law required a plaintiff to prove both causation and damage. While plaintiffs argued that the proof for 2,990 class members was supplied by expert opinion regarding their similarity to 41 representative plaintiffs, the Court remained sceptical: 'The inescapable fact is that the individual claims of 2,990 persons will not be presented. Rather, the claim of a unit

---

[34] *In re Fibreboard Corp.*, 893 F.2d 706 (C.A.5, Tex., 1990), 708–9.

[35] *In re Fibreboard Corp.* (1990), 708–9.

[36] *In re Fibreboard Corp.* (1990), 710. See also *In re Fibreboard Corp.* (1990), 712.

of 2,990 persons will be presented'.[37] The proposed procedure, the Court of Appeals continued, could not adequately determine issues relating to individual causation, but accepted general causation as a sufficient basis for liability, contrary to Texas law.[38] Because the proposed procedure effected a change in the parties' substantive rights under Texas law, the Court granted the petitions for *mandamus* and vacated the District Court's order.

Cimino v. Raymark Industries, Inc.   A few months after the decision in *Fibreboard*, the District Court adopted a modified trial plan,[39] which involved again the use of sampling techniques to determine damages. The main difference between the procedures disapproved in *Fibreboard* and those used in *Cimino* appeared to be that while in *Fibreboard* the 41 cases of allegedly representative and 'illustrative' class members would be presented to the jury to determine an aggregate damage award for the whole class, the *Cimino* process presented to the jury a statistically significant random sample of class claims and awarded each of the non-sample claims the average of the damages awarded in the sample claims.

The sampling methodology involved the following practical steps. First, the Court divided the entire class of 2,298 cases into 5 disease categories and then randomly selected 160 sample cases, some from each type of disease.[40] In determining the sample size for each type of disease, the Court sought a confidence level of 95 per cent, a common standard in statistical sampling. According to the statistical expert retained by the Court, however, the actual confidence level achieved by the samples exceeded the 95 per cent: on the whole, and with two exceptions, a 99 per cent confidence level was achieved.[41]

The damage case of each sample plaintiff was then submitted to a jury and each sample plaintiff was awarded their individual verdict. The Court subsequently calculated the average verdict for each type of disease. These average verdicts constituted the damage award for each non-sample class member. Indeed, once the Court was satisfied that the distribution of variables between the samples and their respective subclasses was comparable, the Court found 'no persuasive evidence why the average damage verdicts in each disease category should not be

---

[37] *In re Fibreboard Corp.* (1990), 711.   [38] *In re Fibreboard Corp.* (1990), 711–12.
[39] *Cimino* v. *Raymark Industries, Inc.*, 151 F.3d 297 (C.A.5, Tex., 1998), 302.
[40] *Cimino* v. *Raymark Industries, Inc.* (1990), 653.
[41] *Cimino* v. *Raymark Industries, Inc.* (1990), 664.

applied to the non-sample claims'.[42] Individual plaintiffs, on the one hand, who received an award that could be different from the one they would have received had their individual case been decided by a jury, waived any objections by agreeing to the procedure. The defendants, on the other, 'cannot show that the total amount of damages would be greater under the Court's method compared to individual trials of these cases', especially since 'the millions of dollars saved in reduced transaction costs inure to defendants' benefit'.[43]

The defendants appealed and in 1998, the Court of Appeals again concluded that the sampling procedure was contrary to Texas law and to the Seventh Amendment right to a jury trial.[44]

Estate of Marcos human rights litigation

In a class action against the Estate of the former President of the Philippines, the District Court used statistical sampling to determine compensatory damages. This time the Court of Appeals upheld the methodology. Since the case offers one of the most comprehensive and far-reaching applications of sampling in domestic litigation, it is worthwhile giving a detailed account of the methodology developed by the District Court and of the reasoning of the Court of Appeals confirming it.

Sampling methodology The class action involved a total of 10,059 individual claims from Philippine nationals seeking damages for human rights abuses committed against them or their decedents. The trial was conducted in three subsequent phases: (1) a first stage in which the jury found defendants liable for the acts of torture, summary execution and disappearance; (2) a second phase in which the jury awarded plaintiffs US $1.2 billion in exemplary damages; and (3) a final phase to determine compensatory damages. It was in the compensatory damages phase that sampling was used.

The District Court first ruled 518 of the claims to be facially invalid. From the remaining 9,541 claims, a sample of 137 claims was randomly selected by computer.[45] The size of the sample was determined to ensure

---

[42] *Cimino* v. *Raymark Industries, Inc.* (1990), 664–5.

[43] *Cimino* v. *Raymark Industries, Inc.* (1990), 665–6.

[44] *Cimino* v. *Raymark Industries, Inc.* (1998), 311. See also the opinion of Judge Reynaldo G. Garza (specially concurring), *Cimino* v. *Raymark Industries, Inc.* (1998), 335–7. For a similar type of reasoning with respect to class action procedure, see *Sterling* v. *Velsicol Chemical Corp.*, 855 F.2d 1188 (C.A.6, Tenn., 1988), 1200.

[45] *In re Estate of Marcos Human Rights Litigation*, 910 F.Supp. 1460 (D. Hawai'i, 1995), 1466.

a confidence level of 95 per cent, i.e. a 95 per cent statistical probability that the results of the review of the sample would be applicable to the totality of the claims filed.[46]

The District Court then appointed a Special Master, who supervised the taking of depositions in the Philippines of the 137 randomly selected claimants and their witnesses. Subsequently, the Special Master reviewed the claim forms and depositions of the class members in the sample, which had been completed under penalty of perjury. He recommended that 6 claims of the 137 in the sample be found invalid.[47] He then proposed the amount of damages to be awarded to the remaining 131 sample claimants.[48]

In a subsequent step, the Special Master made recommendations on damage awards to the other class members. Based on his recommendation that 6 of the 137 claims in the random sample (4.37 per cent) be rejected as invalid, he suggested the application of a five-per-cent invalidity rate to the remaining claims. To determine the award to the class, he multiplied the number of valid remaining claims in each subclass by the average award recommended for the randomly sampled claims in that subclass. Finally, by adding the recommended awards in the randomly sampled cases, the Special Master arrived at a recommendation for a total compensatory damage award in each subclass. Adding together the subclasses, a total of US $767,491,493 was awarded.

A jury trial on compensatory damages was held in January 1995. After five days of deliberation, the jury, contrary to the Master's recommendations, found against only two of the 137 claimants in the random sample.[49] As to the compensatory damages recommended for the sample claims, the jury did not follow the Master's recommendations in 46 instances.[50] For the remaining class members, however, the jury agreed with the Master's methodology.

The District Court subsequently entered judgment for 135 of the 137 claimants in the sample in the amounts awarded by the jury, and for the remaining plaintiffs in each of the three subclasses in the amounts

---

[46] In re Estate of Marcos Human Rights Litigation (1995), 1465.

[47] Hilao v. Estate of Marcos, 103 F.3d 767 (9th Cir. 1996), 783.

[48] Laurens Walker and John Monahan, 'Sampling Liability', Virginia Law Review 85 (1999), 329, 339. In re Estate of Marcos Human Rights Litigation (1995), 1466.

[49] Apparently, this did not result in an alteration of the invalidity rate established by the Special Master (5 per cent). Hilao v. Estate of Marcos (1996), at 784, footnote 10.

[50] Hilao v. Estate of Marcos (1996), 784.

awarded by the jury, to be divided pro rata. In other words, the mechanics of this division are as follows:

- The 135 sample claimants whose claims were found to be valid received the actual amount awarded by the jury.
- The two sample claimants whose claims were held invalid received nothing.
- All remaining 9,404 claimants with prima facie valid claims were eligible to participate in the aggregate award, which was calculated based on a 5 per cent invalidity rate of those claims.

The latter is a principal feature of the sampling methodology employed by the Court. Although the review of the sample claims (which are representative of the total claims population) indicates that a certain percentage of the remaining claims is invalid, *all* 'extrapolated' claimants are awarded compensation. Because of the overall invalidity rate, however, each 'extrapolation' claimant receives an amount that is slightly lower than the average amount the jury awarded to the successful sample claimants, i.e. for each subclass the total award is divided *pro rata* among all subclass members.

Analysis made by the Court of Appeals   In second instance, the Court of Appeals considered whether a representative sample was acceptable to determine which percentage of the total claims was valid[51] and recognised that sampling raised serious issues of due process. Nevertheless, it found this approach to be justified by the unusual nature of the case. According to the Court, '[d]ue process, unlike some legal rules, is not a technical conception with a fixed content unrelated to time, place and circumstances'.[52] To determine whether the requirements of due process were satisfied, the Court of Appeals had to weigh the respective interests involved.[53] In the case at hand, it decided that Estate's interest was

---

[51] *Hilao v. Estate of Marcos* (1996), 784, footnote 11.
[52] Reference to *Cafeteria and Restaurant Workers Union, Local 473* v. *McElroy*, 367 US 886, 895, 81 S.Ct. 1743, 1748, 6 L.Ed.2d 1230 (1961).
[53] *Connecticut* v. *Doehr*, 501 US 1, 10, 111 S.Ct. 2105, at 2112, 115 L.Ed.2d 1 (1991): '[F]irst, consideration of the private interest that will be affected by the [procedure]; second, an examination of the risk of erroneous deprivation through the procedures under attack and the probable value of additional or alternative safeguards; and third, [. . .] principal attention to the interest of the party seeking the [procedure], with, nonetheless, due regard for any ancillary interest the government may have in providing the procedure or forgoing the added burden of providing greater protections.'

confined to the total amount of compensation it had to pay.[54] However, as the sampling procedure provided for a deduction because of invalid claims, the Estate's interest was not negatively affected. The Court of Appeals nonetheless admitted that the sampling methodology presented a somewhat greater risk of error than an adversarial adjudication of each claim. However, this risk was reduced by the fact that each class member had to certify under penalty of perjury that the information provided was true and correct. Moreover, the risk of error was balanced by the plaintiffs' decision to forego compensation for some damages that was not available to the class members.[55]

The Court next turned to the plaintiffs' interest in the use of the statistical method, which it considered to be 'enormous', since adversarial resolution of nearly 10,000 claims would present insurmountable practical hurdles. Furthermore, the similarity in the injuries suffered by many of the class members 'would make such an effort, even if it could be undertaken, especially wasteful, as would the fact that the district court found early on that the damages suffered by the class members likely exceed the total known assets of the Estate'.[56]

Finally, the Court of Appeals held that the judiciary had a substantial ancillary interest in the approach followed, since '9,541 individual adversarial determinations of claim validity would clog the docket of the district court for years'.[57] Consequently, the Court found that the procedure chosen did not violate due process and affirmed the judgment of the District Court.[58]

Blue Cross and Blue Shield v. Philip Morris

A final illustration, albeit in a different context, is found in *Blue Cross and Blue Shield of New Jersey, Inc.* v. *Philip Morris, Inc.*[59] The plaintiff, a health insurer, sued several tobacco companies under the New York consumer protection statute, alleging that these companies had engaged in a scheme

---

[54] *Hilao* v. *Estate of Marcos* (1996), 786: 'The interest of the Estate that is affected is at best an interest in not paying damages for any invalid claims. If the Estate had a legitimate concern in the identities of those receiving damage awards, the district court's procedure could affect this interest. In fact, however, the Estate's interest is only in the total amount of damages for which it will be liable: if damages were awarded for invalid claims, the Estate would have to pay more'.

[55] *Hilao* v. *Estate of Marcos* (1996), 786, footnote 15.

[56] *Hilao* v. *Estate of Marcos* (1996), 786. [57] *Hilao* v. *Estate of Marcos* (1996), 786–7.

[58] Not all judges concurred. See the opinion of J. Rymer, *Hilao* v. *Estate of Marcos* (1996), 788.

[59] For references, see *Blue Cross and Blue Shield of New Jersey, Inc.* v. *Philip Morris, Inc.*, 178 F.Supp.2d 198 (E.D.N.Y., 2001), 206.

to distort public knowledge concerning the risks of smoking, knowing that the public would act on the companies' misinformation.

Unlike in class action claims, the plaintiff was not pursuing the claims of the hundreds of thousands of individual subscribers to the health insurance. Rather, those individual claims constituted evidence of the aggregate injury that the plaintiff itself suffered.

The parties and the Court extensively discussed the concrete aggregation and sampling methodology.[60] Eventually, a sample of 156 deponents was selected. Depositions were taken in person, with standardised questions and without witness preparation. The results were then extrapolated. Other statistical models were used to quantify that portion of smoking-related costs attributable to defendants.[61] In the plaintiffs' view, the sampling procedure ensured that 'the ultimate damages projected by its statistical model will be within 10 per cent (either higher or lower) of the actual damage caused by Tobacco's alleged misconduct'.[62]

A jury found in favour of the health insurer and awarded US $17,000,000 in compensatory damages.[63] The defendants moved to dismiss on the ground that no cause of action was proved. With respect to the use of statistical sampling, the objections of the defendants were largely similar to the challenges discussed in the above-mentioned cases. A few specific elements of the Court's reasoning should nonetheless be mentioned.

First, rejecting the defendants' argument that due process and jury trial rights require individualised evidence, the Court observed that '[t]here is little harm in retaining a requirement for "particularistic" evidence of causation and damages in sporadic individual accidents where there are few medical histories and witnesses'.[64] In mass exposure cases with hundreds of thousands of injured, however, such procedures are hampered by excessive costs and practical impossibilities. Therefore, the consequence of requiring individual proof from each smoker would be 'to allow defendants who have injured millions of people and caused billion of dollars in damages to escape all liability'.

Second, the Court observed that sampling evidence is generally well suited to mass tort actions and particularly appropriate in cases where

---

[60] *Blue Cross and Blue Shield of New Jersey, Inc.* v. *Philip Morris, Inc.* (2001), 254.
[61] *Blue Cross and Blue Shield of New Jersey, Inc.* v. *Philip Morris, Inc.* (2001), 255.
[62] *Blue Cross and Blue Shield of New Jersey, Inc.* v. *Philip Morris, Inc.* (2001), 254.
[63] *Blue Cross and Blue Shield of New Jersey, Inc.* v. *Philip Morris, Inc.* (2001), 206.
[64] *Blue Cross and Blue Shield of New Jersey, Inc.* v. *Philip Morris, Inc.* (2001), 247.

the low financial value of individual claims or the litigation advantages of well-financed defendants may discourage individuals from pressing their claims in court. The Court further noted that in the case at bar, where the plaintiff suffered an aggregated injury, statistical evidence was more accurate and comprehensive than the testimony of millions of smokers. Indeed, according to the Court, '[t]he aggregation of millions of alleged injuries in the instant suit can be expected to yield more accurate results with respect to the causation issue since projections based upon a large statistical base will be available, thus reducing the size of possible error'.[65]

For the Court, sampling would not only increase the accuracy of its decisions, it would also avoid the systematic bias against plaintiffs existing in a traditional case-by-case approach: 'while defendants spread the risk of adverse judgments across all [. . .] trials, each trial decides the fate of each plaintiff party on a single roll of the dice'.[66] Furthermore, a 'defendant who successfully resolves a mass tort dispute with aggregate tools enjoys the economic benefit of a final resolution to all proceedings, not just a single case'.[67]

The Court also found that the use of statistics favours private interests. Defendants admittedly had an interest in not paying for damages in excess of what their alleged misconduct may have caused. However, the litigation costs of requiring individual proof as to hundreds of thousands of claims 'would far exceed any monies saved by avoiding erroneous payments [. . .]'.[68] The plaintiff – a non-profit entity with limited annual income dedicated to covering clients' health costs – had an obvious interest in avoiding these additional litigation costs. The approach furthermore avoided an unnecessary intrusion on the lives of thousands of smoking health plan members.

The District Court concluded that the procedural use of sampling was consistent with New York state law and did not violate defendants' constitutional rights. The tobacco companies appealed. The Court of Appeals found that appellants did not show that either their right to a jury trial or their right to due process had been violated by the use of

---

[65] *Blue Cross and Blue Shield of New Jersey, Inc.* v. *Philip Morris, Inc.* (2001), 248.
[66] *Blue Cross and Blue Shield of New Jersey, Inc.* v. *Philip Morris, Inc.* (2001), 248. Quoting Rosenberg, 'What Defendants Have and Plaintiffs Don't', 430. See also Peterson and Selvin, *Resolution of Mass Torts*, p. 12.
[67] *Blue Cross and Blue Shield of New Jersey, Inc.* v. *Philip Morris, Inc.* (2001), 248–9.
[68] *Blue Cross and Blue Shield of New Jersey, Inc.* v. *Philip Morris, Inc.* (2001), 253.

aggregation and sampling.[69] The appellants *inter alia* argued that their right to a jury trial was violated 'because, by consolidating "snippets" of testimony from a variety of subscribers, [the plaintiff] was able to create a "perfect subscriber" and to litigate the case on that basis'. The Court rejected this argument, stating that the individuals were selected on a random basis, not by the plaintiff.[70]

Preliminary conclusions

The use of sampling in the courtroom remains controversial. The few cases in which sampling was used and upheld by the appellate courts, nevertheless provide useful background for an analysis of the sampling techniques developed by the UNCC. A few preliminary conclusions can be drawn.

Rationale and justification   The argumentation that was given by the courts to justify the use of sampling methodologies ranges from the merely practical to the philosophical.

Some arguments relate to the practicalities of resolving mass claims. The unusual volume of cases made a case-by-case review difficult. The amount of time required to fairly resolve all claims on a one-on-one basis was considered excessive. There were doubts about the manage-ability of the caseload. In the *Marcos* case, the geographical distribution of the potential claimants moreover appeared to have militated against case-by-case litigation.[71]

Other arguments assert that statistical adjudication is more efficient than individualised claims procedures. In *Cimino*, the transaction costs to the parties under a case-by-case procedure were held to be 'unacceptable'.[72] In *Marcos*, the District Court argued that 'it cannot be questioned that a one-on-one trial is more burdensome for the Court than an aggregate trial' and that 'the costs involved in conducting bipolar trials with 9,541 plaintiffs in this case would substantially surpass the costs of an aggregate trial which lasted only about one and one-half weeks'.[73] The same court observed that the similarity in the injuries

---

[69] See *Blue Cross and Blue Shield of New Jersey, Inc.* v. *Philip Morris USA, Inc.*, 344 F.3d 211 (C.A.2, N.Y., 2003), 225.

[70] *Blue Cross and Blue Shield of New Jersey, Inc.* v. *Philip Morris USA, Inc.* (2003), 226.

[71] *In re Estate of Marcos Human Rights Litigation* (1995), 1467.

[72] *Cimino* v. *Raymark Industries, Inc.* (1998), 302.

[73] *In re Estate of Marcos Human Rights Litigation* (1995), 1468.

suffered by the class members would make individual proceedings especially wasteful.[74] The testimony of all plaintiffs would have been repetitive and neither side would benefit from duplication. Moreover, the fact that the damages suffered by the class members were likely to exceed the total known assets of the Estate did not make individualised claims adjudication more meaningful.[75] In *Blue Cross*, it was found that the additional litigation costs required by an individualised approach 'would consume much of any recovery from Tobacco, making continued pursuit of the litigation fruitless'.[76] In short, statistical adjudication saves time and expense, and the courts must take advantage of statistical science.

Furthermore, statistical sampling benefits the plaintiffs. Individualised claims review delays justice for all plaintiffs. Moreover, trying low-value claims individually is costly and discourages claimant from pressing their claims in court.[77] In *Marcos*, the class members were mostly impecunious and the cost of individual trials might have prevented their claims from ever being determined.[78]

Statistical sampling may also increase outcome accuracy. In *Blue Cross*, statistics were held to be more accurate and comprehensive than the testimony of millions of plaintiffs. Statistical tools, when applied properly, can be expected to yield more accurate results since projections based upon a large statistical base reduce the size of possible error.[79] In short, statistical methods provide 'a decent answer – likely a more accurate answer than is possible when addressing the equivalent causation question in a single person's suit'.[80]

Finally, it would be unconscionable to deny relief to persons who have suffered significant damage simply because the number of claims is unmanageable.[81] In *Blue Cross*, it was stated that the 'consequence of requiring individual proof from each smoker would be to allow defendants who have injured millions of people and caused billions of

---

[74] *In re Estate of Marcos Human Rights Litigation* (1995), 1467; *Hilao v. Estate of Marcos* (1996), 786.
[75] *Hilao v. Estate of Marcos* (1996), 786.
[76] *Blue Cross and Blue Shield of New Jersey, Inc. v. Philip Morris, Inc.* (2001), 254.
[77] *Blue Cross and Blue Shield of New Jersey, Inc. v. Philip Morris, Inc.* (2001), 251.
[78] *In re Estate of Marcos Human Rights Litigation* (1995), 1468.
[79] *Blue Cross and Blue Shield of New Jersey, Inc. v. Philip Morris, Inc.* (2001), 248.
[80] *Blue Cross and Blue Shield of New Jersey, Inc. v. Philip Morris, Inc.* (2000), 374.
[81] *In re Estate of Marcos Human Rights Litigation* (1995), 1468, footnote 19.

dollars in damages, to escape all liability'. In a similar vein, it was held that the 'equity in allowing statistical proof [. . .] is underscored by the massive nature of the fraud alleged: if [the plaintiff's] allegations are borne out, the defendants sought to mislead the whole of the American public by distorting the entire body of public knowledge on the lethal and addictive effects of smoking. By carrying out this alleged widespread scheme, it was the defendants themselves who made a claim-by-claim showing virtually impossible'.[82] Moreover, as already mentioned, a traditional case-by-case approach may create a systemic bias against plaintiffs.[83]

Developing a proper sampling methodology   With respect to the choice of an appropriate sampling methodology, three observations emerge from the reviewed case law.

First, the selection of the sample: as the sample must be representative of the overall claims population, it needs to be randomly selected. When sample cases are selected by plaintiffs and defendants, as attempted in certain cases, they may be highly biased, with the very best and the very worst cases.[84] A selection of such extremes cannot constitute a proper basis for extrapolation to the other claims.

Moreover, statistical adjudication is only appropriate when there is a minimal similarity among claims.[85] When the issues are highly individualised and diverse, sampling is less appropriate.

Furthermore, diversity in the claims population can partly be resolved by a 'stratified' sampling technique, which uses a subset of the population that shares at least one common characteristic. In stratified sampling, the court first identifies the relevant strata and their actual representation in the population.[86] A sufficient number of cases from each stratum is then selected at random. Because the claims within each stratum are more homogeneous than the claims in general, stratum-specific estimates will produce more precise results than a simple random sample.

---

[82] *Blue Cross and Blue Shield of New Jersey, Inc.* v. *Philip Morris, Inc.* (2000), 380.

[83] *Blue Cross and Blue Shield of New Jersey, Inc.* v. *Philip Morris, Inc.* (2001), 248.

[84] See also *In re Chevron USA, Inc.*, 109 F.3d 1016 (C.A.5, Tex., 1997), 1019.

[85] Sampling has been used to determine both liability and damages. See Walker and Monahan, 'Sampling Liability', 339.

[86] In the above cases, this was for example done by establishing disease categories within the overall claims population. For an example, see *Hilao* v. *Estate of Marcos* (1996), 784–5.

Evaluating sampling methodologies in a legal context As Judge Parker observed in *Cimino*, perfection is not the benchmark of due process:

> It is apparent from the effort and time required to try these 160 cases, that unless this plan or some other procedure that permits damages to be adjudicated in the aggregate is approved, these cases cannot be tried. Defendants complain about the 1% likelihood that the result would be significantly different. However, plaintiffs are facing a 100% confidence level of being denied access to the courts. The Court will leave it to the academicians and legal scholars to debate whether our notion of due process has room for balancing these competing interests.[87]

He further observed that in the context of mass claims, due process should not be analysed in the narrow, traditional, one-sided view of defendants; instead, it should also 'encompass the impact on plaintiffs and even the obvious societal interest involved'.[88]

Due process in mass claims should not exclusively be seen from the viewpoint of either the defendant's or the plaintiff's right to an individualised claim process. Weighing the interests of the defendants against these of the plaintiffs and the court has substantial merit.[89] The interests of all parties concerned – plaintiffs, defendants and those responsible for or bearing the costs of the adjudication process – should be taken into account.

Sampling in the practice of the UNCC

Facing an unprecedented number of claims, the UNCC was forced to experiment with various statistical methodologies, in particular for small individual claims from Categories "A" and "C", which, for the Governing Council, had to be processed urgently.[90] To ensure uniformity in their treatment, similar claims had to be categorised 'according to, *inter alia*, the type or size of the claims and the similarity of legal and factual issues'.[91] Sampling was authorised by Article 37 of the Provisional Rules. This section provides a detailed overview of the sampling methodologies utilised for Category "A" and "C" claims.[92]

---

[87] *Cimino v. Raymark Industries, Inc.* (1990), 666.
[88] *Cimino v. Raymark Industries, Inc.* (1990), 666.
[89] For a critique, see Charles H. Koch Jr., 'A Community of Interest in the Due Process Calculus', *Houston Law Review* 37 (2000), 635, 636.
[90] UNCC Governing Council, Decision No. 1. [91] UNCC, Provisional Rules, Art. 17.
[92] The overview is based on the relevant Reports of the Commissioners and internal working documents prepared by the UNCC Secretariat, in particular the Secretariat's

Category "A" claims

Category "A" claims concerned departure from Iraq or Kuwait during the time period of the invasion and occupation of Kuwait by Iraq, i.e. from 2 August 1990 to 2 March 1991. Instalments 1 to 3 were largely processed by relying on data matching. For the fourth instalment of Category "A" claims, the Panel designed a sampling methodology to determine whether the evidence attached to the sample claims proved departure from Iraq or Kuwait within the relevant period.[93] The sampling methodology included three successive stages: the design of a representative sample, the review of the sample claims and the extrapolation to the overall population of claims.[94]

Designing the sample

Claims for the fourth instalment had been submitted by sixty-seven countries and by three UN agencies. The Secretariat found significant differences in the claims submitted by different countries and international organisations. Therefore the sampling had to be country-specific, thus increasing the homogeneity and improving the results of the extrapolation.[95]

The size and composition of the samples were guided by two general considerations. The samples had to be representative so that the results could be extrapolated to the overall population of claims per country or international organisation. This required a sufficiently large sample size. However, the size still had to be manageable, because of the urgency to process the Category "A" claims.[96]

Three specific variables helped determining the size of the sample: the prominent proportion of evidence, the chosen margin of error and the desired level of confidence. These, as well as the actual identification of the sample claims, will be analysed hereinafter.

Prominent proportion of evidence The evidence related to the sample claims has to be reviewed and assessed. Consequently, it was essential

---

Memorandum of 18 May 1995, submitted to the Commissioners of Panel "A" to provide background information on the sampling methodology.

[93] UNCC, Report "A" claims, 4th inst., para. 8.

[94] UNCC, Report "A" claims, 4th inst., para. 45.

[95] UNCC, Report "A" claims, 4th inst., para. 46. In practice, a sample was selected for each of the countries and organisations that submitted over 100 claims. If a country submitted less than 100 claims, all claims were reviewed individually.

[96] UNCC, Report "A" claims, 4th inst., para. 47.

that the sample reflected the types of evidence in the relevant claims population.[97] The percentages of the respective types of evidence could be determined through the claims database.[98] The statisticians had to compile a sample that reflected this distribution. In determining the proper sample size, the experts relied on the 'prominent proportion of evidence'. This proportion is 'determined from the percentages of the types of evidence submitted and serves as an estimate of the heterogeneity of the types of evidence in the population of claims from a particular country or international organisation'.[99] When the percentage of a particular type of evidence is close to either 0 or 100, the population has a high level of homogeneity with respect to that type of evidence. A percentage close to 50 reflects a very high degree of heterogeneity. The 'prominent proportion of evidence', which determines the sample size, should be based on the type of evidence presenting the highest degree of heterogeneity. In this way, the selected sample also takes account of the lack of homogeneity in the other types of evidence.

The UNCC statisticians determined the sample size by examining the percentage of each type of evidence and selecting the percentage proportion closest to 50 – i.e. the 'prominent proportion' – in order to maximise the likelihood that the sample would be representative. For instance, if the data showed that 90 per cent of the claims from a particular country have 'Visa/passport stamp', 26 per cent have 'Used tickets', and 40 per cent have 'Statement', the size of the sample was determined on the basis of the 40 per cent proportion (this being the closest to 50 per cent). In this way, not only would the 26 per cent proportion of 'Used tickets' be reflected in the sample, but so also would the 'Visa/passport stamp' proportion of 90 per cent.[100]

For large claims populations, the sample size is relatively independent of the total number of claims, because the main criterion in the sampling is not the number of claims, but the percentage of evidence that is critical to determine the sample size. Adding more claims to a sample that adequately reflects the prominent proportion of evidence would neither increase the representativeness of the sample nor the accuracy of the extrapolation.[101]

---

[97] UNCC Secretariat, Memorandum, at 4.   [98] UNCC, Report "A" claims, 4th inst., para. 50.
[99] UNCC, Report "A" claims, 4th inst., para. 49. In sampling, the higher the degree of heterogeneity in the population, the larger must be the sample size to maximise the likelihood that the sample is representative of the population.
[100] Example taken from the Panel's report, para. 50.
[101] UNCC Secretariat's Memorandum, at 5–6.

Chosen margin of error and the confidence level   The margin of error is the amount of acceptable variation with respect to the results obtained from the sample review.[102] Put simply, the margin of error is an expression of the range of error that one is willing to accept. It is typically expressed as a numerical range around the proportion of claims in the sample satisfying the sampling criteria. For a given level of confidence, the smaller the margin of error, the larger must be the size of the sample. Similarly, the higher the margin of error, the smaller the sample size may be. In determining the size of the Category "A" samples, the UNCC applied the standard margin of error, used in many statistical estimations, of plus or minus 5 per cent.

Any margin of error is associated with a level of confidence, i.e. the probability that the proportion of claims in the sample satisfying the relevant criteria reflects the whole claims population.[103] While the margin of error quantifies how precise the results are, the confidence level relates to the probability that the examined sample is representative of the overall claims population. There is a trade-off between the margin of error and the confidence level. Thus, to obtain a higher level of confidence for the same sample size, one must be willing to accept a higher margin of error, or increase the size of the sample. The smaller the margin of error and the higher the desired level of confidence, the larger the sample size must be. The most commonly used confidence level in statistics is '19 times out of 20', i.e. there is a 95 per cent probability that for a chosen margin of error the sample drawn is representative and a 5 per cent chance that it is not.[104]

For the sampling of Category "A" claims, the UNCC calculated the sample size for a 95 per cent confidence level. In other words, the size of the sample ensured that there was a 95 per cent probability that the selected sample would be representative within a 5 per cent margin of error. In reality, however, as the UNCC was in a position to verify whether a selected sample was representative of the overall population of that country's claims, the distribution of evidence in the sample could be compared to the distribution of evidence in the larger claims population. Where the percentages of evidence in the sample corresponded accurately to those in the overall population, the '19 times out of 20'

---

[102] UNCC, Report "A" claims, 4th inst., para. 51.
[103] In other words, the confidence level concerns the probability that the sample actually reflects the population. See Saks and Blanck, 'Justice Improved, 824, footnote 68.
[104] UNCC, Report "A" claims, 4th inst., para. 55.

was no longer applicable and became a 100 per cent certainty within a 5 per cent margin of error.[105]

Identification of sample claims   Based on the above criteria, the required size of the samples could be calculated with a standard statistical formula. To ensure that the chosen sample claims were sufficiently representative of the overall population, the sample had to be selected on a random basis.[106] The actual selection took place through a computerised random number generator. Once the sample claims were selected, each Government or organisation was asked to submit to the UNCC the paper claim forms with the attached evidence.

Assessment of the sample claims

The selected sample claims and the evidence attached thereto were reviewed individually to ascertain whether the claimant departed from Iraq or Kuwait during the relevant period. The purpose of the manual review was to evaluate the quality of the evidence attached to the claims and to determine whether it met the appropriate evidentiary standard.[107]

The Category "A" claim form lists the types of documents that the claimant could submit in support of their claim and provides tick boxes for each type: a copy of official identification issued by Iraq or Kuwait, used tickets, visa or passport stamps, boarding pass, receipts or bills and other documents. Moreover, claimants had to submit a statement including the address of last residence and the last place of work in Iraq or Kuwait and to describe how they travelled from Iraq or Kuwait to their ultimate destination.[108]

The Secretariat reviewed the seven evidence types in the sample claims, pursuant to the general determinations made by the Commissioners regarding the evidentiary value of the respective records and documents. Each evidence received an evidentiary value, represented by stars. For instance, items that proved presence in Iraq or Kuwait were assigned one star. Items that proved presence in Jordan or in another border country or demonstrated entry into or exit from any other country were assigned two stars. Items that proved by themselves

---

[105] UNCC, Report "A" claims, 4th inst., para. 57–58; UNCC Secretariat's Memorandum, at 9.
[106] UNCC, Report "A" claims, 4th inst., para. 59.
[107] UNCC Secretariat's Memorandum, at 2. The UNCC Provisional Rules (Art. 35, 2 (a)) provided that 'simple documentation of the fact and date of departure from Iraq or Kuwait' was sufficient to be eligible for compensation under Category "A".
[108] UNCC Secretariat' Memorandum, at 14.

departure from Iraq or Kuwait during the relevant time period were assigned three stars. A worksheet was then developed, on which paralegals, supervised by lawyers, recorded all relevant details of the reviewed sample claims. The Panel then assessed the claim to be 'conclusive', 'possible' or 'insufficient'.[109]

Claims were assessed as 'conclusive' if the attached evidence clearly proved departure from Iraq or Kuwait within the jurisdictional period and had a total value of three stars: either one three-star item of evidence or the combination of one two-star item and one one-star item.[110] Three one-star items or two two-star items did not add up to a total value of three stars in this assessment, since such combination did not establish the basic fact of departure.

'Possible' claims had evidence attached that was not assessed as 'conclusive', but was more than 'insufficient'. Their evidence only demonstrated presence in Iraq, Kuwait, Jordan or another border country or entry in and exit from a non-border country.

Finally, 'insufficient' claims had no evidence attached, or the only evidence manifestly disproved, or was irrelevant to the fact of, departure from Iraq or Kuwait within the relevant timeframe.

Extrapolation of the results of the sample review to the total population

The Secretariat used 'selective sampling', i.e. 'a country-specific and evidence-specific methodology that involves the assessment of evidence attached to the sample from each country or international organization by type of evidence so as to extrapolate the conclusions from this assessment, by type [of evidence], over the whole population of claims submitted by each country or international organization'.[111]

Before extrapolating the sample results, the UNCC verified whether the sample was representative of the overall population of Category "A" claims submitted by the country or organisation at stake. When the percentages for the distribution of types of evidence in the sample corresponded to those in the statistics from the claims database, the sample was confirmed as representative. If the percentages did not match, further efforts were made to find out whether there was a particular explanation

---

[109] UNCC, Report "A" claims, 4th inst., paras 72–5.
[110] UNCC Secretariat's Memorandum, at 20.
[111] UNCC, Report "A" claims, 4th inst., para. 78.

for the discrepancy in the percentages.[112] If there was no reasonable explanation, re-sampling was needed. The first sample had then to be enlarged until the sample was representative of the overall population, or until a reasonable explanation was found.

Once found representative, the sample results were extrapolated on the basis of the 'conclusive' claims within each type of evidence. When the percentage of 'conclusive' claims within a particular type of evidence was judged to be sufficiently high, the Panel concluded that all the claimants from that country or organisation who submitted that particular type of evidence were entitled to compensation. If, on the contrary, the Panel determined that the percentage of 'conclusive' claims within a particular type of evidence was not sufficiently high or if a type of evidence existing in the claims database was not represented in the sample, the Panel requested the submitting entity to provide the paper claim forms and evidence for further individual review. The claims for which the claims database indicated that no evidence at all had been provided were also requested for individual review.[113]

Whether the percentage of 'conclusives' within an evidence type or the general percentage of 'conclusive' evidence in the sample was regarded as sufficiently high to recommend for compensation all claimants who attached that type of evidence depended on various factors. There was no standard or threshold percentage applicable across the board.[114]

Results

Based on sampling, the Panel of Commissioners recommended compensation for 217,513 claims in the fourth instalment. The total recommended amount of compensation for the fourth instalment was US $771,531,000.[115] Relying on the same procedure, a further 217,520 claims were recommended for compensation in the fifth instalment, totalling US $784,076,500.[116]

---

[112] UNCC Secretariat's Memorandum, at 28.

[113] Some claimants had submitted evidence, but did not tick the relevant check-box on the claim form. Some claims were altered when being data-captured. In this way, these claimants will not be prejudiced for such involuntary modifications, since their claims will be given further consideration on a case-by-case basis. UNCC, Report "A" claims, 4th inst., para. 82.

[114] UNCC, Report "A" claims, 4th inst., paras 85–87.

[115] UNCC, Report "A" claims, 4th inst., para. 90.

[116] UNCC, Report and Recommendations Made by the Panel of Commissioners Concerning the Fifth Instalment of Claims for Departure from Iraq or Kuwait (Category "A" Claims), 13 December 1995, UN Doc. S/AC.26/1995/5, para. 9.

The remaining Category "A" claims included in the sixth instalment were verified either through sampling or through individual examination. When claims were reviewed individually, they were immediately categorised as either 'conclusive' or 'insufficient'.[117] On this basis, the Panel recommended for payment of compensation another 80,456 claims. The overall recommended amount of compensation for the sixth instalment totalled US $319,730,500.

Finally, a total of 18,899 claims had been verified both through the sampling procedure and through individual review and were found not to be eligible for compensation.[118]

Category "C" claims

Category "C" claims were individual claims for damages up to US $100,000 sustained as a result of Iraq's unlawful invasion and occupation of Kuwait. They included twenty-one different types of losses. The UNCC received approximately 420,000 Category "C" claims submitted by eighty-five Governments and three international organisations, seeking approximately US $9 billion in compensation. In addition, the Central Bank of the Government of Egypt submitted a consolidated Category "C" claim on behalf of over 800,000 workers in Iraq for the non-transfer of remittances by Iraqi banks to beneficiaries in Egypt. This consolidated Category "C" claim comprised 1,240,000 individual claims with an asserted value of approximately US $491 million.

Category "C" claims had to 'be documented by appropriate evidence of the circumstances and amount of the claimed loss' and the standard of evidence was to 'be the reasonable minimum that is appropriate under the particular circumstances of the case'.[119] The Governing Council determined that "C" claims were considered urgent claims and accordingly allowed for the processing of these categories of claims 'on an expedited basis', including by 'checking individual claims on a sample basis, with further verification only if circumstances warranted'.[120]

---

[117] The latter included claimants who did not attach any evidence to their claim form, claimants who attached evidence that manifestly disproved their departure or that was considered to have no probative value.

[118] UNCC, Report and Recommendations Made by the Panel of Commissioners Concerning the Sixth Instalment of Claims for Departure From Iraq or Kuwait (Category "A" Claims), 16 October 1996, UN Doc. S/AC.26/1996/3, para. 51.

[119] UNCC, Provisional Rules, Art. 35, 2(c).

[120] UNCC Governing Council, Decision No. 1, para. 8. See also UNCC, Provisional Rules, Art. 37(b).

The diversity of types of loss within the Category "C" claims necessitated the development of tailor-made processing methodologies for each type of loss. For some loss, the "C" Panel relied on statistical sampling to render practical and simple justice.[121] Two examples will be reviewed.[122]

Loss type "C1": Departure and relocation claims

Loss type "C1" covered damages arising from departure, inability to leave or return, a decision not to return, hostage-taking or other illegal detention and where costs for transportation, food, lodging, relocation expenses and similar costs were claimed.[123]

Departure and relocation claims were probably among the most diverse claims before the "C" Panel in terms of facts, items claims and amounts asked for.[124] Certain patterns became nevertheless clear from the review of a sample. Claimants from the same country appeared to claim for similar items and amounts, reflecting perhaps the involvement of their respective governments in the preparation of the claims. Individuals from the same country often travelled by the same modes of transportation and by the same routes to similar destinations, and incurred similar costs reflecting these common patterns. Also claimants' family status and socio-economic background apparently determined the type and level of costs claimed.[125]

Taking into consideration the high number of "C1" claims, the factual diversity in the claims, their urgent character, and the potential for multiple recovery under Categories "A" and "C", the Panel processed the claims as follows.

Claims presenting similar factual and legal issues were grouped together, making maximum use of the UNCC's elaborate claims databases. Computer searches enabled the Secretariat to determine the size of the groups and the actual claims included therein, the number of claims per country as well as the number of claims within a group presenting certain substantive features (type and level of evidence, etc.).[126]

---

[121] UNCC, Report "C" claims, 2nd inst., para. 9.

[122] The "C" Panel applied statistical sampling methodologies to a number of other loss types. See for instance, UNCC, Report and Recommendations Made by the Panel of Commissioners Concerning the Fifth Instalment of Individual Claims for Damages up to US$ 100,000 (Category "C" Claims), 25 June 1997, UN Doc. S/AC.26/1997/1, paras 12–13; UNCC, Report "C" claims, 1st inst., p. 148.

[123] UNCC, Report "C" claims, 1st inst., p. 59.   [124] UNCC, Report "C" claims, 1st inst., p. 68.

[125] UNCC, Report "C" claims, 1st inst., p. 70.

[126] UNCC, Report "C" claims, 1st inst., p. 46.

A sample was then selected from the various groups. The size of the sample depended on a number of variables, including the number of claims in a particular group, the complexity of the factual and legal issues, the homogeneity of the group, the margin of error and the confidence level.

The sample claims were reviewed to determine the following elements: (1) whether claimants were present or resident in Iraq or Kuwait prior to the invasion; (2) whether the losses or the events giving rise to the losses took place during the relevant jurisdiction period; (3) whether the claimants departed from Iraq or Kuwait during this period; and (4) whether their losses were caused by the Iraqi invasion and occupation of Kuwait.[127]

With the help of statisticians, the Panel then verified whether the sample claims were representative of the totality of departure and relocation claims. This included checking the homogeneity of a grouping of claims in order to apply the results to the non-sampled claims in the particular grouping.[128] The Panel also determined whether application of the evaluation and compensation criteria with respect to all similarly situated claims would lead to a fair and equitable result.

Once the Panel was satisfied, the results of the sample review were extrapolated to the remainder of the "C1" claims. The "C" Reports unfortunately provide no further details regarding the precise method of extrapolation.

Claims for mental pain and anguish

Statistical sampling was also used to process the "C1-MPA" claims, i.e. claims for mental pain and anguish resulting from hostage-taking, illegal detention or forced hiding. The "C" Panel used steps similar to those outlined above regarding sampling.[129] They will be reviewed briefly.

A sufficient number of sample claims were randomly selected. While exact representativeness is seldom achievable, the Panel emphasised that a properly designed sample should make it possible 'to obtain a reliable estimate of the proportion of the population that holds the characteristics under consideration'.[130] The Panel added that '[a] sample that is randomly selected and relatively large is more likely to be representative. At the same time, the sample should not be so large as to undermine the very purpose for which the sampling exercise is being conducted: time

---

[127] UNCC, Report "C" claims, 1st inst., p. 73.   [128] UNCC, Report "C" claims, 1st inst., p. 47.
[129] UNCC, Report "C" claims, 2nd inst., para. 28.
[130] UNCC, Report "C" claims, 2nd inst., para. 26.

savings and cost effectiveness'.[131] These considerations eventually led to the selection of two separate samples: one for claims filed by Kuwaiti nationals and a second one for claims by nationals of OECD countries.[132]

The UNCC Secretariat then reviewed the sample claims pursuant to the criteria established by the Panel and found that approximately 94 per cent of the claims filed by nationals of OECD countries for hostage taking or illegal detention for more than three days satisfied the Panel's criteria.[133] Furthermore, all claims by nationals of OECD countries and 99.5 per cent of claims by Kuwaiti nationals regarding claims for being forced to hide on account of a manifestly well-founded fear for one's life, satisfied the Panel's criteria.[134] These results were consistent with United Nations reports describing incidents and identifying patterns of hostage taking, detention and forced hiding during the relevant time period.[135]

These results were deemed sufficiently high to warrant extrapolation to all similar claims. The Panel thus concluded that *all* Kuwaiti nationals with claims for forced hiding, and nationals of OECD countries with claims for forced hiding, hostage taking or illegal detention for more than three days, should be compensated for their respective "C1-MPA" losses.[136] The sample review also allowed the Panel to determine that the number of days of detention or hiding mentioned by the claimants in their claim forms provided a sufficiently reliable basis to determine the amounts of compensation to be awarded.[137]

Analysis of the UNCC's recourse to sampling

Not surprisingly, Iraq vigorously protested against the use of statistical claims processing techniques. It formally objected that the UNCC's use of statistical sampling favours 'speed rather than justice' and 'is not the approved procedure under international law which requires proof and causation in respect to every claim'.[138]

---

[131] UNCC, Report "C" claims, 2nd inst., para. 27.
[132] UNCC, Report "C" claims, 2nd inst., para. 31.
[133] UNCC, Report "C" claims, 2nd inst., para. 32, footnote 32.
[134] UNCC, Report "C" claims, 2nd inst., para. 32. In the recommendations on the fifth instalment of "C" claims, the Commissioners arrived at similar conclusions based on sampling. UNCC, Report "C" claims, 5th inst., paras 10–11.
[135] UNCC, Report "C" claims, 2nd inst., para. 32, footnote 32.
[136] UNCC, Report "C" claims, 2nd inst., para. 32.
[137] UNCC, Report "C" claims, 2nd inst., para. 32.
[138] Presentation of the Delegation of the Republic of Iraq in the Dialogue with the Secretary-General of the United Nations, 26–7 February 2001, p. 26.

This section seeks to evaluate statistical adjudication against the backdrop of three fundamental values, i.e. efficiency, outcome accuracy and procedural participation.[139] Although the analysis focuses primarily on the UNCC's sampling methodologies, it applies more generally to all statistical approaches to adjudication. The central question is whether statistical adjudication is capable of furthering the substantive goals of mass claims procedure, i.e. to provide compensation and/or restitution to numerous victims of wrongful acts within a reasonable period of time, and if so, at what cost?

The analysis deliberately avoids any unnecessarily positivist legal perspectives. Obviously, international and domestic procedural law, as they stand today, have had too little experience with aggregative and sampling procedures to posit firm rules against which the appropriateness of statistical adjudication can be assessed in a positivist legal sense. By necessity, the analysis also remains wary of traditional 'proceduralist' dogmas and views, at least to the extent that these take the supremacy of the individualised case-by-case model for granted.[140]

Efficiency

The UNCC received approximately 2.6 million claims, the largest caseload ever dealt with by an international claims programme. Approximately 2.5 million claims were from individuals, spread over 90 different countries, the vast majority of which were developing countries. The adjudication of the many small claims was considered urgent for humanitarian reasons. Obviously, procedural efficiency was critical. The many victims of Iraq's unlawful invasion and occupation were entitled to a timely remedy. Iraq also had a substantial interest in the efficiency of the UNCC claims procedure, since it had to pay the direct costs of running the claims process.[141]

---

[139] In part, the analysis builds upon existing literature in the US concerning adjudication by sampling and class actions under Rule 23(b)(3) of the US Federal Rules of Civil Procedure. Adjudication by sampling has much in common with class actions. See Bone, 'Statistical Adjudication', 569.

[140] See also Mary J. Davis, 'Toward the Proper Role for Mass Tort Class Actions', *Oregon Law Review* 77 (1998), 157, 160.

[141] See the Report of the Secretary-General of 2 May 1991, para. 8 and 29: 'The expenses of the Commission, including those of the Governing Council, the commissioners and the secretariat, should in principle be paid from the [Compensation] Fund,' which was financed by Iraq.

Direct costs

The UNCC's sampling methodologies were designed to reduce the direct cost, i.e. the costs of making decisions. The grouping of similar claims and the use of statistical sampling within these homogeneous groups allowed the UNCC to avoid redundant repetition and the tremendous delays that individualised adjudication would inevitably involve.[142]

Measuring exactly the money saved through statistical methods is difficult. Nevertheless, there is little doubt that the transaction costs associated with the individual processing of over 1.3 million Category "A" and "C" claims would substantially exceed the costs of statistical sampling.[143] To handle 1.3 million claims, the UNCC appointed only 12 Commissioners, all on a part-time basis. It can be roughly estimated that, in order to adjudicate 1.3 million claims by case-by-case methods in roughly ten years, a minimum of 178 adjudicators would be required, each working seven days a week and resolving an average of 2 claims per day. Moreover, this would necessitate drastic increases in the staffing levels in the Secretariat – compared to the 230 staff members employed – and additional investments in terms of office space, equipment and services.

Nevertheless, these efficiency gains must be weighed against the investment required to process claims by statistical means. This includes in particular the cost of information technology and scientific expertise. For a very small caseload, these costs might be prohibitive. As long as the claim population is large enough to justify these investments, however, statistical sampling remains efficient.[144]

Private costs

Private litigation costs Private litigation costs include claims registration fees, legal representation, presenting evidence, obtaining expert testimony etc. In an administrative claims model, such as the UNCC,

---

[142] See Heiskanen ('The United Nations Compensation Commission', 298–9) arguing that statistical methods 'were designed to expedite processing the urgent claims'. See also, McGovern ('The Intellectual Heritage', 188) arguing that 'the political demands on the UNCC have focused on low transaction costs and high speed'.

[143] McGovern ('The Intellectual Heritage', 188) estimates that a case-by-case review of the Category "C" claims alone 'would necessitate at least 416,384 work days or over eight years for a staff of one hundred translators and one hundred lawyers'. For another estimate of the time and resources required to process the "C" claims individually, see Gibson, 'Using Computers', 171.

[144] Bone, 'Statistical Adjudication', 597.

private costs are obviously much lower than in a litigation or adversarial model. However, given the socio-economic background of the claimants before the UNCC and the relatively small values claimed in Category "A", the private costs remained an important element in the discussion on UNCC procedures.

Statistical adjudication clearly reduces the private litigation costs for the claimants. If claims are reviewed individually, each claimant needs to invest in the preparation of their case. If claims are aggregated and decided on the basis of a representative sample, a substantial part of the costs is only incurred by the claimants included in the sample. If the costs to the sample claimants are pro-rated over all claimants,[145] the per-claimant private costs will be substantially less than in individualised claims adjudication.

The economic gain resulting from aggregation is most prominent for claimants. The respondent in a mass claims situation exploits economies of scale to invest more cost-effectively in preparing its side of the case than claimants can in preparing their side.[146] Faced with numerous claims presenting common legal and factual issues, the respondent naturally prepares one defence for all of those claims. Even in a system that relies on individualised claims processing, the respondent is able to spread the private investments made for one claim across all claims and as such he always enjoys the advantages of economies of scale.[147] Individual claimants, on the other hand, are compelled in a case-by-case system to make the costs of wastefully repetitive investments. Unless the claims resolution facility somehow aggregates the claims and spreads the costs among the claimant population, claimants do not enjoy the advantages of economies of scale.[148]

In the case of the sampling methodologies utilised by the UNCC, however, this cost-reducing effect for claimants was not clearly seen, since the UNCC had already minimised the cost to the claimants in

---

[145] The benefit only accrues to the claimants who are not included in the sample. Arguably, this would necessitate a type of burden- or cost-sharing mechanism to spread the costs incurred by the sample claimants over the entire claims population. In the context of mass tort claims in the United States, see for instance Francis E. McGovern, 'Resolving Mature Mass Tort Litigation', *Boston University Law Review* 69 (1989), 659, 671; Rosenberg, 'What Defendants Have and Plaintiffs Don't', 415–16.

[146] For an analogy with mass tort claims in the United States, see Rosenberg, 'What Defendants Have and Plaintiffs Don't', 393.

[147] Rosenberg, 'What Defendants Have and Plaintiffs Don't', 393–4, 400–1.

[148] Rosenberg, 'What Defendants Have and Plaintiffs Don't', 412.

the "A", "B" and "C" Categories. Because of the socio-economic profile of claimants, the UNCC had made claims registration as straightforward as possible, developed inquisitorial procedures that limited claimant participation to a minimum, relaxed the evidentiary standards and made it possible to pursue claims without legal representation. The private costs for claimants were already minimal, regardless of whether a statistical methodology or a case-by-case approach was taken.

Delay costs Claimants are entitled to a timely remedy. Long delays in providing remedies are universally seen as unfair to claimants. Procedures must ensure 'some minimally fair level of actual recovery net of litigation and delay costs'.[149]

If the claims population is large, individualised approaches to mass claims inevitably entail extremely long waiting periods for most claimants. If the claims population is enormous, as was the case in the UNCC, the delay cost of individualised processes will become so large that the eventual remedy falls below the minimum required by fairness.[150]

Statistical adjudication is capable of delivering remedies to all claimants much more quickly than traditional case-by-case methods.[151] The UNCC's results in Categories "A" and "C" are eloquent on this point. Between 1993 and 1996, the UNCC resolved all Category "A" claims.[152] With a few exceptions, the review of Category "C" claims was finalised by mid 1999.

Small value claims

By reducing the transaction costs, sampling procedures make it economically feasible to adjudicate claims with a low economic value.[153] A distinction must be made in this respect between the private costs to the claimants and the direct costs of running the claims process.

In a traditional claims adjudication system, the private costs to the claimants – i.e. the cost of filing the case, hiring legal representation etc. – play an important (though not necessarily decisive) role in the claimants' decision whether or not to submit a claim. Claimants with

---

[149] Bone, 'Statistical Adjudication', 601.   [150] Bone, 'Statistical Adjudication', 602.
[151] Gibson, 'Using Computers', 171.
[152] Fred Wooldridge and Olufemi Elias, 'Humanitarian Considerations in the Work of the UNCC', *International Review of the Red Cross* 85 (2003), 555, 567.
[153] The small economic value of category "A" claims has been referred to as one of the justifications for using statistics. See for instance Wühler, 'A New Contribution', 261.

small value claims generally have little incentive to come forward when private costs are high. When their costs exceed the value of the outcome, claimants have in fact a clear economic incentive *not* to make use of the claims procedure.

Even if the system succeeds in effectively taking away the economic incentive for small claimants *not* to submit their claims, it is quite possible that the per-claim transaction cost remains higher than the economic value of a small claim. This creates specific economic dilemmas for the adjudicator. Two situations need to be considered.

In the first situation, compensation is paid from a capped fund, from which the direct costs are also paid. If the claims population includes a large proportion of low value claims, the direct costs associated with processing these claims might quickly exhaust the fund. As a consequence, the net benefits for claimants will be reduced and many of them will be denied meaningful compensation.

Second, if the compensation fund is a so-called open fund, as was the case for the UNCC, then a large proportion of small claims might operate to the detriment of the respondent party. The respondent is liable to pay the proper amount of compensation to all eligible claimants. If the per claim transaction cost is high, however, and if there are many small value claims, the respondent will also have to bear transaction costs that are entirely disproportionate to the amount of compensation paid.

By significantly reducing the transaction costs, statistical adjudication avoids these dilemmas and makes it possible to process large numbers of small value claims in a cost-effective way. This can be applauded as one of the most important advantages of statistical adjudication: it makes the remedies offered by international law accessible to large numbers of people, even if the economic value of their claims is modest. In this sense, statistical adjudication furthers the 'democratisation' of international claims practice.[154]

In order to fully assess procedural efficiency, however, the impact of statistical sampling upon the transaction costs must be considered in conjunction with its effect on the error costs. Procedural techniques that minimise direct costs but result in increased error costs are not

---

[154] For similar conclusions, see Carmel Whelton, 'The United Nations Compensation Commission and International Claims Law: A Fresh Approach', *Ottawa Law Review* 25 (1993), 607, 623 and 627.

considered efficient. Outcome accuracy is therefore a key value to be considered in this analysis.

Outcome accuracy

A mass claims process, as any other legal process, has to ensure accurate and rational outcomes. An outcome is accurate if it reflects a correct determination of the facts and the law and a correct application of law to fact. One outcome is more accurate than another 'if the error risk associated with the former is less than the error risk associated with the latter, where risk of error measures the probability that the outcome is erroneous'.[155]

This section provides first a general assessment of the outcome accuracy guaranteed by sampling methodologies and focuses subsequently on the sampling methodologies used by the UNCC.

Sampling compared to individualised claims adjudication: A general assessment

In an individualised adjudication system, each claim is examined in detail in order to receive a specific outcome tailored to that, and only that, claim.[156] The outcome is based on the particulars of the case, as presented by the claimant or the claimant's lawyer and as they appear from all available information.

It is often said that statistical adjudication cannot ensure as accurate a result as traditional claims resolution procedures. How could an award, arrived at by extrapolation from an average of other cases, possibly be as accurate as an award made by an adjudicator on the basis of the particulars of each individual case?[157]

For Saks and Blanck, statistical sampling, if conducted properly, produces outcomes that are more accurate than case-by-case approaches: 'In fact, aggregation adds an important layer of process which, when done well, can produce more precise and reliable outcomes.'[158] While their argumentation focuses on the use of sampling to determine damages – and not eligibility, as was the case in some of the sampling applied by the UNCC – it deserves to be analysed in some detail.

---

[155] Bone, 'Statistical Adjudication', 577.   [156] McGovern, 'The Intellectual Heritage', 190.
[157] Saks and Blanck, 'Justice Improved', 833.
[158] Saks and Blanck, 'Justice Improved', 815.

According to Saks and Blanck, it is incorrect to assume that the estimate based upon a sample's average is in all likelihood an over- or under-compensation. Indeed, an individual award is also an estimate:

> To regard an individualized damages determination as *the* correct amount is nothing more than a potent – and often desirable – illusion resulting largely from the fact that more is invisible than evident about the measurement process that underlies the legal process. Let us consider one important nonobvious feature of the process. Every verdict is itself merely a sample from the large population of potential verdicts. That 'population of verdicts' consists of all the awards that would result from trying the same case repeatedly for an infinite number of times. We can remind ourselves that the exact same case could have been tried repeatedly in different contexts: before the same jury, before different juries, or by different lawyers using exactly the same facts. Or, the case could have been tried using different permutations of the same facts or different facts and arguments that could have been assembled out of the same basic case. Clearly, any given trial of a case is but a single instance from among thousands of possible trials of that same basic case.[159]

Put differently, each individual decision is only a sample from all possible case outcomes. For Saks and Blanck, one should conceive the 'true' award as the average of the population of possible awards.[160] The fact that we normally see only one award obscures the entire range of possible awards from which that particular award was drawn. By taking just the one award that results from a single trial, we are accepting the likelihood of some error. Traditional individualised claims resolution always accepts this 'measurement error'.[161] According to Saks and Blanck, repeated trials of the same case can help to make the true award visible.[162] Indeed, if the same case were tried a hundred times, the average of the hundred outcomes will more closely approximate the correct damages figure than any of the hundred outcomes separately. The reason is simply that the average cancels out much of the extreme variation, eliminating unusually high and unusually low outcomes.

Saks and Blanck underscore a common misconception when sampling is compared to individualised decision making. The tailor-made

[159] Saks and Blanck, 'Justice Improved', 833–4.
[160] Saks and Blanck, 'Justice Improved', 834.
[161] Saks and Blanck, 'Justice Improved', 834, footnote 137.
[162] Saks and Blanck, 'Justice Improved', 834–5.

and fully individualised awards to which the latter appears to lead, are in reality only approximations. Even if the law is correctly applied to the facts, the exact same case, if tried repeatedly in different contexts, may lead to different outcomes. In the same vein, Abraham and Robinson argue that the right to individualised treatment produces disparate outcomes that cannot be accounted for by intrinsic differences in the underlying claims:

> Critics have often remarked that the common law system of tort claims adjudication is an unprincipled lottery. Whether or not that character-ization is completely accurate, it can hardly be denied that there is ran-domness in outcomes and this randomness is in substantial degree a function of insisting that each claim be valued in isolation from any other. Any such randomness must be seen as a flaw in the system that under-mines the system's accuracy and fairness.[163]

Indeed, different lawyers will present the same case in radically different ways. Different adjudicators may assess the merits of a particular argu-ment or the strength of certain evidence differently.[164] Moreover, their opinion on a particular issue may change over time. Formal or procedural issues have an impact upon the trial and may affect the outcome of the case. Much evidence, furthermore, only establishes some degree of probability.[165] In addition, a case-by-case approach risks being subjective, biased or irrational. Individualised approaches may recognise 'differences that are either not grounded in objective reality or should not be recognized'.[166]

In short, both systems – individualised and statistical adjudication – provide only approximations of the actual losses suffered by the claimant. Which approach then gives the best insight into the actual losses?[167]

---

[163] Abraham and Robinson, 'Aggregative Valuation of Mass Tort Claims', 147.

[164] See for instance Reiner, 'Burden and General Standards of Proof', 340: 'Two arbitrators applying the same 'standard' of proof, or I should rather say: the same 'standard-of-proof formula', may come to different results.'

[165] See the remarks with respect to 'particularistic evidence' by David Rosenberg, 'The Causal Connection in Mass Exposure Cases: A 'Public Law' Vision', *Harvard Law Review* 97 (1984), 849, 870: ' "Particularistic" evidence [. . .] is no less probabilistic than is the statistical evidence that courts purport to shun. All knowledge of past as well as future events is probabilistic.' In the same vein, see Abraham and Robinson, 'Aggre-gative Valuation of Mass Tort Claims', 143–4: 'The objections to probabilistic proof rest on an exaggerated distinction between general probability and "particularistic" evi-dence. In all but the simplest case, determinations about particular facts depend on inferences drawn from generalized knowledge and hence on general probability.'

[166] Abraham and Robinson, 'Aggregative Valuation of Mass Tort Claims', 147, footnote 30.

[167] See also Bone, 'Statistical Adjudication', 577.

For Saks and Blanck, statistical sampling is better equipped to identify the true award than an individualised case-by-case approach. If claims are homogeneous, the average of a hundred sample outcomes will more closely approximate the correct damages for any case in the population than the verdict from an individual trial of that case.

> Suppose that in an aggregation of cases, every one of 1000 were identical, and from those, 100 were drawn at random for trial. By trying these 100 cases and taking the average award, the court [. . .] will have far more accurately measured the correct damages than is usually done in individualized cases. By granting the mean award to each of the 100 cases, the court awards a more nearly correct amount than if each case received the award assigned by its jury. By awarding the same amount to each of the remaining 900 plaintiffs, the court also does better, in terms of accuracy of award, than it would if it conducted 900 individualized trials. The goals of corrective justice are better achieved: defendants pay to each plaintiff an amount that is [more] correct than could otherwise be accomplished.[168]

Aggregation and sampling may help exclude random and systematic error – i.e. irrationality and bias – while preserving the core of the decision's logic: 'The aggregation process refines the decision by averaging out of existence the undesirable variations and bringing the systematic and legally relevant relationships into sharper relief.'[169] Saks and Blanck conclude that 'any given award in a traditional trial is likely to be an over- or under-award relative to the true, or population, mean of awards for that trial'.[170] Sampling, on the other hand, is capable of surmounting this defect: 'in aggregated trials people recognize that the problem exists and they begin to think about how to minimize it. [. . .] More importantly, the aggregation procedure itself provides a device for minimizing the problem and producing a more accurate estimate of the true award'.[171]

However, sampling can only be more accurate than an individualised approach when (1) the claims population is homogenous and (2) the statistical system is able to capture all variables that are relevant in deciding the claim. In practice, however, no two cases are identical and a claims population is rarely perfectly homogeneous. For Saks and Blanck, the above conclusions hold true as long as the variation is not excessive.

---

[168] Saks and Blanck, 'Justice Improved', 835–6.
[169] Saks and Blanck, 'Justice Improved', 836.
[170] Saks and Blanck, 'Justice Improved', 836.
[171] Saks and Blanck, 'Justice Improved', 836.

The more the claims differ from each other in legally relevant ways, the 'more we move away from aggregation's accuracy-producing benefits and move toward its error-producing harms'.[172] At some point, aggregation 'ceases to improve the accuracy of traditional trials and becomes a vitiation'.[173]

This part of the Saks and Blanck reasoning may be problematic.[174] The less homogeneous the population is with respect to all legally relevant parameters, the less accurate the sampling. Without perfect homogeneity, trying a sample of a hundred cases is not equivalent to trying any individual case in the population a hundred times. The slightest variation among claims will imply that statistical adjudication may produce a result that is inferior to the result achieved by an individualised trial. The more distant a case from the population mean on the distribution curve, the more likely that an individualised decision in that case will be a better estimate of actual damages than the sample average. As Bone suggests, the cut-off point in the heterogeneity–homogeneity continuum, where statistical adjudication ceases to improve accuracy, is more easily reached than Saks and Blanck suggest.[175] For a non-homogeneous population of claims, it does not take much variation before statistics produce an estimate of the actual damages that is inferior to the approximation produced by an individualised claims review, at least for some cases.

Arguably, this problem can partially be addressed by increasing the homogeneity of the population and by eliminating extreme cases from the population. Stratified sampling, for instance, can be used to increase the homogeneity within the population. Even then, however, 'perfect' homogeneity may rarely be achievable in practice. Moreover, the elimination of extreme cases from the population requires the capacity to identify extreme cases without going through an individual examination of all cases.[176] And, as Bone argues, the more subgroups are created, the smaller each subgroup will be and the less reliable the sampling procedure

---

[172] Saks and Blanck, 'Justice Improved', 836.
[173] Saks and Blanck, 'Justice Improved', 837.
[174] See also the critique formulated by Bone, 'Statistical Adjudication', 577–84.
[175] Bone, 'Statistical Adjudication', 580.
[176] Saks and Blanck ('Justice Improved', 836–7) recognise this. The UNCC was in some cases capable of identifying extreme cases. See for instance the discussion of 'outlier claims' in UNCC, Report and Recommendations Made by the Panel of Commissioners concerning the Sixth Instalment of Individual Claims for Damages up to US $100,000 (Category "C" Claims), 2 July 1998, UN Doc. S/AC.26/1998/6, paras 103–11.

will be. At some point further refinement into subgroups will cost more in lost reliability than it gains in increased homogeneity.[177]

Finally, in any event, statistical adjudication requires that all relevant variables are known in advance and are adequately reflected in the design of the statistical technique.

Outcome accuracy in the UNCC's sampling methodology

Before having a closer look at each of the factors that affect outcome accuracy, a few preliminary observations are called for.

Preliminary remarks   Iraq's liability for losses resulting directly from its invasion and occupation of Kuwait had already been established by the Security Council. Moreover, the Government of Iraq had expressly, though reluctantly, accepted its liability.[178] The Security Council therefore 'started from the assumption that Iraqi responsibility was already established under international law' and set up the UNCC with the primary purposes of examining individual claims and evaluating losses.[179]

Specifically for Category "A" claims, it was presumed that any departure from Iraq or Kuwait during the relevant time period was causally linked to Iraq's invasion and occupation of Kuwait. No proof of causation was required. Sampling only had to establish the fact of departure within the relevant period. The UNCC did not rely on statistical sampling to determine the amount of damages for successful Category "A" claimants, since the UNCC Governing Council had set fixed compensation amounts. However, for Category "C" claims, the UNCC relied on statistical

---

[177] Bone, 'Statistical Adjudication', 584. See also Saks and Blanck, 'Justice Improved', 845.

[178] The Permanent Representative of Iraq addressed two identical letters to the UN Secretary-General and the President of the Security Council on 6 April 1991 (UN Doc. S/22456). In these letters, Iraq criticised the text of Resolution 687 (1991), calling it 'unjust' and alleging that it constituted 'an unprecedented assault' on its sovereignty and rights. Nonetheless, the letters continued, Iraq had no choice but to accept the Resolution's provisions. In a subsequent letter dated 10 April, Iraq transmitted the text of a decision taken by the Iraqi National Assembly on 6 April formally accepting Resolution 687 (1991). The Security Council promptly notified Iraq that its acceptance of liability was 'irrevocable and without qualifying conditions' and was legally binding on the Republic of Iraq. See also Boutros Boutros-Ghali, *The United Nations and the Iraq-Kuwait Conflict: 1990–1996* (New York: UN Department of Public Information, 1996), United Nations Blue Book Series, Vol. IX, paras 109–10.

[179] Andrea Gattini, 'The UN Compensation Commission: Old Rules, New Procedures on War Reparations', *European Journal of International Law* 13(1) (2002), 161, 167.

sampling in combination with other techniques, including statistical modelling, to value various types of losses.[180]

To the extent that sampling was used to determine eligibility rather than the amount of compensation, it requires a slightly different type of analysis than the one suggested by Saks and Blanck. Indeed, the latter focus primarily on the accuracy of outcomes that vary in a wide range, while eligibility determination is binary: a claimant is either eligible or not. Sampling of eligibility concerns the probability that the respondent is liable to a particular claimant (and not an estimate of the damages to which a claimant is entitled).

Increasing homogeneity by using selective or stratified sampling
Representativeness is the touchstone of good sampling.[181] The representativeness of a sample is determined by various factors, one of which is the degree of homogeneity of the overall population. The more homogeneous a population, the more likely the sample is representative for the whole population.

As mentioned before, stratified sampling increases accuracy by selecting samples separately for each homogeneous sub-group. The UNCC relied on two types of stratified sampling.

First, the UNCC's sampling methodologies were country-specific. Separate samples were selected for each submitting country and the conclusions were extrapolated country by country, because the quality of the claims submitted by individuals from different countries was different.[182] The availability and materiality of supporting evidence depended, for instance, on the precise evacuation routes used by the claimants and thus on the particular country to which they were returning. Moreover, some governments had offered extensive assistance and guidance to their claimants, while others merely transmitted their citizens' claims to the UNCC.

Is stratified sampling compatible with the requirement of equality and consistency? As argued above, equality and consistency only require that 'like cases' are treated alike. Objective differences in the starting position of claimants may necessitate corrections. In this respect, different standards for different groups of claimants are justified, and even called for, in order to neutralise the undesirable impact of unequal access to evidence among claimant groups.

---

[180] Statistical modelling techniques are studied in Chapter 12.
[181] Saks and Blanck, 'Justice Improved', 841.
[182] Gibson, 'Mass Claims Processing', 169–71.

Second, for Category "A" claims, the sampling methodology was stratified by type of evidence. Evidence attached to the sample claims from a given country was assessed by type of evidence so as to extrapolate conclusions, again by type of evidence, over the whole population of Category "A" claims submitted by that country. As such, an evidence-specific sampling is a compromise between individualised proceedings, where the evidence for every claim is scrutinised, and general sampling where the type of evidence submitted by the claimant plays no significant role.

Margin of error and the level of confidence   The margin of error and the level of confidence have a direct bearing upon the sampling results. The UNCC applied a margin of error of plus or minus 5 per cent and a 95 per cent confidence level.[183] Because the overall population of claims was known with unusual completeness, however, the UNCC could ensure in many cases a 100 per cent confidence level.[184] Unfortunately, neither the Commissioners' Report, nor the secretariat's Memorandum specifies in how many cases the 100 per cent confidence level was actually reached.

For the samples with a 95 per cent confidence level and a margin of error of 5 per cent, the correct interpretation of the sample results is as follows: if 95 per cent of the claimants in a particular sample were found to be eligible, there was a 95 per cent probability that the true percentage of eligible claimants within the larger population from which the sample was drawn, lies between 90 and 100 per cent.

Regarding samples with a 100 per cent confidence level and a 5 per cent margin of error, if 95 per cent of the claimants in a particular sample were eligible, it is 100 per cent *certain* that the true percentage of eligible claimants within the larger population lies between 90 and 100 per cent.

In both situations, the use of statistical sampling inevitably accepts the *possibility* of errors in individual outcomes. This becomes clear if we consider the best possible scenario, i.e. a margin of error of 5 per cent combined with a confidence level of 100 per cent and 100 per cent of the sample claimants are found to be eligible. Even in this best possible

---

[183] UNCC, Report "A" claims, 4th inst., para. 53.
[184] For each member of the population, the electronic claims database recorded all the details that were considered legally relevant. This means that the degree to which the sample was representative of the overall population could be checked. For a similar reasoning in relation to mass torts in the United States, see Saks and Blanck, 'Justice Improved', 841 (arguing that mass torts represent 'a sampling theorist's dream').

situation, it can only be concluded that a *minimum* of 95 per cent of the claimants in the larger population are eligible. In other words, even in the best possible scenario, the true percentage of eligible claimants lies somewhere between 95 and 100 per cent. In this sense, statistical sampling – based on probability, not certainty – inherently implies the possibility of errors in some individual decisions.

Percentage of conclusive claims within a sample The accuracy of the results obviously also depends on the number of eligible claimants within a sample that is considered sufficient to award compensation to all claimants in the population. To the extent that the UNCC Commissioners accepted an eligibility rate of less than 95 per cent of the sample claims, it should be noted that the sampling methodology went beyond accepting a mere *possibility of errors*, and implied acceptance of a *mathematical certainty of errors*.

For reasons unknown, the Commissioners of the "A" Panel decided against making public the actual percentages of conclusive claims. Instead, they merely stated that whether a percentage was sufficiently high was a 'country-specific determination'[185] that 'depended on various factors' and for which the 'Panel had various resources available to it'. These resources included, in particular, reports for each country describing the socio-economic background and evacuation routes of the foreign worker communities, legal briefs and other background information submitted by various governments describing 'their national claims programmes and particular characteristics relevant to their claimant communities', as well as the results obtained through data matching.[186] Likewise, the "C" Panel did not disclose the percentages used in the sampling procedure for departure and relocation claims. Only with respect to claims for mental pain and anguish resulting from hostage-taking, illegal detention or forced hiding, were the actual percentages (i.e. 94, 99.5 and 100 per cent) disclosed in a footnote in the Report.[187]

This approach is regrettable. Knowledge of the precise percentages is key to evaluating the appropriateness of the sampling methodology. Indeed, these percentages largely determine the overall accuracy of the claim outcomes.

---

[185] UNCC, Report "A" claims, 4th inst., para. 85.
[186] UNCC, Report "A" claims, 4th inst., paras 85–7.
[187] UNCC, Report "C" claims, 2nd inst., para. 32, footnote 32.

Consider the following hypothetical scenario. If a representative sample demonstrates that 100 per cent of the claims with a particular type of evidence are considered 'conclusive', no major objections should exist against extrapolating the sample results to all claims with this type of evidence. For some, 95 per cent would be equally acceptable: given the numbers involved and the practical constraints inherent in processing hundreds of thousands of claims, a 5 per cent invalidity rate is not entirely unreasonable. The problem is simple. Somewhere along this line, there is a critical point below which most of us will agree that the gains – i.e. speed and economy – no longer justify the losses in terms of accuracy. A procedure in which too much accuracy is sacrificed for the sake of judicial economy, loses its integrity and credibility. Such a procedure is also no longer considered efficient: while the direct cost has been minimised, the error cost has become excessive.

By not making the accepted percentages public in each case, the UNCC Commissioners failed to communicate where they placed this critical juncture for each of the various samples. At least Iraq, the respondent party in the UNCC proceedings, was entitled to this critical information, since the percentages had a direct bearing upon the extent of Iraq's liability. The claimants who fell through the cracks and were not awarded compensation based on the sampling were likewise entitled to information regarding the percentages judged insufficient to extrapolate the sample results. The Governing Council, which had to approve the Commissioners' recommendations, also had an interest in knowing the precise percentages. Even more generally, the claims process would most certainly have benefited from more transparency and openness on this particular point.

This issue is of fundamental importance to the assessment of the outcome accuracy guaranteed by the sampling procedure. The precise impact of the percentages of eligible claims in a sample upon the accuracy of the UNCC claims outcomes can best be explained by way of hypothetical examples.

Let us assume that a Panel of Commissioners reviews a particular sample, the representativeness of which has been confirmed (i.e. a confidence level of 100 per cent). The Commissioners find that 95 per cent of the sample claims are eligible for compensation. Taking into account the 5 per cent margin of error, this means that it is certain that the true percentage of eligible claimants within the larger population lies somewhere between 90 and 100 per cent. If the Commissioners decide that this eligibility rate is sufficient to award compensation to all claimants in the larger group, then they accept a mere possibility that a proportion between 0 and 10 per cent of the compensated claimants are in reality not eligible.

If, in the same hypothetical situation, the sample review demonstrates that 94 per cent of the sample claims are eligible for compensation, then the true percentage of eligible claimants within the larger population lies between 89 and 99 per cent. Put differently, a minimum of 89 per cent of the claimants and a maximum of 99 per cent are eligible. If the Commissioners nevertheless decide that this rate is sufficiently high to award compensation to all claimants in the larger group, then it can be concluded with mathematical certainty that at least 1 per cent of the claimants who receive compensation are in reality not eligible. In this case, the Commissioners accept not only a 10 per cent range of possible error, but also the statistical certainty that 1 per cent of the awards are inaccurate.

In this sense, with a 100 per cent confidence level and a 5 per cent margin of error, the acceptance of an eligibility rate of less than 95 per cent necessarily implies the acceptance of actual errors in the awards. Some claimants included in the group are not eligible but will nevertheless be awarded compensation. This was the case, for instance, with the claims filed by OECD nationals for hostage taking or illegal detention for more than three days, for which the Panel accepted 94 per cent of eligible sample claims as sufficiently high to warrant extrapolation.

As the Saks and Blanck argumentation demonstrated, the possibility of inaccuracies is present both in individualised and in aggregative procedures, in the sense that both accept the *possibility* of an inaccurate approximation of the 'true' damages. In other words, in both systems the parties risk receiving a somewhat inaccurate decision. Various tools can be used to minimise the risk of inaccuracies, but the risk is nevertheless there in both systems. To the extent, however, that a *certainty* of errors is accepted, concrete sampling offers less accuracy than individualised claims resolution. To this extent, it imposes a risk upon the parties that is not present in individualised decision making.

In itself, more inaccuracy is not a sufficient reason to reject the concrete sampling developed by the UNCC, which can still be justified on other grounds. Nor is it a sufficient reason to discard statistical adjudication in general: as explained above, the acceptance of certain and known errors depends entirely on the concrete design and application of the sampling methodology. Moreover, as the following section will demonstrate, even if sampling sacrifices outcome accuracy, this does not necessarily have to be unjust to the parties.

Offsetting inaccuracies

Whereas the previous section focused on identifying the impact of statistical sampling on outcome accuracy, this section explores how possible inaccuracies can be dealt with to avoid injustices to the respondent.

Inaccuracy cost and requirements of fairness

The concrete sampling methodology developed by the UNCC could not exclude the possibility that a marginal percentage of claimants would receive compensation even though they were not eligible under the applicable rules. By doing so, the respondent paid more than what he was liable for. This can be referred to as the inaccuracy (or error) cost to the respondent.[188] In order to ensure fairness to the respondent, a mass claims process that makes use of statistical tools needs to counterbalance possible inaccuracies resulting in increased liability. This can be achieved in different ways, as will be demonstrated below.

In a mass claims process, it may be assumed, as it was in the *Marcos Human Rights Litigation*[189], that the respondent party is not interested in the identities of those claimants receiving compensation, but only in the total amount of compensation he owes. This assumption may seem awkward from a traditional perspective of bipolar justice. It certainly contradicts the currently prevailing theories of corrective or restorative justice, which hold that the respondent must pay the full measure of compensation to the specific plaintiff they have wronged.[190] Nonetheless, this assumption seems justified in a situation of widespread damages caused by a respondent's harmful behaviour, which was directed at the public or at a population group and not at specific individuals. In such a situation, the relationship between the respondent and the claimants is a distant and impersonal one and no meaningful distinctions can be made between various cases based on that relationship.[191]

---

[188] In some situations, the inaccuracies associated with sampling might also present a cost to some claimants. This occurs, for instance, when eligible claimants are refused compensation or when they are offered an amount lower than the true value of their losses. The inaccuracy cost to claimants is not included in the present analysis, since it is not an issue in the context of the UNCC. If a claim could not be resolved by sampling, the UNCC reviewed it manually.

[189] *Hilao* v. *Estate of Marcos* (1996), 786.   [190] Bone, 'Statistical Adjudication', 604.

[191] For a similar argument in the context of mass torts, see Davis, 'Mass Tort Class Actions', 165.

Offsetting lost accuracy by reductions in the
level of compensation

One will recall that in the *Estate of Marcos Human Rights Litigation*, the jury found that two of the sample claims were invalid because of insufficient proof, but decided to award compensation to all claimants, thus accepting that a small percentage of ineligible claimants would receive compensation. To counterbalance this loss of accuracy, the jury worked with an invalidity rate to calculate the aggregate award. Knowing that 2 out of every 137 claims were invalid, they calculated the total amount of compensation for the entire class by first deducting a 5 per cent invalidity rate from the total number of claims and subsequently multiplying the remaining number of claims by the average awards in each category. The total award was then divided pro rata among all class members. In this way, the respondent's overall liability was not distorted in any significant way and their rights were not violated by the sampling. The UNCC did not counterbalance the inaccuracies associated with statistical sampling by reducing the amounts of compensation.

However, such a reduction raises some problems as it sanctions the claimants who are fully eligible and will not receive full compensation. The claimants with a valid claim bear the cost of the system. Moreover, since the available compensation is divided pro rata, the cost falls most heavily upon those claimants who have suffered the greatest losses.

This problem can be solved to some extent by requiring the consent of all participating claimants, as happened in the *Cimino* litigation in the US, where the plaintiffs had waived their rights to more accurate damage determinations.[192] However, requiring the consent of claimants is delicate. To qualify as a voluntary waiver, the claimant's consent needs to reflect a deliberate decision to forego the right to full compensation.[193] The critical question is then whether claimants had a reasonable opportunity to 'opt out' and seek a more accurate determination of their losses elsewhere.[194] Moreover, the reduction in the compensation for each

---

[192] *Cimino* v. *Raymark Industries, Inc.* (1990), 664–5. The issue was raised also in *Hilao* v. *Estate of Marcos* (1996), 785, footnote 13.

[193] Bone, 'Statistical Adjudication', 601.

[194] In the UNCC's case, the only alternative for claimants would have been to submit a claim against Iraq before a national court. The delay and litigation costs associated with individual trials, however, mean that this was not an effective option for many claimants. See Bone ('Statistical Adjudication', 601): 'When delay costs become so large that actual recovery falls below the minimum floor required by fairness, plaintiffs no longer have a reasonable opportunity to exercise their procedural rights.'

claim is proportionate to the number of invalid claims within the overall population. However, the precise invalidity rate and, hence, the rate of reduction, remains unknown until the sample has been reviewed, and claimants are therefore consenting to a reduction without knowing its precise size.

In addition, those with a claim of above-average economic value may financially be better off refusing consent and opting out of the statistical adjudication system.[195] If statistical adjudication cannot offer full compensation, they have a clear economic incentive to pursue an individual action and seek full compensation elsewhere. While driving out the high-value claims, the system simultaneously attracts low-value and deficient claims. Indeed, a claimant who has suffered minor losses has no economically viable alternative to statistical adjudication.[196] Likewise, claimants who face serious problems of proof, or who simply do not meet all the eligibility requirements, gain by submerging themselves within the larger population.[197]

As the system drives out the high-value claims and simultaneously attracts low-value claims, the composition of the population obviously becomes very biased. The percentage of eligible claimants in the sample group decreases, and the overall award as well as the individual awards is likewise reduced. The higher the number of ineligible claimants within the population and, hence, within the sample, the more significant the reductions of compensation awards will be. If compensation is reduced excessively, it will no longer approximate the actual losses suffered.

In conclusion, a reduction of compensation to counter-balance the cost of inaccuracies should be handled with great caution. Unless the system is very carefully managed, 'bad' claimants might drive out the 'good' ones, resulting in a highly biased claimant population and excessive reductions in compensation for eligible claimants.

Bringing the transaction costs into the equation

Although not explicitly mentioned in the various UNCC Reports, Iraq's increased liability may have been compensated by the savings in transaction costs, equally borne by Iraq.[198] As explained above, Categories

---

[195] John C. Coffee, 'The Regulation of Entrepreneurial Litigation: Balancing Fairness and Efficiency in the Large Class Action', University of Chicago Law Review 54 (1987), 877, 879.

[196] Coffee, 'The Regulation of Entrepreneurial Litigation', 906.

[197] Coffee, 'The Regulation of Entrepreneurial Litigation', 906.

[198] See the Report of the Secretary-General of 2 May 1991, paras 8 and 29: 'The expenses of the Commission, including those of the Governing Council, the commissioners and the

"A" and "C" included a total number of over 1.3 million claimants spread over more than 60 different countries. The costs of over a million bipolar proceedings would have substantially exceeded the costs of processing the claims through statistical sampling. Iraq's savings by avoiding the litigation costs of hundreds of thousands of small-value claims far exceeded what it spent on erroneous payments to some of these claimants.[199] From a fairness point of view, statistical sampling is justified only to the extent that the respondent's savings in transaction costs outweigh their costs because of inaccurate decisions. The litigation costs that sampling saves should offset the inaccuracies it produces.

Procedural due process and the participation of the parties

Statistical sampling clearly restricts the participation of the parties. Their entitlement to a due process cannot be reconciled with sampling of claims and statistics.

Procedural participation of the respondent

Iraq's participation in the UNCC claims procedures   Iraq's participation in the UNCC claims process varied according to the categories of claims. For the mass claims in Categories "A", "B" and "C", Iraq's participation was restricted to reacting to the UNCC's periodic reports, which the Executive Secretary prepared in accordance with Article 16 of the Provisional Rules. The reports listed the total number of claims covered, the relevant category and the total amount of compensation sought, and summarised all significant factual and legal issues raised by the claims under review. The reports were made available to the Government of Iraq, which was invited to present additional information and views within particularly short deadlines: thirty days for Categories "A", "B" and "C" and ninety days for the other categories. Iraq's views were then transmitted to the relevant Panels to be taken into account for recommendations to the Governing Council.[200]

Iraq had more opportunities to participate in the processing of larger Category "D", "E" and "F" claims, which were decided on a case-by-case

---

secretariat, should in principle be paid from the [Compensation] Fund,' which was financed by Iraq.

[199] Compare with the reasoning in *Blue Cross and Blue Shield of New Jersey, Inc.* v. *Philip Morris, Inc.* (2001), 253, and in *Cimino* v. *Raymark Industries, Inc.* (1990), 665.

[200] In addition, the reports are circulated to the Governing Council and all countries and organisations that have submitted claims. See UNCC, Provisional Rules, Art. 16 (3).

basis. In such large or complex claims, the Panel could make claim files available to the Government of Iraq and request additional written submissions.[201] In fact, in Decision No. 114, the Governing Council encouraged the Panels to make claims files available to Iraq prior to the formal commencement of the review of an instalment of claims and to be flexible with Iraq's six-month deadline to submit a response.[202] Moreover, the Council recommended that Iraq should be given an additional six months to respond to claims with an asserted value of US $1 billion or more. Moreover, in large cases, the Panel could also invite Iraq to present its views in oral proceedings. Although such occurrences were rare in the initial phases of the UNCC's work, they were more frequently used later on.

Contextual analysis The Government of Iraq criticised the lack of full procedural rights, claiming that the UNCC's work 'is purely political, lacks any element of fairness and ignores the principle of due process of law required by natural justice'.[203] Scholars voiced similar criticisms, arguing that 'Iraq's right to be heard is not just violated, it has simply not been foreseen. The basic concept on which the system is built assumes that there is no need for Iraq to be heard.'[204]

This criticism is not without merit. For the numerous small claims, Iraq's role in the claims review process was, by any standard, minimal. It had no access to the claim files, nor did it receive detailed information on the individual claims. It could not present written comments with respect to individual claims, let alone a detailed legal defence. Nor was it entitled to a public hearing or adversarial trial. The UNCC justified these restrictions on Iraq's participation on two grounds.

First, it argued that the participation of Iraq (as well as of the claimants) in the proceedings was only required to the extent that it was necessary for the Commissioners to make just determinations.[205] Indeed, it was the responsibility of the Commissioners to establish the

---

[201] Caron and Morris, 'The UN Compensation Commission', 192.

[202] UNCC Governing Council, Decision No. 114, para. 14.

[203] Presentation of the Delegation of the Republic of Iraq in the Dialogue with the Secretary-General of the United Nations, 26–27 February 2001, p. 26.

[204] Michael E. Schneider, 'How Fair and Efficient is the UNCC System? A Model to Emulate?', *Journal of International Arbitration* 15(1) (1998), 15, 18. For similar criticisms, see Elyse J. Garmyse, 'The Iraqi Claims Process and the Ghost of Versailles', *New York University Law Review* 67 (1992) 840, 843; Bernhard Graefrath, 'Iraqi Reparations and the Security Council', *Heidelberg Journal of International Law* 55 (1995), 1, 51–2.

[205] Wühler, 'A New Contribution', 261, 267.

facts and evaluate the claims. The claims process was inquisitorial rather than adversarial. It thus was up to the Commissioners to seek the necessary information and documentation to arrive at fair decisions. Panels, especially those dealing with larger claims, were well aware of their task in the light of Iraq's limited participation.[206]

Second, the claimant's right to a timely and effective remedy should not be frustrated by the parties' participation in the proceedings. In a mass claims situation, the need to provide a speedy remedy to claimants must balance in the human rights equation together with the procedural rights of parties. The UNCC would not be able to process claims expeditiously by hearing the parties, it would take many years to complete its work, leaving its hundreds of thousands of claimants without an effective remedy in the meantime. Such delays would effectively amount to a denial of justice for many claimants.[207] In this respect, the ECHR has for instance accepted in social security cases that the claimants' rights to a decision within a reasonable time may prevail over the right to be heard.[208]

The ultimate justification for the restrictions of Iraq's rights to participate is found in the massive nature of the damages and injuries caused by Iraq's behaviour. By causing widespread damages to millions of individuals, it was Iraq itself who made a claim-by-claim approach impossible. Full procedural rights for Iraq, including the possibility to

---

[206] See for instance UNCC, Report and Recommendations Made by the Panel of Commissioners Concerning Part One of the First Instalment of Individual Claims for Damages Above US $100,000 (Category "D" Claims), UN Doc. S/AC.26/1998/1, para. 76.

[207] See Heiskanen, 'The United Nations Compensation Commission', 315:

> [. . .] Iraq's right to participate in the process has to be balanced against the claimants' countervailing right to have their claims heard within a reasonable period of time. Given the scope of losses caused by Iraq's invasion and occupation of Kuwait and given the number of claims filed with the UNCC [. . .], Iraq's right to participate in the process cannot be considered in isolation of the context within which the process takes place. In an international mass claims context [. . .], the respondent's right to due process cannot be applied in a manner that would effectively undermine the claimants' corresponding right to have their claims heard within a reasonable period of time. Overlooking the time aspect would effectively amount to a denial of justice – justice delayed is justice denied.

[208] See ECHR, *Case of Schuler-Zgraggen* v. *Switzerland*, 24 June 1993, No. 14518/89, para. 58: '[. . .] in this sphere the national authorities should have regard to the demands of efficiency and economy. Systematically holding hearings could be an obstacle to 'the particular diligence required in social-security cases' [. . .] and could ultimately prevent compliance with the 'reasonable time' requirement of Art. 6 para. 1 [. . .]'. For another illustration, see ECHR, *Case of Golder* v. *UK*, 21 February 1975, No. 4451/70, para. 38.

examine and argue each case before the Panels of Commissioners would result in excessive delays for claimants and allow Iraq to escape liability in many cases. As one author stated:

> It turns judicial integrity on its head to suggest that the greater and more widespread the harm caused the greater protections we provide to the institutional defendant and the harder we make it for individuals to have their day in court. [. . .] It is precisely because the harm caused is so widespread and because it comes from a common course of defendant conduct that the defendants should not be entitled to rely on the individualized adjudication model that provides the greatest likelihood of successfully defending these claims.[209]

Of course the respondent's right to be heard should not be arbitrarily curtailed. Its participation in the procedure may only be restricted insofar as such restrictions are necessary to protect the claimants' right to a timely remedy. Moreover, a mass claims process may not abandon all due process guarantees to expedite the claims processing. The respondent's due process rights may not be restricted in such a way or to such an extent that the very essence of due process is impaired.[210] The restrictions must be necessary to provide a speedy remedy to a large number of claimants. The restrictions of the respondent's participation rights must pursue a legitimate aim and must be proportionate to the aim they seek to achieve. These are two conditions that have been used by human rights courts and they should also apply in this context.[211]

Procedural participation and statistical adjudication   If mass claims are resolved on an aggregative basis, e.g. through statistical sampling, it is necessary to refuse the respondent any opportunity to dispute the merits of individual claims on a case-by-case basis. Indeed, sampling simply cannot work unless the respondent is forced to participate at the level of the aggregation and not at the level of the individual claims.

   If Iraq had been granted a right to review each and every individual claim and to present its views on each of them, long delays would have been inevitable. Moreover, any opportunity for Iraq to comment on individual claims would need to be matched with a corresponding opportunity for individual claimants to respond to Iraq's comments.

---

[209] Davis, 'Mass Tort Class Actions', 225–6.
[210] Compare with ECHR, *Ashingdane* v. *United Kingdom*, 28 May 1985, No. 8225/78, para. 57.
[211] ECHR, *Ashingdane* v. *United Kingdom*.

Allowing the respondent and the claimants to discuss individual cases would undo the efficiency of statistical adjudication and inevitably bring us back to individualised claims resolution.

Moreover, allowing the respondent to formulate comments on individual claims is not effective after statistical sampling. Even if the respondent identifies a few claims for which an individualised review might lead to a different conclusion, this would not be sufficient to reject sampling, which accepts some error and inaccuracy.

Defining the proper role for the respondent in statistical mass claims adjudication The respondent in a mass claims process should play a role at the level of the methodology rather than at the level of the merits of individual claims.[212] The respondent should, for instance, be able to dispute the scientific and legal validity of the proposed sampling methodology. The respondent should receive detailed information on the proposed sampling methodology and be invited to submit comments to the adjudicators before the methodology is adopted. They should be allowed to recruit their own scientific experts and challenge the scientific techniques or findings proposed by the claims facility. This would best be accompanied by unfettered access to the electronic claims database so that the respondent's experts can run their own selections and extrapolation reports. The respondent should also be heard on the selection and the representativeness of the sample claims and on the extrapolation of the sample results.

Such participation would contribute to the development of a balanced and fair methodology and ensure a higher degree of transparency. If managed properly, it would not result in unacceptable delays. Moreover, moving the respondent's participation from the individualised claim level to the aggregate level would meet the requirements of legitimacy and proportionality. The aim pursued – ensuring a timely remedy for mass claimants – is legitimate, and the respondent's participation is only restricted to the extent that this is necessary to achieve this goal. Of course, the adjudicators must exercise strong managerial direction to steer the respondent's input away from the individual claims and direct it towards methodological questions.

How then should Iraq's role in the UNCC's mass claims procedures be assessed in light of these findings? While the Article 16 reporting

---

[212] In the context of US mass tort litigation, see Laurens Walker and John Monahan, 'Sampling Damages', *Iowa Law Review* 83 (1998), 545, 564.

mechanism steered Iraq's input away from the individual claims and towards the aggregate claims, it also appears to limit Iraq's role to receiving a short summary of thousands of claims and to submitting general comments on the summary within an even shorter period of time. Iraq was apparently not given any detailed information regarding the proposed sampling methodology, nor was it invited to present comments in this respect. It was not heard on the design of the samples or the extrapolation of the sample results. These restrictions of Iraq's procedural due process rights could be considered unnecessary and disproportionate.

Procedural participation of claimants

This subsection presents a similar analysis of claimant participation in mass claims processes generally, and in systems relying on sampling in particular.

Claimant participation in a mass claims situation   Adjudication by sampling cannot be reconciled with participation opportunities for *all* claimants. Based on a review of representative claims only, the use of statistical sampling falls short of the ideal of a 'personal day-in-court' for each claimant.

Nevertheless, in mass claims, the ideal of full claimant participation necessarily conflicts with the right to a timely remedy. Procedural participation for tens or hundreds of thousands individuals costs time and resources. If the claims facility affords full procedural rights or a case-by-case approach to each claimant, it cannot guarantee a timely remedy for all claimants. While a few claimants may receive full procedural due process within a reasonable period of time, many more will either have no day in court, or only so after years of waiting.[213] Likewise, if the claimants are spread all over the globe, many will be unable to effectively participate. In the case of the UNCC, for instance, the 2.6 million individual claimants were distributed over 90 different countries, mostly in the developing world. With limited funds to run the claims process, most of these claimants would never have received a fair trial, even with an individualised type of procedure.

The protection of the claimants' right to a timely remedy not only justifies proportionate restrictions of the respondent's participation in the process, but also of the claimants' participation.[214] The mass claims

---

[213] See also Saks and Blanck, 'Justice Improved', 839.
[214] See Bone, 'Statistical Adjudication', 620.

body may restrict the participation of all claimants as the UNCC did. Alternatively, it may be preferable in some situations, to provide full procedural rights to the claimants included in the sample, and none to the remaining claimants. Both approaches will be briefly reviewed.

Claimant participation in the UNCC In the UNCC, individual claimants (Categories "A", "B" and "C") were granted only one opportunity to 'tell their story', i.e. through the statement of claim.[215] However radical, such a restriction meets the test of proportionality. In order to guarantee a timely remedy to 2.6 million claimants, the process simply could not provide any meaningful form of claimant participation. Even conducting hearings for only a tiny fraction of these claimants would have taken decades.

Moreover, the UNCC had no exclusive jurisdiction to decide compensation claims against Iraq.[216] At least in theory, claimants had a choice: they could either submit their claims to domestic courts and pursue individualised justice in a traditional adjudicatory system or submit their claim to the more expeditious but less individualised processes of the UNCC, or do both.

Claimant participation and sampling Alternatively, the claimants' participation in the proceedings can be restricted by allowing only the 'sample' claimants to fully participate. A full trial – possibly with oral hearings and cross-examination – is then conducted for the sample claimants, and the results are extrapolated to the remaining claims, without offering the other claimants similar opportunities. Arguably, this is only fair if each claimant has an equal chance of being included in the sample.[217] The only acceptable way of achieving this is an entirely random distribution by lot.[218] Obviously, the participation of

---

[215] In some cases, a subsequent notification requested additional information from claimants.

[216] See Report of the Secretary-General of 2 May 1991, para. 22. Parallel procedures have occurred in countries where Iraqi assets were frozen after the invasion as part of national measures or in implementation of the trade embargo against Iraq. See Wühler, 'A New Contribution', 260.

[217] In the abstract, various ways can be imagined to distribute participation opportunities in a system relying on sampling. See Bone, 'Statistical Adjudication', 638. For instance, 'if there is not enough to go around, the justification for sampling must turn on the answer to a question of distributive justice: What is a fair way to distribute limited litigation opportunities?' (Bone, 'Statistical Adjudication', 620.)

[218] Bone, 'Statistical Adjudication', 621 and 642.

the sample claimants must be matched by a corresponding opportunity for the respondent party to argue and to be heard on these specific cases.

Towards the proper role for statistical sampling in mass claims procedure

Based on the above analysis, this section seeks to define a proper role for statistical adjudication in international mass claims procedure. Should the international legal order embrace sampling techniques as a convenient and practicable way of achieving 'rough' justice in a mass claims situation? If so, is their use justified in all mass claims processes or only in particular situations? Or is statistical adjudication simply too risky and should we remain wary, as some have suggested, of the siren song of the numerical display?[219]

Statistical adjudication and corrective justice

Sampling must be examined in the light of the corrective justice goals pursued by international mass claims. Statistical adjudication and corrective justice ideals obviously have some points of contact.[220]

First, a claims process relying on statistical adjudication does not seek to provide some general 'insurance' for claimants nor are payments based simply on humanitarian need. On the contrary, claims are processed with a view to determining, as precisely as possible, the scope of the losses or damages caused by the respondents.[221] Second, claimants receive compensation in an amount that bears some relationship to the respondent's wrong. Although exceptions exist, the ideal remains compensation in the amount of the actual losses or damages suffered by each claimant, and sampling is designed to achieve that ideal as closely as possible.

Of course sampling cannot guarantee perfect accuracy of all decisions. This should not prevent it from operating within a corrective justice framework. In fact, if corrective justice would require perfect accuracy in every case, most decisions from traditional individualised systems would

---

[219] See *In re Fibreboard Corp.* (1990), 710.
[220] See in this respect Bone, 'Statistical Adjudication', 607–8.
[221] Bone, 'Statistical Adjudication', 608.

not fit either.[222] The 'random error' associated with sampling is a 'background risk' that corrective justice accepts:

> [C]orrective justice theory in most of its contemporary forms treats background risks as morally legitimate; only 'unreasonable' risks qualify as wrongful. Background risks are those risks that all persons can fairly be required to bear as part of the morally just baseline distribution of benefits and burdens that corrective justice is meant to preserve. Thus, background risks are defined by whatever theory of justice allocates initial benefits and burdens. It is sensible to include as part of the baseline distribution, and thus within background risk, not only 'real world' risks but also ordinary error risks associated with existing systems of procedure. [...] If the error ordinarily associated with individual trials defines the morally acceptable baseline of procedural risk, the random error created by sampling should easily pass muster.[223]

If neither system can guarantee absolute accuracy in all cases, the question is to know *when* statistical adjudication is better capable of achieving corrective justice for mass claims.

Defining the proper role for statistical adjudication in international mass claims procedure

This section suggests a few general guidelines to determine when the use of statistical techniques is appropriate for mass claims.

Number of claims and degree of homogeneity

The claimant population must be large enough to warrant the initial investment in computer technology and know-how. Sophisticated statistical applications are not an option for a few thousand claims. With tens or hundreds of thousands, however, the efficiency gains will easily outweigh the required investment.

The homogeneity of the claims is a second element to be taken into account. Sampling is inappropriate when the elements to be assessed are inherently subjective, imprecise and individualised. As indicated above, when mass claims are homogeneous with respect to all relevant variables, statistical adjudication is justified. When the claims are not

---

[222] As Bone notes, it 'is extremely doubtful that any corrective justice theorist would hold a procedural system to such an impossible accuracy standard' (Bone, 'Statistical Adjudication', 613).

[223] Bone, 'Statistical Adjudication', 608.

homogeneous enough, it may still be possible to reach homogeneity by creating subgroups, by eliminating extreme cases and by relying on stratified sampling techniques.

Even if perfect homogeneity is not achievable, sampling can be a normatively defensible approach, despite its adverse effects upon outcome accuracy, because of its comparative advantages. In all cases, however, there must be a minimum degree of homogeneity within the claims population. When the determination of the fact and the scope of the losses break down into what may be characterised as virtually a mechanical task, then sampling is well suited to guarantee an appropriate level of outcome accuracy. If the issues are inherently subjective, imprecise and wholly individualised, on the other hand, sampling is inappropriate.

Direct costs as a proportion of available compensation resources

Even if perfect homogeneity is not achievable, the use of sampling can be justified – despite its adverse effects upon outcome accuracy – when the direct costs of a case-by-case approach would consume a significant proportion of the available compensation resources. Whenever this is the case, traditional case-by-case approaches risk rending 'accurate' awards that are nevertheless meaningless or ineffective in practice. If statistical techniques succeed in reducing the direct costs, their use is justified to ensure more effective relief (i.e. full compensation) for eligible claimants.

Private costs compared to economic value of the claims

Similarly, when case-by-case approaches entail excessive private costs to the parties, and when the economic value of the claims is relatively low, they might make it impossible to assure a positive net recovery or a minimally acceptable level of compensation to claimants. If private costs are high, many will never claim and the respondent prevails merely because pursuing a claim costs too much and not because of the merits as established by the law. Since statistical adjudication significantly reduces these private costs, its use is justified in such situations to guarantee an acceptable compensation to eligible claimants.

Excessive delay costs

When the caseload is enormous, case-by-case approaches will not be capable of guaranteeing a timely remedy to all claimants. If delay costs are excessive, individualised approaches cannot offer to each eligible claimant an individual remedy early enough to assure a positive net recovery or an amount of compensation above a minimally acceptable level. When this risk is real, sampling is justified to protect the claimants' right to a timely and effective remedy.

Minimum requirements

The particular sampling technique that is used to process mass claims has to meet a number of minimum requirements.

Minimising scope of inaccuracies

While sampling can never exclude the possibility of errors, any sampling methodology designed for the adjudication of mass claims must nevertheless minimise the scope of possible inaccuracies by making use of established statistical techniques. Moreover, the sample must be so selected that it ensures the highest degree of representativeness.[224] The selection of the sample claims should not be left to the parties, as this may result in a selection of only the very best and only the very worst cases. Random selection of sample claims is critical.

In addition, the lowest possible margin of error and the highest possible level of confidence should be achieved. As a minimum, the margin of error and the level of confidence must conform to the standards ordinarily set in statistical applications, i.e. a margin of error of 5 per cent and a confidence level of '19 times out of 20'. A higher margin of error or lower confidence level should not be acceptable.

Finally, the adjudicators should be cautious with the acceptable rate of invalid claims in a sample. A small percentage of claims that are inconclusive or invalid in the sample should not necessarily prevent awarding compensation to all claimants in the larger population. In determining what constitutes an acceptable invalidity rate, however, the adjudicators should balance the efficiency gains and the extent to which they compensate the respondent and the inaccuracy cost.

Is consent of claimants required?

The degree of homogeneity within the population and the precise sampling technique employed may disadvantage some claimants. In this sense, it is tempting to require claimants' consent for sampling.[225]

---

[224] Compare: *In re Chevron USA, Inc.* (1997), 1020–1.
[225] See the discussion in Bone, 'Statistical Adjudication', 600.

As already briefly mentioned, however, requiring the claimants' consent is delicate.[226] To be effective, such a requirement needs to be matched by a realistic opportunity for all claimants to opt out of the statistical process. In reality, this opt-out opportunity only exists for certain claimants, in particular those with a high value claim and with strong evidence in support of their claim. For them, individualised justice is more adequate: they can offset the long delay and high private costs against the amount of recovery and do not need to fear rejection of their claim on the basis of insufficient evidence. On the other hand, claimants with a below-average claim have little to gain from an individualised process associated with high private costs and long delays: the latter costs will consume most, if not all, of their expected recovery.[227] Likewise, claimants with insufficient evidence can be expected to opt for statistical adjudication.[228]

The statistical adjudication might thus be applied to an extremely biased claimant population consisting largely of low-value and poorly supported claims. This composition will be reflected in the sample outcomes. If the remaining claimant population includes a substantial proportion of poorly supported or simply invalid claims, the validity or eligibility rates will drop, making it difficult to extrapolate the sample results to the overall group. Moreover, if a significant number of claimants take an individualised route to justice, the efficiency gains associated with sampling will be lost. In short, requiring the consent of claimants might very well jeopardise the goals and values of statistical sampling. The benefits of statistical adjudication would then have to be clearly communicated to potential claimants and the opt-out procedure well regulated.

In reality, the problem might not be so important. Indeed, if there are extreme variations within the claims population, sampling should not be used. If there are no extreme variations, on the other hand, few claimants will opt out and the above problems will not significantly affect the efficiency and reliability of sampling.

A more radical approach would be to submit all claimants to statistical analysis in a first stage.[229] Among all those who have suffered losses,

---

[226] Bone, 'Statistical Adjudication', 601 and 623.   [227] Bone, 'Statistical Adjudication', 575.

[228] See the analysis of reductions in the level of compensation as a way to offset inaccuracies, in the part on 'Offsetting inaccuracies' in Chapter 11. See also Coffee, 'The Regulation of Entrepreneurial Litigation', 906.

[229] This would require that the jurisdiction of the mass claims programme is exclusive at first instance level.

injuries or damages as a result of the respondent's behaviour, a truly representative sample of the 'victim' population can be selected. The results of the sample review will thus reflect the characteristics of the overall victim population, and lead to fairer and more accurate outcomes for the overall group and for individual claimants. The efficiency gains resulting from sampling will be maximised. Claimants with above-average evidence or claims could then have access to some limited type of second instance procedure to claim the surplus afterwards through an individualised appeals process.

Such a radical collectivisation of claims adjudication is likely to raise controversy. However, once it is accepted that statistical adjudication is better equipped to bring corrective justice in a specific mass claims context, it is not as radical a step as it may seem at first glance.

Compensating for inaccuracies

To the extent that the concrete sampling methodology cannot exclude a marginal number of claimants with invalid claims being awarded compensation, this inaccuracy cost to the respondent needs to be outweighed by other savings. In particular, the economic savings that the respondent realises by avoiding the litigation costs of an individualised process should exceed the inaccuracy cost to the respondent (i.e. the money spent on erroneous payments to some of these claimants). As a minimum requirement, therefore, the use of statistical sampling should generate litigation cost savings that offset the inaccuracies it produces.

12

Regression analysis

Regression analysis estimates the value of a dependent variable on the basis of two or more independent variables. In the field of mass claims resolution, regression analysis can be used to evaluate the value of claimed losses against an objective standard. Again, it is in the context of the UNCC that this technique has been tested for the first time in international mass claims adjudication.

Since most of the conclusions and suggestions formulated with respect to the use of sampling are equally valid when applied to regression analysis, the following paragraphs focus on what distinguishes regression analysis from sample averaging. A first section briefly outlines the statistical concept of regression analysis and illustrates its use in the legal sphere by referring to national practice. A second section explains how regression analysis was used in the UNCC. A final section discusses the values that are served by this technique by comparing it with two alternative valuation methodologies.

General overview

Concept

Regression analysis is a statistical technique used to find and understand relationships between two or more variables for the purpose of predicting future values.

A 'simple regression' is a regression equation that includes only one independent variable. 'Multiple regression' has two or more independent variables. The term 'regression equation' expresses the relationship between two (or more) variables algebraically. In particular, it indicates the extent to which one can predict some variables by knowing others, or the extent to which some are associated with others.

Multiple or multivariate regression analysis therefore involves a variable to be explained – the *dependent* variable (e.g. in our context, the value of a claim) – and variables relevant to explaining the dependent variable. The latter are known as *independent* or *explanatory* variables and may be qualitative or quantitative.[1] A regression model attempts to combine the values of the explanatory variables in order to obtain expected values for the dependent variable.

Linear regression analysis is based upon the assumption that the dependent variable can be expressed as a linear combination of a given set of explanatory variables.[2] The challenge is to obtain from the data the optimum combination of variables. Through multiple trials, coefficients or 'weightings' are assigned to each explanatory variable included in the analysis in order to obtain the closest possible approximation of the dependent variable.[3]

In the field of mass claims resolution, regression analysis can be used to assess the value of claimed losses. A regression model aims to express the value of a particular claim on the basis of a number of variables that are considered to be determinative of the claim outcome. The principal idea underlying linear regression analysis in this context can be summarised as follows: 'if it is possible to isolate the key variables that drive the outcome of [a claim], then it is possible to measure the relative strength of each variable in determining a particular outcome'.[4] Consequently, it must be possible also to predict claim values with a high degree of accuracy and confidence.

National practice

Multiple regression analysis has been increasingly used in US courts over the past decades. Especially in sex and race discrimination cases as well as antitrust violation, data obtained through regression analysis are frequently admitted as evidence.[5]

---

[1] An advantage of regression analysis is that it enables qualitative factors to be taken into account to explain a quantitative value (i.e. the dependent variable). See UNCC, Technical Description of Statistical Modelling, Annex I to Report and Recommendations Made by the Panel of Commissioners Concerning the Second Instalment of Individual Claims for Damages up to US $100,000 (Category "C" Claims), 29 April 1996, UN Doc. S/AC.26/1996/R.3/Add.1, para. 3.

[2] To the extent that this linearity assumption is not satisfied, mathematical transformations of the data may be used to make the data more linear. UNCC, Technical Description, para. 4.

[3] UNCC, Technical Description, para. 4.

[4] McGovern, 'The Intellectual Heritage', 193.

[5] See the examples offered by Judge Parker in *Cimino* v. *Raymark Industries, Inc.* (1990), 661–3.

The potential value of regression analysis for mass torts has not gone unnoticed. In the *Dalkon Shield* litigation, regression analysis was used effectively to settle mass claims.[6] This litigation involved approximately 200,000 personal injury claims filed against the A. H. Robins Company because of alleged defects in its Dalkon Shield intra-uterine device. The claims varied widely in value and severity. In order to value the entire population of claims, the court took a sample of 2,000 previously resolved cases, which were analysed on the basis of a data collection instrument with 150 questions.[7] After computerising the responses to each of these variables, software was developed to determine correlations among these variables and the outcomes and values of the claims. Strong statistical relationships were found between certain variables and the values of the cases.[8] At the same time, the court collected the answers to the same 150 questions for 8,000 pending cases. The statistical relationships were used to design a statistical model that could predict values for the pending cases.

Abraham-Robinson proposal

The concept of regression analysis and its potential for mass torts attracted academic attention. A brief review of the Abraham-Robinson proposal, which promotes a more extensive use of 'claims profiles' in mass tort cases, highlights the main directions that are taken in the academic debate about regression analysis in the US.

Abraham and Robinson suggest 'to promote settlement of claims by presenting information to the parties on the valuation of similar claims in prior settlements and/or adjudications'.[9] Claims profiles should indicate the amounts paid in judgment or settlement to different categories of claimants. The profiles would be developed on the basis of only legally relevant factors, i.e. 'the characteristics of claims or claimants that the finder of fact in any individual trial may consider in making determinations of liability, causation and damages'.[10] These claims

---

[6] McGovern, 'The Intellectual Heritage', 193; McGovern, 'Resolving Mature Mass Tort Litigation', 675–88; Hensler and Peterson, 'Mass Personal Injury Litigation', 983. For a detailed account of the *Dalkon Shield* litigation, see Kenneth R. Feinberg, 'The Dalkon Shield Claimants Trust', *Law and Contemporary Problems* 53 (1990), 79.

[7] McGovern, 'Resolving Mature Mass Tort Litigation', 683–4.

[8] McGovern, 'The Intellectual Heritage', 193.

[9] Abraham and Robinson, 'Aggregative Valuation of Mass Tort Claims', 140.

[10] Abraham and Robinson, 'Aggregative Valuation of Mass Tort Claims', 141–2: 'In contrast, it would be impermissible to define the profiles by reference to legally irrelevant factors such as the race, gender, or religion of the claimant [. . .].'

profiles could be used also in formal adjudication as 'statistical evidence' that the adjudicator could consider in evaluating the claim.[11] Moreover, according to Abraham and Robinson, it would be possible also to give the claims profiles the weight of rebuttable presumptions, which 'would be only marginally more radical than allowing them to be used simply as evidence' and can be justified 'by the conventional criteria for the use of presumptions: a combination of probative power, judicial convenience, and public policy'.[12]

As a further step, the claims profiles could also be used to dispose of individual cases: 'The rebuttable presumption then becomes a fixed schedule of damages – in effect an irrebuttable or conclusive pre-sumption about the value of the plaintiff's claim. Under this further limitation, the jury's only job would be to determine which profile best represents a particular claim.'[13]

While the feasibility of the Abraham–Robinson proposal within a national legal context is of little interest for international mass claims, its methodology can be criticised on three points.

First, accurate outcomes for the totality of claims require that the regression equation is built upon representative samples, which thus must be selected randomly. However, the Abraham–Robinson proposal selects samples in the chronological order in which claims are filed and decided or settled. As Bone argues, '[i]f factors such as severity of injury, amount of litigation resources, and likelihood of success correlate with early filing and disposition, then regression could produce skewed damage awards. Furthermore, the defendant may have strong incentives to skew the initial cases toward the low end [. . .], thereby exacerbating the sampling problem'.[14]

Second, the proposal includes trial verdicts as well as settlements to determine a market value for the claims.[15] However, 'settlements are influenced by a number of factors other than the expected trial verdict, including the transaction costs of trial versus settlement and the parties' relevant bargaining power and strategic skill' and 'the only proper measure of damages is the trial verdict because only the trial verdict reflects the considered judgment of neutral decisionmakers about "true" damages'.[16]

[11] Abraham and Robinson, 'Aggregative Valuation of Mass Tort Claims', 141.
[12] Abraham and Robinson, 'Aggregative Valuation of Mass Tort Claims', 146–7.
[13] Abraham and Robinson, 'Aggregative Valuation of Mass Tort Claims', 149.
[14] Bone, 'Statistical Adjudication', 587, footnote 74.
[15] Abraham and Robinson, 'Aggregative Valuation of Mass Tort Claims', 145–6.
[16] Bone, 'Statistical Adjudication', 587, footnote 74.

Third, the proposal treats differently early and later claims. 'Of necessity the early claims would have to be resolved by current procedures, because there would be no previously resolved claims from which a set of claim categories could be constructed'.[17] By contrast, later claims would be determined by reference to the outcomes of the earlier claims. Though the practical reasons for such different treatment are obvious, it introduces an inequality between early and late claims.

These pitfalls should be avoided when regression analysis is designed in the international claims adjudication sphere.

Regression analysis in the practice of the UNCC

In the UNCC, regression analysis was used, *inter alia*, to value certain loss types in Category "C", where an individualised valuation was impossible because of the vast numbers of claims, the diverse nature of the losses, the lack of evidentiary support and the requirement of 'expedited' processing. In this situation, regression analysis was regarded as a means to 'provide a level of objectivity and consistency while taking into account individual characteristics relevant to the determination of compensation awards'.[18]

The regression model developed for the "C" Panel made it possible to compare the amounts claimed by any claimant to the amounts claimed by alike claimants, while still taking into account individual characteristics that were likely to have made the claimant more or less susceptible to have borne the allegedly suffered loss.[19]

The following overview provides some examples of how the UNCC relied on regression analysis to determine the value of certain loss types.

Assessing the value of personal property losses

Rationale

The UNCC received over 350,000 claims for losses of personal property directly resulting from Iraq's unlawful invasion and occupation of Kuwait.[20] The asserted value of the personal property claims was approximately US $36 million. The most frequently claimed items

---

[17] Abraham and Robinson, 'Aggregative Valuation of Mass Tort Claims', 150.
[18] UNCC, Report "C" claims, 5th inst., para. 14.
[19] UNCC, Technical Description, para. 10.
[20] UNCC, Report "C" claims, 1st inst., pp. 134, 136.

included losses of clothing (85 per cent) and of household furnishings (88 per cent).

Any methodology based on a claim-by-claim review would have required excessive processing time – between 11 and 15 years, according to the secretariat's estimate[21] – which was excluded in view of the need for an urgent settlement. The "C" Panel therefore designed an innovative methodology entailing:

- the grouping of claims presenting similar factual and legal issues;
- an individualised review of sample claims;
- the analysis of statistical data regarding the evidentiary patterns and amounts claimed;
- the extrapolation of its findings from sample claims to non-sampled claims;
- additional verification of individual claims only where deemed absolutely necessary.

The Panel took into account the difficulties of proving ownership of personal property in the difficult circumstances prevailing at the time of the invasion and occupation. Based on the relaxed standards of proof set by the Governing Council, it accepted a broad range of documents, including receipts, invoices, witness statements, itemised lists and personal statements, as sufficient evidence.

The scarcity of supporting evidence was even more outspoken with respect to the value of the claimed losses. Less than 15 per cent of claimants submitted primary evidence, i.e. receipts, invoices, bills or similar documentation, of the value of the claimed losses. When primary evidence was provided, usually only partial and rarely faithful amount was claimed.[22] Many claimants submitted secondary evidence, such as itemised lists, personal statements and witness statements, which might provide detailed information relevant for the valuation of their claim, including the make, model, year of purchase, purchase price etc. Others, however, only provided very scant details. Claimants also used different valuation bases and methods for similar items. The Panel was unable to establish general valuation standards on the basis of the sample claims, principally because the amounts claimed for similar items varied considerably.

---

[21] UNCC, Report "C" claims, 1st inst., p. 138, footnote 262.
[22] UNCC, Report "C" claims, 1st inst., p. 142.

In short, because of the diversity of the evidence, the lack of detail and the number of claims involved, the Panel was unable to value the claimants' personal property losses solely on the basis of the evidence submitted.

Design of statistical model

A statistical model was constructed to estimate the 'amount each claimant might reasonably have been expected to claim based on (1) the amounts claimed by similarly situated claimants in the claimant population, and (2) certain individual characteristics of the claimant relevant to predicting that claimant's property accumulation behaviour, and hence, property losses'.[23]

The model was based on various personal characteristics and property accumulation indicators, including:

(i)   Claimed amount: The amount claimed by each claimant for personal property losses was entered into the model. The Panel verified whether the amount reflected generally the value of property the average Kuwaiti and non-Kuwaiti household was deemed to have owned prior to the invasion.

(ii) Nationality: Each claimant's nationality was entered into the model to reflect characteristics that are deemed to have a bearing upon the composition of personal property and to capture the variations in property ownership and accumulation patterns that existed among the various nationalities resident in Iraq and Kuwait.

(iii) Family status: The model also included the claimant's family situation while in Iraq or Kuwait. Expatriate workers who resided in Iraq or Kuwait with their families were indeed likely to have owned more personal property than those who travelled without their families.

(iv) Country of residence and duration of stay: The model took into account the place of residence in order to capture differences in the cost of living between Iraq and Kuwait, and variations in the propensity of claimants in the two countries to accumulate property. The number of months spent in Iraq or Kuwait prior to the invasion was also a relevant property accumulation indicator.

(v)   Age: Claimants' ages also affected variations in property accumulation. On average, older claimants were expected to have accumulated more personal property and to claim higher amounts than young claimants.

---

[23] UNCC, Report "C" claims, 1st inst., pp. 143–4.

(vi) Household furnishings: When expatriates claimed for household furnishings, claimant-specific variations such as duration of stay, professional and economic status, family status were taken into account. Claimants who had filed a household furnishings claim were likely to have resided for a longer period of time in Iraq or Kuwait or to have been accompanied by their families.

A number of other variables, such as the claimants' pre-invasion monthly income, the fact of claiming for clothing, personal effects, motor vehicles, the value of bank account losses and external property accumulation data, were also taken into account.[24]

Application of the model

The model generated an estimate for each claimant 'reflecting the individual qualities of the claimant that are likely, on average, to have made him or her more or less susceptible to the amount of personal property losses alleged to have been suffered'.[25]

When applied to the caseload, the model indicated that approximately 57 per cent of the claimants had claimed a lower amount than the estimate provided by the model. According to the Panel, this was due to several factors, *inter alia:*

- the invasion had affected claimants differently;
- the amount, value and type of property differed significantly;
- claimants did not claim for all of the losses actually suffered;
- some claimants submitted for only a portion of their losses as Category "C" claim, and claimed the balance as a Category "D" claim;
- claimants undervalued their claims for a variety of reasons, such as cultural and socio-economic factors.

As the Panel was highly confident in the accuracy of the amounts provided by the model, it awarded claimants claiming an amount lower than the estimate generated for them by the model, the amount claimed.

The remaining 43 per cent, who claimed an amount exceeding the estimate from the model, only received the estimated amounts determined by the model.

---

[24] For a complete list, see UNCC, Technical Description, para. 14.
[25] UNCC, Report "C" claims, 1st inst., p. 146.

Assessing the value of C1-Money claims

Similar statistical models were used to value 'C1-Money' claims, i.e. claims for the costs of departure, transportation, food, lodging and relocation, where the evidence attached to the claims did not provide a sufficiently clear and consistent valuation basis.[26] The number and the diversity of the claims excluded a case-by-case approach. Consequently, the Panel applied a statistical model:

> where lack of time and paucity of information inhibit a more individu-
> alized processing approach, statistical tools such as regression analysis
> provide a means for taking into account individual characteristics relevant
> to the determination of compensation awards. Statistical methods also
> introduce a level of objectivity and consistency into the determinative
> process of resolving thousands of claims presenting a myriad of valuation
> and other issues.[27]

The regression analysis for C1-Money claims was based upon the proposition that claimants' departure- and relocation-related losses reflected various factors, such as patterns of departure, extent of third-party assistance, cost of living, and family status and size.[28] The amount claimed by a claimant was compared to the amounts claimed by all other similarly situated claimants, taking into account each claimant's personal situation and other relevant characteristics.[29]

The formula used was largely similar to the one described above. In a first phase, the largest possible representative sample of available claims had 'to determine the parameters of the model, i.e. the weightings to be given to each of the variables included in the analysis'.[30] The respective impact of the various parameters was then established to arrive at the best approximation of the amount claimed.

In a second phase, the model was applied to the claims from a particular instalment. The Panel verified on a sample basis the evidence submitted in support of these claims. Claims were compensated for either the amount claimed or the amount generated by the modelling

---

[26] UNCC, Report "C" claims, 2nd inst., para. 33.
[27] UNCC, Report "C" claims, 2nd inst., para. 34.
[28] UNCC, Technical Description, para. 11.
[29] UNCC, Report "C" claims, 2nd inst., para. 35.
[30] UNCC, Report "C" claims, 2nd inst., para. 37. So-called 'outliers', i.e. claims that do not resemble similarly situated claims, were excluded from the modelling data-sets and reviewed individually. See also UNCC, Report "C" claims, 5th inst., para. 16.

process, whichever was the lower. For the Panel, this valuation methodology was justified as it reflected the patterns in the amounts claimed by all claimants in the population: '[. . .] by compiling and comparing information about groups of claims, statistical sampling and modelling methods provide results that are efficient and, based on presumptions of normalcy and on the reduction of individual bias, reasonable'.[31]

Analysis

The impact of regression analysis on efficiency, outcome accuracy and due process is similar to the effect of sampling. This section therefore discusses the pros and cons of regression analysis by contrasting it with the two classic valuation models: the individualised valuation system and the standardised grid approach.

Valuing losses in traditional case-by-case procedures

If the parties present adequate evidence of the precise scope of the claimed losses, international adjudicators generally have few problems to assess the value of the claim. However, especially after armed conflicts or similar circumstances, practical and evidentiary difficulties complicate the valuation of claimed losses.

Once the occurrence of the loss or damage has been proved, international adjudicators do not refuse damages merely because the precise scope of the damages remains uncertain. If the evidence is unreliable, imprecise or otherwise inadequate, they simply 'estimate' the value of the losses without much explanation.[32]

Historical examples

A few examples illustrate the difficulties experienced by claims commissions in the past.[33] In the *Compagnie Générale of the Orinoco Case*, for example, the French–Venezuelan Mixed Claims Commission awarded compensation although there was very little evidence with respect to the value of the claim. The Arbitrator stated that '[a]pproximate equity is all

---

[31] UNCC, Report "C" claims, 5th inst., para. 21.

[32] See in this respect the celebrated decision of the French–Mexican Claims Commission, *Georges Pinson (France)* v. *United Mexican States*, Decision No. 1, 19 October 1928, 5 *UN Reports of International Arbitral Awards* 323, 414.

[33] For additional examples, see Christine D. Gray, *Judicial Remedies in International Law* (Oxford, Clarendon, 1987), pp. 19–20, 44–5.

that can be required and all that can be gained from a case so indefinite in many of its important facts'.[34] In the *Theodorou Case*, the Anglo–Italian Conciliation Commission concluded that 'the loss has in principle been proved, but [. . .] the exact amount cannot be established or is difficult to determine, partly because of the same events which caused the damage, and partly by reason of the fact that the evidence adduced is not sufficiently precise'.[35] In these circumstances, the Commission merely estimated the claimant's losses. The French–Italian Conciliation Commission decided in the *Sandron Case* that the claimant had not submitted any credible evidence of the value of the losses and, moreover, found the claimed sum of almost 100,000 Italian lire 'manifestly exaggerated'.[36] Without any explanation, the Commission nevertheless awarded compensation in the amount of 70,000 lire.

The Iran–US Claims Tribunal

More recently, the Iran–US Claims Tribunal was faced with numerous cases in which the parties failed to present evidence of the precise value of their losses.[37] In these instances, the adjudicators merely tried to make the best possible approximations of the actual amount of damages. In *Dames and Moore*, for example, the Tribunal concluded that 'because of [the] gap in the evidence and the difficulties in quantifying the actual amount of damages in this respect with any precision, the Tribunal is justified in estimating such amount'.[38] In *Sea-Land Service*, the Tribunal held that '[i]n view of the scanty evidence submitted', the assessment of the level of compensation 'will, of necessity, be an approximation'.[39] In *Starret Housing Corporation*, the Tribunal stated that 'the practice of the Tribunal supports the principle that when the circumstances militate against calculation of a precise figure, the Tribunal is obliged to exercise

---

[34] Mixed Claims Commission France–Venezuela, *Company General of the Orinoco Case*, 31 July 1905, 10 *UN Reports of International Arbitral Awards* 184, 284.

[35] Anglo–Italian Conciliation Commission, *Theodorou Case*, Decision No. 190, 25 July 1961, 14 *UN Reports of International Arbitral Awards* 53, 64.

[36] French–Italian Conciliation Commission, *Sandron Case*, Decision No. 53, 13 May 1950, 13 *UN Reports of International Arbitral Awards* 210, 211.

[37] For additional illustrations of approximate valuation in the practice of the Iran–US Claims Tribunal, see Allahyar Mouri, *The International law of Expropriation as Reflected in the Work of the Iran–US Claims Tribunal* (Dordrecht: Nijhoff, 1994), 496–500.

[38] Iran–US Claims Tribunal, *Dames and Moore*, 20 December 1983, 4 *US Claims Tribunal Reports* 222, 224. See also Brower and Brueschke, *The Iran–US Claims Tribunal*, p. 610.

[39] Iran–US Claims Tribunal, *Sea-Land Service, Inc.*, 20 June 1984, 6 *Iran–US Claims Tribunal Reports* 149, at 172.

its discretion to "determine equitably" the amount involved'. The Tribunal added that '[i]t is generally recognized that international tribunals have a wide margin of appreciation to make reasonable approximations in such circumstances'.[40]

The European Court of Human Rights

In the case of *Akdivar and Others* v. *Turkey*, in which the European Court of Human Rights had found that Turkish security forces were responsible for the burning of the applicants' houses, the applicants claimed compensation for the losses incurred.[41] However, only three out of nine houses were registered in the municipal property records. For these three houses, the Court calculated compensation on the basis of the surface area, as registered in the records, and a base rate per square metre that the parties had agreed upon. There was no official documentation with respect to the surface or the value of the six remaining houses. The absence of reliable evidence, however, did not prevent the Court from awarding compensation, even though the valuation of the losses would 'inevitably involve a degree of speculation'.[42] The Court simply took 50 per cent of the surface area claimed by the applicants as the basis for its award because the three applicants whose houses were registered had claimed surface areas of twice the size that was registered in the property records.[43] The Court thus implicitly assumed that the other applicants had also exaggerated the surface area of their houses and, therefore, took 50 per cent of the claimed surface area as the basis for its calculation of the appropriate compensation amount.[44] The Court applied the same arbitrary methodology – basing its award on 50 per cent of the claimed surface area – in a later case, which involved similar facts but which was not directly related to the *Akdivar* case.[45]

---

[40] Iran–US Claims Tribunal, *Starrett Housing Corporation, et al.*, 14 August 1987, 16 *Iran–US Claims Tribunal Reports* 112, para. 339.

[41] ECHR, *Case of Akdivar and Others* v. *Turkey* (*Article 50*), 1 April 1998, No. 99/1995/605/693.

[42] ECHR, *Case of Akdivar and Others* v. *Turkey* (*Article 50*), para. 19.

[43] ECHR, *Case of Akdivar and Others* v. *Turkey* (*Article 50*), paras 16–17.

[44] With respect to household property, the Court simply accepted the estimates suggested by the Government experts, without any explanation, even though the applications claimed higher losses. ECHR, *Case of Akdivar and Others* v. *Turkey* (*Article 50*), paras 27–9.

[45] ECHR, *Case of Mentes and Others* v. *Turkey* (*Article 50*), Judgment of 24 July 1998, No. 58/1996/677/867, para. 13. In *Loizidou* v. *Turkey*, the Court took a far more balanced approach. See ECHR, *Case of Loizidou* v. *Turkey* (*Article 50*), Judgment of 28 July 1998, No. 40/1993/435/514, paras 31–4.

The fairness and wisdom of this approach – based on an extremely small sample, with no guarantees of representativeness – can be questioned.

Conclusion

These examples illustrate the practical and evidentiary difficulties to value losses in traditional individualised proceedings. If the supporting evidence is unreliable, incomplete or otherwise inadequate, a case-by-case procedure cannot ensure an objective, consistent and accurate valuation. Indeed, 'to regard an individualized damages determination as the correct amount is nothing more than a potent – and often desirable – illusion'.[46]

Standardised grid approach

The most radical solution to these difficulties is the introduction of fixed amounts of compensation for particular types of losses and per category of claim. In a standardised grid approach, the values of losses and damages are estimated on the basis of a predetermined grid of awards, consisting of mutually exclusive and inflexible categories. Individual claims are placed in the appropriate category and assigned an amount of compensation corresponding to the grid location.

The fixed compensation sums are irrebuttable presumptions of the value of claims, based upon the proposition that all like claims have equal value.[47] Standardised grids have been used occasionally in mass claims settlements in the US[48] and in international mass claims processes. Both the German Forced Labour Compensation Programme and the Holocaust Victim Assets Programme used fixed compensation sums. The UNCC used fixed compensation sums in Categories "A" and "B".[49]

Fixed compensation amounts score highly in terms of efficiency and consistency. They reduce the inefficiencies of individualised valuation and ensure that all claimants who are eligible receive a minimum amount of compensation.

Since fixed compensation amounts eliminate the cost of collecting individualised information, they are particularly appropriate when

---

[46] Saks and Blanck, 'Justice Improved', 833.

[47] Abraham and Robinson, 'Aggregative Valuation of Mass Tort Claims', 151.

[48] An example is found in the initial settlement reached in the DDT litigation in Alabama. See Hensler and Peterson, 'Mass Personal Injury Litigation', 1006.

[49] With respect to the use of fixed compensation sums in the UNCC, see McGovern, 'The Intellectual Heritage', 197.

the losses are very similar and the cost of collecting individualised information is high. Indeed, if the claims process requires the claimants to establish the precise value of their losses, the respondent might prevail simply because it costs the claimant too much to gather the relevant information. In such a situation, fixed compensation amounts are a convenient way of to minimum justice.

However, fixed compensation grids abandon any pretence of accuracy in the valuation of the loss.[50] They place a premium on consistency and efficiency.

Regression analysis

Against the backdrop of these two radical alternative systems, regression analysis scores highly in terms of efficiency, consistency and accuracy.

Although the economic gains associated with regression analysis are somewhat lower than those of fixed compensation, both systems reduce the time and resources needed to arrive at individual value assessments. If the claims population is large enough to justify the investment in equipment and expertise, regression analysis avoids outcomes that are driven by the cost of collecting individualised information.

Both systems also promote consistency among similarly situated claimants.[51] Unlike fixed compensation sums, the use of a statistical model allows the adjudicator to take into account the claimants' individual circumstances and characteristics in so far as they are relevant.[52] For each specific claimant the model generates a compensation standard reflecting the individual qualities that are likely, on average, to have made the claimant more or less susceptible to losses. Consequently, regression analysis ensures higher outcome accuracy than fixed compensation grids do.

Perfect outcome accuracy, however, cannot be achieved with regression analysis. Three types of error may occur. First, as a regression equation is built on a sample rather than on the entire population, it is

---

[50] As such, a system of fixed awards is more difficult to reconcile with the goals of corrective justice. Compare with the analysis of sampling and corrective justice, in the part on 'Statistical adjudication and corrective justice' in Chapter 11.

[51] See UNCC, Report "C" claims, 2nd inst., para. 34: 'Statistical methods also introduce a level of objectivity and consistency into the determinative process of resolving thousands of claims.'

[52] UNCC, Report "C" claims, 2nd inst., para. 34: 'statistical tools such as regression analysis provide a means for taking into account individual characteristics relevant to the determination of compensation awards'.

subject to 'sampling error'.[53] Second, regardless of the size of the sample, the fact that no set of independent variables can possibly explain all of the relevant variation may lead to an 'unexplained error'. The only way to reduce unexplained error is by including more variables in the regression equation. If more variables are included, however, a third type of error, namely the 'measurement error', becomes relevant: 'The more variables one includes, the more measurements one must make, and the more measurements, the greater the measurement error and the higher the cost.'[54]

It is impossible to say with confidence that regression analysis produces at least as accurate an outcome as individual trials. Much depends on 'the particular regression equation and the distribution of damages and trial error in the population'.[55]

In general terms, however, regression analysis offers a few clear benefits for mass claims. First, since it is built on the basis of damage-related variables only, it ignores all legally irrelevant variations that may inadvertently play a role in individualised approaches.[56] It excludes bias and subjectivity and generally ignores all variables that may account for randomness in individualised decision making.[57] Second, within the parameters of a mass claims process and especially where the documentary evidence is not fully adequate, the use of a statistical model based upon all similarly situated claims introduces a 'presumption of normalcy' against which individual claims can be evaluated.[58] As such, it protects against excessiveness in the amounts. Third, statistical modelling promotes consistency across claim outcomes and achieves a higher level of equality among claimants than any group of adjudicators can ensure.

On this basis, the use of regression analysis may be preferable to a case-by-case approach, particularly in situations when evidence of the scope and quantum of losses is costly or impossible to obtain.

Minimum requirements

The previous chapter proposed a few minimum requirements for sampling techniques. These suggestions are equally valid with respect to regression analysis, which is also based on a sample of the population.

---

[53] Bone, 'Statistical Adjudication', 585.   [54] Bone, 'Statistical Adjudication', 585–6.
[55] Bone, 'Statistical Adjudication', 586.
[56] See also Abraham and Robinson, 'Aggregative Valuation of Mass Tort Claims', 147.
[57] Abraham and Robinson, 'Aggregative Valuation of Mass Tort Claims', 147, footnote 30.
[58] UNCC, Report "C" claims, 1st inst., pp. 79–80.

Moreover, in order to minimise unexplained error, the regression equation must take into account all independent variables that are relevant to the determination of the claim value. If some of these variables are ignored, the resulting unexplained error may very well exceed individual trial error. Furthermore, accurate values must be assigned to the independent variables. Each of them must be measured with precision to determine its relative value in the determination of compensation.

In this respect, finally, a trade-off may exist between economy and outcome accuracy. In some cases, the measurement of all independent variables may require extensive factual investigations: '[a]ny regression procedure that significantly reduces costs would have to ignore variables that are difficult to measure without an expensive factual inquiry'.[59] Similar to sample averaging, regression analysis therefore 'purchases litigation economy at the price of larger error'.[60]

---

[59] Bone, 'Statistical Adjudication', 586.
[60] Bone, 'Statistical Adjudication', 584.

PART IV

General conclusions

13

New prospects for the international justice system

The emergence and continuous expansion of international mass claims processes in recent years gives the international justice system the opportunity to experiment with new concepts and to consider what is feasible and fair in the face of large-scale conflicts, widespread harms or systematic violations of individuals' rights.[1]

The establishment of these mass claims facilities has been triggered by a sense that traditional courts and tribunals are a too expensive and time-consuming process for resolving mass claims. Traditional adjudicative procedures, designed to achieve corrective justice goals in a simple two-party setting, are not necessarily adequate to impose liability upon those who have caused harms on a wider scale and to deliver timely remedies to mass victims.

International law has made unprecedented progress over the last fifty years with respect to the development and codification of international legal rules for the protection of individuals. The main challenge today lies in ensuring respect for these rights and laws.[2] Large groups of people continue to suffer because of armed conflicts or at the hands of abusive governments. The growing recognition and acceptance of an individual right to reparation for victims of international human rights violations and violations of international humanitarian law are meaningless if they are not accompanied by the creation of effective mechanisms to enforce such rights.

Mass claims processes can be used in specific situations to meet this challenge. They are a vehicle to provide all victims of a mass harm, however numerous they are, with easy and equal access to reparations. A well-considered use of such processes will help avoid the perception

---

[1] See also Heiskanen, 'The United Nations Compensation Commission', 392.
[2] Emanuela-Chiara Gillard, 'Reparation for Violations of International Humanitarian Law', *International Review of the Red Cross* 85 (2003), 529, 529.

that international justice is largely unresponsive to the basic needs of individual victims. Simultaneously, it will help ensure that those responsible for mass harms will not escape liability merely because of the system's inadequacy to handle large numbers of individual claims. Moreover, by pooling many similar claims, persons with claims that are too small to justify individual litigation can vindicate their rights through an inexpensive and straightforward collective process. As such, mass claims processes assist in the democratisation of international claims practice.

A new functionalism

This study has identified and analysed several new techniques that present-day mass claims processes have developed to resolve numerous claims in an expeditious, efficient and consistent manner. The growing use of these techniques is indicative of a new functionalism in international mass claims practice. Recently established mass claims processes are goal-oriented. Their design, both in terms of evidence and procedure, starts from the social goals that the process seeks to accomplish – mainly compensation, but also optimal enforcement of the law and public control of harmful activities – and an assessment of how well these goals can be achieved under alternative approaches. Specific evidentiary and procedural techniques are selected, not for their intrinsic value, but because of their respective cost, their direct and indirect consequences and their effect on the underlying substantive issue.

This new functionalism, which is apparent both with respect to evidence and claims processing, underscores the need for more research on the role of these techniques and their impact on various social values. This study provides a first step in this direction; its main conclusions can be summarised as follows.

Evidence

Supporting evidence is scarce in mass claims processes. Various factors – including the war conditions prevalent at the time of the losses, the lapse of time since the losses occurred, the loss of records or their poor quality and reliability, the parties' unequal access to evidentiary sources, the humanitarian and socio-economic condition of the claimant population, and the nature of the claims – tend to make it particularly difficult for claimants to offer sufficient evidence. Based upon the *probatio diabolica* theory, historical claims tribunals and commissions have occasionally agreed to relax the evidentiary requirements for claimants. This ad hoc approach has been abandoned by present-day mass claims processes, which have addressed the problem of scarce evidentiary support by developing written rules, which apply across the board to all alike claims.

Easing the claimant's burden of proof

The optimal allocation of the burden of proof in a mass claims context depends on the probable merits of the claims, the relative costs of presenting evidence and the social costs associated with different types of errors. In ordinary situations, the weighing of these three factors will put the burden of proof upon the claimant. Because of the difficulties for claimants to access and present evidence, however, departures from the general rule are required in some mass claims situations.

When the adjudicator has superior access to the evidence, strengthening the adjudicator's fact-finding role will minimise the total costs of the litigation and thus enhance its efficiency. This will be the case, for instance, when the outcome of the claims depends on evidentiary sources that are not within the control of the parties, such as official records kept by outside bodies. Especially when these records can be computerised or exist already in electronic format, the adjudicator may exploit economies of scale and spread the initial costs of gathering the evidence over all claims, significantly reducing per-claim transaction cost.

Compelling the respondent to share certain evidence with the claimants or to disclose it to the tribunal is appropriate when the respondent's costs of producing the evidence are much lower than the claimants' or the adjudicator's cost. Burden sharing is used especially when the relevant evidence is in the possession or under the control of the respondent party.

Shifting the burden of proof on a particular issue to the respondent party is a more radical intervention that enhances efficiency only in two situations. First, if evidence is scarce and if there is a high probability that the claimant's position on the issue is correct, the total error costs will decrease if the respondent bears the burden of proof (i.e. the risk of losing the case when no evidence is presented). Second, when evidence is scarce and the social costs associated with false negatives are higher than the social costs of false positives, the total error costs will decrease only if the respondent carries the burden of proof.

Relaxing the standard of evidence

Concerned with the difficulties for individual claimants to prove their losses, several mass claims processes have introduced relaxed standards of evidence. Under the standard of plausibility, the claimants need to produce all documentation and information that they can reasonably be expected to submit. The effect of the plausibility standard is to impose a duty upon the adjudicator to determine the probative weight of the evidence and information submitted by the parties in accordance with the difficulties they faced and the efforts they undertook to obtain better evidence. It integrates the *probatio diabolica* doctrine in the adjudicative framework and ensures its consistent application across all claims.

In a situation of scarce evidence, relaxed standards of evidence reduce the risk of issuing false negatives. Simultaneously, however, they also increase the chances that meritless claims are erroneously compensated, thus resulting in a higher number of false positives. While under a high standard of evidence the error cost is predominantly borne by the claimants (assuming that they bear the burden of proof), it is the respondent who will bear the cost of errors under a relaxed standard of evidence. Relaxed standards of evidence therefore reflect a clear policy choice and their appropriateness should be assessed on the basis of the specific circumstances.

Using presumptions and inferences

Based on probability, judicial convenience and public policy, presumptions and inferences allow the adjudicator to fill the gaps in the evidence and to arrive at a sound and fair conclusion through logic and reasoning. Present-day mass claims adjudication has abandoned the reluctance shown by some traditional claims commissions and makes maximum use of presumptions and inferences.

Probability-based presumptions are based upon clear and objectively verifiable indicia that usually attend the occurrence of the presumed fact. If the indicia are strong, clear and concordant, the adjudicator *must* rely upon the presumption in order to maximise outcome accuracy. Failing to do so will result in increased error costs.

Presumptions and inferences based upon public policy are not explained by the desire to maximise outcome accuracy. Rather, they deal with uncertainty in a way that the community finds most desirable.

It is important, however, that presumptions and inferences are formulated in sufficiently precise and detailed terms. Presumptions with too general a scope will have an adverse impact upon outcome accuracy and create new injustices.

Mass claims processing techniques

Precedent-setting and common issue determination

Common issue determination and precedent-based procedures are aimed at resolving common questions on a wholesale basis rather than on a case-by-case basis. Both techniques reduce the direct cost of making decisions by avoiding duplicative litigation. Moreover, their use does not result in an increase of the error costs. On the contrary, by curbing arbitrariness and subjectivity in decision making, these techniques increase outcome accuracy. The net result is a significant increase in efficiency.

The proper use of common issue determination and precedent setting also ensures a high degree of equality and consistency. In a mass claims setting, a system with strong precedential constraint is preferable and is likely to strengthen the credibility of the process. Because of the similarity of the claims, this is arguably achievable without affecting outcome accuracy.

Computerised data-matching techniques

Computerised data matching compares information alleged by the claimant with information stored in objective and trustworthy sources of evidence. It may reduce direct costs, enhance efficiency and improve outcome accuracy. The option to invest in data matching should be made on the basis of a proper analysis of the needs and functions of the claims process. The economic savings – both in terms of money and time – will depend on various elements, including the complexity of the verification rules, the number of claims, the number of variables within each claim, and the ease of collecting the verification data in a computerised format.

Use of statistics

Sampling

There is nothing in the inherent structure of statistical adjudication that prevents it from operating in mass claims processes. On the contrary, in specific situations, sampling may be better capable of furthering the goals of corrective justice than individualised case-by-case methodologies. Four guidelines have been suggested to determine whether the utilisation of sampling is called for in a given mass claims situation:

(1) If the claims population is (or can be made) perfectly homogeneous, sampling will provide more accurate approximations of the true losses suffered by the claimants than the traditional case-by-case approach.
(2) If the traditional case-by-case approach entails excessive direct costs and risks consuming a substantial portion of the funds available for compensation, adjudication by sampling is justified in order to increase the level of compensation for eligible claimants and to ensure effective relief.
(3) Similarly, when the value of individual claims is low in comparison to the parties' private cost under a case-by-case procedure, the use of statistical sampling is justified in order to assure a positive net recovery or a minimally acceptable level of compensation for all claimants.
(4) Finally, if a traditional case-by-case procedure entails excessive delay costs, statistical sampling may offer each claimant an individual remedy early enough to ensure a positive net recovery.

In each of these situations, individualised claims processing undermines the effectiveness of the remedies and reduces the net recovery. Sampling, if conducted properly, will then achieve a higher level of justice than can be reached in traditional claims resolution approaches. In this sense, statistical sampling pursues 'effective justice' in a mass claims context.[3]

In order to achieve an acceptable compromise between efficiency and accuracy, sampling must minimise the scope of inaccuracies, compensate for possible inaccuracies, and distribute participation opportunities fairly (i.e. randomly) among claimants.

Regression analysis

Even though regression analysis cannot ensure perfect outcome accuracy, its use may be justified in case of numerous claims for similar losses and where supporting evidence of the scope and quantum of losses is impossible or costly to obtain. In such situations, a regression equation makes abstraction of all irrelevant variations that may inadvertently play a role in individualised approaches. By providing an objective standard

---

[3] UNCC, Report "A" claims, 4th inst., para 9.

against which all similar claims can be evaluated, it promotes consistency among claim outcomes and achieves more equality than any
individualised approach. Moreover, if the claims population is large
enough to warrant the investment in the development of the model,
regression analysis results in significant efficiency gains.

Conclusion

Further innovation and improvement are needed. Even then, statistical
adjudication will require compromise and a rethinking of some of the
basic values on which our understanding of justice is built. In itself,
however, this is an insufficient reason to fear the use of statistical
techniques in mass claims processes. Even though our perception of
justice is based on individualised adjudication, it does not also have to
accept that the larger the number of victims of a particular harm, the
more difficult it is to obtain redress.[4] The failure to recognise the
potential value of statistical adjudication for international mass claims
programmes may deny many victims of mass harms – armed conflicts,
mass displacement, systematic human rights violations, environmental
wrongs and others – the chance to obtain meaningful redress. International procedural law must be sufficiently flexible to integrate new and
sophisticated techniques that help make substantive international law
enforceable in a timely and effective way.[5]

---

[4] See the argument with respect to the class action device, in Davis, 'Mass Tort Class
Actions', 232.
[5] As Davis writes, '[j]udicial integrity is a valuable asset only if it is achieved not for the sake
exclusively of the judiciary as an institution, but also, and most importantly, for the sake
of the timely and meaningful vindication of rights and the enforcement of
responsibilities'. (Davis, 'Mass Tort Class Actions', 232.)

BIBLIOGRAPHY

Books

Aldrich, George H., *The Jurisprudence of the Iran–United States Claims Tribunal* (Oxford: Clarendon, 1996).

Bayles M. D., *Procedural Justice: Allocating to Individuals* (Dordrecht: Kluwer, 1990).

Boutros-Ghali, Boutros, *The United Nations and the Iraq–Kuwait Conflict: 1990–1996* (New York: UN Department of Public Information, 1996), United Nations Blue Book Series, Vol. IX.

Brower, Charles N. and Brueschke, Jason D., *The Iran–United States Claims Tribunal* (The Hague: Nijhoff, 1998).

Cheng, Bin, *General Principles of Law* (London: Stevens and Sons, 1953).

Cooter, Robert and Ulen, Thomas, *Law & Economics*, 3rd edn (Reading MA: Addison-Wesley, 2000).

Cross, R. and Harris, J. W, *Precedent in English Law* (Oxford: Clarendon Press, 1991).

De Schutter, Olivier, *Fonction de juger et droits fondamentaux: Transformation du contrôle juridictionnel dans les ordres juridiques américain et européen* (Bruxelles: Bruylant, 1999).

Dworkin, Ronald, *Taking Rights Seriously* (Cambridge MA: Harvard University Press, 1977).

Fix-Fierro, Hector, *Courts, Justice and Efficiency: A Socio-Legal Study of Economic Rationality in Adjudication* (Oxford and Portland: Hart Publishing, 2003).

Fleming, James and Hazard, Geoffrey C., *Civil Procedure*, 2nd edn (Boston: 1977).

Friedenthal, Jack H., Kane, Mary Kay and Miller, Arthur R., *Civil Procedure*, 3rd edn (St Paul, MN: West, 1999).

Garner, Bryan A. (ed.), *Black's Law Dictionary*, 6th edn (St Paul: West Group, 1990).

Gray, Christine D., *Judicial Remedies in International Law* (Oxford:, Clarendon, 1987).

Herzog, Peter and Weser, Martha, *Civil Procedure in France* (The Hague: Nijhoff, 1967).

Heydon, J. D, *Cases and Materials on Evidence* (London: Butterworths, 1975).

Kazazi, Mojtaba, *Burden of Proof and Related Issues: A Study on Evidence before International Tribunals* (The Hague: Kluwer Law International, 1996).

Lillich, Richard B. (ed.), *Fact-Finding Before International Tribunals – Eleventh Sokol Colloquium* (Ardsley, NY: Transnational, 1992).

MacCormick, N., *Legal Reasoning and Legal Theory* (Oxford: Clarendon, 1978).

Morgan, Edmund M., *Some Problems of Proof Under the Anglo-American System of Litigation* (New York: Columbia University Press, 1956).

Mouri, Allahyar, *The International Law of Expropriation as Reflected in the Work of the Iran–US Claims Tribunal* (Dordrecht: Nijhoff, 1994).

Niyungeko, Gérard, *La preuve devant les juridictions internationales* (Bruxelles: Université Libre de Bruxelles, 1988).

Pellonpää, Mattie and Caron, David D., *The UNCITRAL Arbitration Rules As Interpreted and Applied: Selected Problems in Light of the Practice of the Iran–US Claims Tribunal* (Helsinki: Finnish Lawyers' Publishing, 1994).

Perelman, Chaïm, *Justice et raison*, 2eme édn (Bruxelles: Ed. de l'Université de Bruxelles, 1972).

Peterson, Mark A. and Selvin, Molly, *Resolution of Mass Torts: Toward a Framework for Evaluation of Aggregative Procedures* (Santa Monica, CA: Rand Corporation, 1988), RAND Note N-2805-ICJ.

Reuter, Paul, *Le développement de l'ordre juridique international: Écrits de droit international* (Paris: Economica, 1995).

Salmon, Jean (edn), *Dictionnaire de droit international public* (Bruxelles: Bruylant, 2001).

Sandifer, Durward D., *Evidence Before International Tribunals* (Charlottesville, NY: University Press of Virginia, 1975).

Shelton, Dinah, *Remedies in International Human Rights Law* (Oxford: Oxford University Press, 1999).

Sir Fitzmaurice, Gerald, *The Law and Procedure of the International Court of Justice* (Cambridge: Grotius, 1986), Vol. II.

Wasserstrom, Richard A., *The Judicial Decision: Toward a Theory of Legal Justification* (Stanford, CA: Stanford University Press, 1961).

Articles in journals and chapters in books

Abraham, Kenneth S. and Robinson, Glen O., 'Aggregative Valuation of Mass Tort Claims', *Law and Contemporary Problems* 53 (1990), 137.

Alford, Roger P., 'The Claims Resolution Tribunal and Holocaust Claims Against Swiss Banks', *Berkeley Journal of International Law* 20(1) (2002), 250.

Arndt, Karl, 'Arbitral Commission on Property, Rights and Interests in Germany', in Rudolf Bernhard (ed.), *Encyclopedia of Public International Law* (Amsterdam: North-Holland, 1981), Vol. I.

Asgarkhani, Abumohammad, 'Compromise and Cooperation at the Iran–United States Claims Tribunal', *Arbitration International* 19(2) (2003), 149.

Florence, B. Thomas and Gurney, Judith, 'The Computerization of Mass Tort Settlement Facilities', *Law and Contemporary Problems* 53 (1990), 189.

Ball, Markham, 'The Iraq Claims Process – A Progress Report', *Journal of International Arbitration* 9(1) (1992), 37.

Bederman, David J., 'Historic Analogues of the UN Compensation Commission', in Richard B. Lillich (ed.), *The United Nations Compensation Commission – Thirteenth Sokol Colloquium* (Irvington, NY: Transnational, 1995).

Belton, Robert, 'Burdens of Pleading and Proof in Discrimination Cases: Toward a Theory of Procedural Justice', *Vanderbilt Law Review* 34 (1981), 1205.

Berglin, R. Haklan, 'Treaty Interpretation and the Impact of Contractual Choice of Forum Clauses on the Jurisdiction of International Tribunals: The Iranian Forum Clause Decisions of the Iran–United States Claims Tribunal', *Texas International Law Journal* 21 (1985), 39.

Bodansky, Daniel, Crook, John R. and Shelton, Dinah, 'Righting Wrongs: Reparations in the Articles on State Responsibility', *American Journal of International Law* 96 (2002), 833.

Bone, Robert G., 'Statistical Adjudication: Rights, Justice, and Utility in a World of Process Scarcity', *Vanderbilt Law Review* 46 (1993), 561.

Born, Hans Peter, 'Awarding the millions, eyes closed' (on file with the author).

Brower, Charles N., 'Evidence Before International Tribunals: The Need for Some Standard Rules', *The International Lawyer* 28(1) (1994), 47.

'Lessons to be Drawn from the Iran–US Claims Tribunal', *Journal of International Arbitration* 9(1) (1992), 51.

Buergenthal, Thomas, 'Judicial Fact-finding: Inter-American Human Rights Court', in Richard B. Lillich (ed.), *Fact-Finding Before International Tribunals – Eleventh Sokol Colloquium* (Ardsley-on-Hudson, NY: Transnational, 1992).

Carbonneau, Thomas E., 'Darkness and Light in the Shadows of International Arbitral Adjudication', in Richard B. Lillich (ed.), *Fact-Finding Before International Tribunals – Eleventh Sokol Colloquium* (Ardsley-on-Hudson, NY: Transnational, 1992).

Caron, David D., 'The UNCC and the Search for Practical Justice', in Richard B. Lillich (edn), *The United Nations Compensation Commission – Thirteenth Sokol Colloquium* (Irvington, NY: Transnational, 1995).

Caron, David D. and Morris, Brian, 'The UN Compensation Commission: Practical Justice, Not Retribution', *European Journal of International Law* 13(1) (2002), 183.

Clermont, Kevin M. and Sherwin, Emily, 'A Comparative View of Standards of Proof', *American Journal of Comparative Law* 50 (2002), 243.

Coffee, John C., 'The Regulation of Entrepreneurial Litigation: Balancing Fairness and Efficiency in the Large Class Action', *University of Chicago Law Review* 54 (1987), 877.

Coons, John E., 'Consistency', *California Law Review* 75 (1987), 59.

Cox, Marcus, 'The Right to Return Home: International Intervention and Ethnic Cleansing in Bosnia and Herzegovina', *International & Comparative Law Quarterly* 47 (1998), 599.

Cox, Marcus and Garlick, Madeline, 'Musical Chairs: Property Repossession and Return Strategies in Bosnia and Herzegovina', in Scott Leckie (ed.), *Returning Home: Housing and Property Restitution Rights of Refugees and Displaced Persons* (Ardsley, NY: Transnational, 2003), p. 65–81.

Cramton, Roger C., 'Individualized Justice, Mass Torts, and 'Settlement Class Actions': An Introduction', *Cornell Law Review* 80 (1995), 811.

Crook, John R., 'The United Nations Compensation Commission – A New Structure to Enforce State Responsibility', *American Journal of International Law* 87 (1993), 144.

Damaska, Mirjan, 'Truth & Its Rivals: Evidence Reform and the Goals of Evidence Law', *Hastings Law Journal* 49 (1998), 289.

Das, Hans, 'Restoring Property Rights in the Aftermath of War', *International & Comparative Law Quarterly* 53 (2004), 429.

Davis, Mary J., 'Toward the Proper Role for Mass Tort Class Actions', *Oregon Law Review* 77 (1998), 157.

Demougin, Dominique and Fluet, Claude, 'Preponderance of Evidence', CIRANO Scientific Series, No. 2002s-61 (2002) (available at www.cirano.qc.ca/pdf/publication/2002s-61.pdf (visited October 2007)).

Devèze, Jean, 'Contribution à l'étude de la charge de la preuve en matière civile' (Grenoble: Service de reproduction des thèses de l'Université des sciences sociales de Grenoble, 1980).

Dodson, Alan and Heiskanen, Veijo, 'Housing and Property Restitution in Kosovo', in Scott Leckie (ed.), *Returning Home: Housing and Property Restitution Rights of Refugees and Displaced Persons* (Ardsley, NY: Transnational, 2003).

Dolzer, Rudolf, 'The Settlement of War-Related Claims: Does International Law Recognize a Victim's Private Right of Action? Lessons after 1945', *Berkeley Journal of International Law* 20(1) (2002), 296.

Feinberg, Kenneth R., 'The Dalkon Shield Claimants Trust', *Law and Contemporary Problems* 53 (1990), 79.

Frowein, Jochen A., 'Fact-Finding by the European Commission on Human Rights', in Richard B. Lillich (ed.), *Fact-Finding Before International Tribunals – Eleventh Sokol Colloquium* (Ardsley, NY: Transnational, 1992).

Garlick, Madeline, 'Protection for Property Rights: A Partial Solution? The Commission for Real Property Claims of Displaced Persons and Refugees (CRPC) in Bosnia and Herzegovina', *Refugee Survey Quarterly* 19 (2000), 68.

Garmyse, Elyse J., 'The Iraqi Claims Process and the Ghost of Versailles', *New York University Law Review* 67 (1992), 840.

Garth, B. G., 'Improvement of Civil Litigation by Lessons Derived from Administrative Procedures: General Report', in W. Wedekind (ed.), *Justice and Efficiency: General Reports and Discussions. The Eighth World Conference on Procedural Law* (Deventer: Kluwer Law and Taxation., 1989).

Gattini, Andrea, 'The UN Compensation Commission: Old Rules, New Procedures on War Reparations', *European Journal of International Law* 13(1) (2002), 161.

Gibson, Christopher S., 'Mass Claims Processing: Techniques for Processing over 400,000 Claims for Individual Loss at the UNCC', in Richard B. Lillich, *The United Nations Compensation Commission – Thirteenth Sokol Colloquium* (Irvington, NY: Transnational, 1995).

Gibson, Christopher, 'Using Computers to Evaluate Claims at the United Nations Compensation Commission', *Arbitration International* 13 (1997), 167.

Gillard, Emanuela-Chiara, 'Reparation for Violations of International Humanitarian Law', *International Review of the Red Cross* 85 (2003), 529.

Gold, Steve, 'Causation in Toxic Torts: Burdens of Proof, Standards of Persuasion, and Statistical Evidence', *Yale Law Journal* 96 (1986), 376.

Graefrath, Bernhard, 'Iraqi Reparations and the Security Council', *Heidelberg Journal of International Law* 55 (1995), 1.

Hay, Bruce L., 'Allocating the Burden of Proof', *Indiana Law Journal* 72 (1997), 651.

Hay, Bruce L. and Spier, Kathryn E., 'Burdens of Proof in Civil Litigation: An Economic Perspective', *Journal of Legal Studies* 26 (1997), 413.

Heiner, Ronald A., 'Imperfect Decisions and the Law: On the Evolution of Legal Precedent and Rules', *Journal of Legal Studies* XV (1986), 227.

Heiskanen, Veijo, 'The United Nations Compensation Commission', *Collected Courses of the Hague Academy of International Law* 296 (2002), 255
  'Innovations in Mass Claims Dispute Resolution: Speeding the Resolution of Mass Claims Using Information Technology', *Dispute Resolution Journal* 58 (2003), 79.

Hensler, Deborah R., 'Assessing Claims Resolution Facilities: What We Need to Know', *Law and Contemporary Problems* 53 (1990), 175

Hensler, Deborah R. and Peterson, Mark A., 'Understanding Mass Personal Injury Litigation: A Socio-Legal Analysis', *Brooklyn Law Review* 59 (1993), 961.

Holtzmann, Howard M., 'Fact-Finding by the Iran–United States Claims Tribunal', in Richard B. Lillich (ed.), *Fact-Finding Before International Tribunals – Eleventh Sokol Colloquium* (Ardsley, NY: Transnational, 1992).
  'Mass Claims Settlement Systems: Potentials and Pitfalls', in The International Bureau of the Permanent Court of Arbitration (ed.), *Institutional and Procedural Aspects of Mass Claims Settlement Systems* (The Hague: Kluwer, 2000).

Kaplow, Louis, 'The Value of Accuracy in Adjudication: An Economic Analysis', *Journal of Legal Studies* 23 (1994), 307

Kazazi, Mojtaba, 'An Overview of Evidence Before the UNCC', *International Law Forum* 1 (1999), 219.

Kazazi, Mojtaba and Shifman, Bette E., 'Evidence before International Tribunals – Introduction', *International Law Forum* 1(4) (1999), 193.

Koch Jr., Charles H., 'A Community of Interest in the Due Process Calculus', *Houston Law Review* 37 (2000), 635.

Laughlin, Charles V., 'The Location of the Burden of Persuasion', *University of Pittsburgh Law Review* 18 (1956), 3.

Lind, E. Allan, Maccoun, Robert J., Ebener, Patricia A., Felstiner, William L. F., Hensler, Deborah R., Resnik, Judith, Tyler, Tom R., 'In the Eye of the Beholder: Tort Litigants' Evaluations of Their Experiences in the Civil Justice System', *Law and Society Review* 24 (1990), 953.

Masse, Claude, 'La compensation des victimes de désastres collectifs au Québec', *Windsor Yearbook of Access to Justice* 9 (1989), 3.

McCallion, Kenneth F., 'Institutional and Procedural Aspects of Mass Claims Litigation and Settlement: The Exxon Valdez and Bhopal Gas Disaster Cases', in The International Bureau of the Permanent Court of Arbitration (edn), *Institutional and Procedural Aspects of Mass Claims Settlement Systems* (The Hague: Kluwer, 2000).

McGovern, Francis E., 'Resolving Mature Mass Tort Litigation', *Boston University Law Review* 69 (1989), 659.

'Claims Resolution Facilities and the Mass Settlement of Mass Torts: Foreword', *Law and Contemporary Problems* 53 (1990), 1.

'The Intellectual Heritage of Claims Processing at the UNCC', in Richard B. Lillich (edn), *The United Nations Compensation Commission – Thirteenth Sokol Colloquium* (Irvington, NY: Transnational, 1995).

Miller, Nathan, 'An International Jurisprudence? The Operation of 'Precedent' Across International Tribunals', *Leiden Journal of International Law* 15 (2002), 3.

Peterson, Mark A., 'Giving Away Money: Comparative Comments on Claims Resolution Facilities', *Law and Contemporary Problems* 53 (1990), 113.

Posner, Richard A., 'An Economic Approach to Procedure and Judicial Administration', *Journal of Legal Studies* 2 (1973), 399.

'An Economic Approach to the Law of Evidence', *John M. Olin Law & Economics Working Paper No. 66* (1999).

Project on Internationl Courts and Tribunals, 'Internationalised Criminal Courts and Tribunals: Practice and Prospects', *PICT Conference, Amsterdam*, 2002.

Radin, Max, 'Case Law and Stare Decisis: Concerning Präjudizienrecht in Amerika', *Columbia Law Review* 33(2) (1993), 199.

RAND Institute for Civil Justice, 'Asbestos Litigation Costs and Compensation – An Interim Report' (RAND, 2002).

Redfern, Alan, 'The Practical Distinction Between the Burden of Proof and the Taking of Evidence – An English Perspective', *Arbitration International* 10 (3) (1994), 317.

Reed, Lucy, 'Institutional and Procedural Aspects of Mass Claims Settlement Systems: The Iran–United States Claims Tribunal', in The International Bureau of the Permanent Court of Arbitration (ed.), *Institutional and Procedural Aspects of Mass Claims Settlement Systems* (The Hague: Kluwer, 2000).

Reiner, Andreas, 'Burden and General Standards of Proof', *Arbitration International* 10(3) (1994), 328.

Robinson, Glen O., 'Multiple Causation in Tort Law: Reflections on the DES Cases', *Virginia Law Review* 68 (1982), 713.

Roodt, Monty J., 'Land Restitution in South Africa', in Scott Leckie (ed.), *Returning Home: Housing and Property Restitution Rights of Refugees and Displaced Persons* (Ardsley, NY: Transnational, 2003).

Rosenberg, David, 'The Causal Connection in Mass Exposure Cases: A "Public Law" Vision', *Harvard Law Review* 97 (1984), 849.

'Class Actions for Mass Torts: Doing Individual Justice By Collective Means', *Indiana Law Journal* 62 (1987), 561.

'Mass Tort Class Actions: What Defendants Have and Plaintiffs Don't', *Harvard Journal On Legislation* 37 (2000), 393.

Saks, Michael J., 'Enhancing and Restraining Accuracy in Adjudication', *Law and Contemporary Problems* 51 (1988), 243.

Saks, Michael J. and Blanck, Peter D., 'Justice Improved: The Unrecognized Benefits of Aggregation and Sampling in the Trial of Mass Torts', *Stanford Law Review* 44 (1990), 815.

Schauer, Frederick, 'Precedent', *Stanford Law Review* 39 (1987), 571.

Schneider, Michael E., 'How Fair and Efficient is the UNCC System? A Model to Emulate?', *Journal of International Arbitration* 15(1) (1998), 15.

Schwartz, Gary T., 'The Ethics and Economics of Tort Liability Insurance', *Cornell Law Review* 75 (1990), 313.

Seidl-Hohenveldern, Ignaz, 'Conciliation Commissions Established Pursuant to Art. 83 of the Peace Treaty with Italy of 1947', in Rudolf Bernhard (ed.), *Encyclopedia of Public International Law* (Amsterdam: North-Holland, 1992), Vol. 1.

Sethi, Gobind Singh, ' "The European Court of Human Rights" Jurisprudence on Issues of Forced Disappearances', *Human Rights Brief* 8(3) (2000), 29.

Sir Eveleigh, Edward, 'General Standards of Proof in Litigation and Arbitration Generally', *Arbitration International* 10(3) (1994), 354.

Solum, Lawrence B., 'You prove it! Why should I?', *Harvard Journal of Law and Public Policy* 17 (1994), 691.

Stamm, Luzi, 'Amerika wo bleibt dein Rechtsstaat? Skandalöse Vorgänge beim Verteilen der Holocaust-Gelder', *Schweizer Zeit* Nr. 16, 28 June 2002, available at www.schweizerzeit.ch/1602/rechtsstaat.htm (visited October 2007).

Stavropoulou, M., 'Bosnia and Herzegovina and the Right to Return in International Law', in Michael O'Flaherty and Gregory Gisvold (eds), *Post-war Protection of Human Rights in Bosnia and Herzegovina* (The Hague: Nijhoff, 1998).

Stein, Ted L., 'Jurisprudence and Jurists' Prudence: The Iranian-Forum Clause Decisions of the Iran–US Claims Tribunal', *American Journal of International Law* 78 (1984), 1.

Sylvain Beauchamp, 'The New Claims Resolution Tribunal for Dormant Accounts in Switzerland: Distribution Organ, Mass Claims Adjudicative Body or Sui Generis Entity?', *Journal of World Investment* 3(6) (2002), 999.

Thibaut, John and Walker, Laurens, 'A Theory of Procedure', *California Law Review* 66 (1978), 541.

Tyler, Tom R., 'A Psychological Perspective on the Settlement of Mass Tort Claims', *Law and Contemporary Problems* 53 (1990), 199.

Van der Auweraert, Peter, 'The Practicalities of Forced Labor Compensation. The Work of the International Organisation for Migration as One of the Partner Organisations under the German Foundation Law', in Peer Zumbansen (ed.), *NS-Forced Labor: Remembrance and Responsibility* (Wiesbaden: Nomos, 2002).

Van Haersolte-van Hof, Jacomijn J., 'Innovations to Speed Mass Claims: New Standards of Proof', *PCA/ICDR Forum*, Brussels, 28 May 2003.

'Issues of Evidence in the Practice of the Claims Resolution Tribunal for Dormant Accounts', *International Law Forum* 1 (1999), 216.

Van Houtte, Hans, 'Mass Property Claim Resolution in a Post-War Society: The Commission for Real Property Claims in Bosnia and Herzegovina', *International & Comparative Law Quarterly* 48 (1999), 625.

Walker, Laurens and Monahan, John, 'Sampling Damages', *Iowa Law Review* 83 (1998), 545.

'Sampling Liability', *Virginia Law Review* 85 (1999), 329.

Wassgren, Hans, 'The UN Compensation Commission: Lessons of Legitimacy, State Responsibility, and War Reparations', *Leiden Journal of International Law* 11 (1998), 473.

Westen, Peter, 'The Empty Idea of Equality', *Harvard Law Review* 95 (1982), 537.

Whelton, Carmel, 'The United Nations Compensation Commission and International Claims Law: A Fresh Approach', *Ottawa Law Review* 25 (1993), 607.

Witenberg, J.-C., 'La théorie des preuves devant les juridictions internationales', *Recueil des Cours de l'Académie de Droit International de La Haye* 56 (1936), 1.

'Onus probandi devant les juridictions arbitrales', *Revue Générale de Droit International Public* 55 (1951), 321.

Wooldridge, Fred and Elias, Olufemi, 'Humanitarian Considerations in the Work of the United Nations Compensation Commission', *International Review of the Red Cross* 85 (2003), 555.

Wühler, Norbert, 'Causation and Directness of Loss as Elements of Compensability Before the United Nations Compensation Commission', in Richard B. Lillich (edn), *The United Nations Compensation Commission – Thirteenth Sokol Colloquium* (Irvington, NY: Transnational, 1995).

'Mixed Arbitral Tribunals', in Rudolf Bernhard (ed.), *Encyclopedia of Public International Law* (Amsterdam: North-Holland, 1997), Vol. III.

'The United Nations Compensation Commission: A New Contribution to the Process of International Claims Resolution', *Journal of International Economic Law* 2 (2) (1999), 249.

International instruments, agreements and treaties

Agreement between the United States and Austria and Hungary for the determination of the amounts to be paid by Austria and by Hungary in satisfaction of their obligations under the Treaties concluded by the United States with Austria on 24 August 1921, and With Hungary on 29 August 1921, signed 26 November 1924, reprinted in 6 *UN Reports of International Arbitral Awards* 199.

Treaty of Peace between the Allied and Associated Powers and Italy, signed at Paris on 10 February 1947, 49 *United Nations Treaty Series 1*.

Convention on the Settlement of Matters Arising Out of the War and the Occupation, signed at Bonn on 26 May 1952 (as amended by Schedule IV to the Protocol on the Termination of the Occupation Regime in the Federal Republic of Germany, signed at Paris on 23 October 1954), *United Nations Treaty Series No. 4762* (1959).

Declaration of the Government of the Democratic and Popular Republic of Algeria Concerning the Settlement of Claims by the Government of the United States of America and the Government of the Islamic Republic of Iran, 19 January 1981, *American Journal of International Law* 75 (1981), 422.

General Framework Agreement for Peace in Bosnia and Herzegovina, initialled in Dayton on 21 November 1995 and signed in Paris on 14 December 1995 (commonly known as the 'Dayton Peace Agreement'), *International Legal Materials* 35 (1996), 75.

African Commission on Human Rights and People's Rights, Principles and Guidelines on the Right to a Fair Trial and Legal Assistance in Africa, November 1999, available at www.achpr.org (visited October 2007).

Agreement between the Government of the United States of America and the Government of the Federal Republic of Germany concerning the Foundation 'Remembrance, Responsibility and the Future', 17 July 2000, available at www.compensation-for-forced-labour.org/english_home.html (visited October 2006).

Miscellaneous documents
Iran–US Claims Tribunal

Iran–US Claims Tribunal Rules of Procedure (3 May 1983) (available at www.iusct.org/tribunal-rules.pdf (visited October 2007)).

CRT-I

Independent Committee of Eminent Persons, Report on Dormant Accounts of Victims of Nazi Persecution in Swiss Banks (commonly known as the 'Volcker Report'), 6 December 1999.

Board of Trustees of the Independent Claims Resolution Foundation, Rules of Procedure for the Claims Resolution Process (commonly referred to as the 'CRT-I, Rules of Procedure'), adopted on 15 October 1997, available at www.crt-ii.org/_crt-i/frame.html (visited October 2007).

CRT-I, Final Report on the Work of the Claims Resolution Tribunal for Dormant Accounts in Switzerland (CRT-I), 5 October 2001.

CRT-II

Settlement Agreement in the US District Court for the Eastern District of New York, Chief Judge Edward R. Korman presiding, *In re Holocaust Victim Assets Litigation (Swiss Banks)*, 4 November 2002, CV-96–4849, available at www.swissbankclaims.com/PDFs_Eng/exhibit1toPlanofAllocation.pdf (visited October 2007).

Final Order and Judgment of the court approving the Settlement Agreement of 26 July 2000 (as corrected on 2 August 2000), available at www.swissbank-claims.com/PDFs_Eng/FinalOrder.pdf (visited October 2007).

Plan of Allocation and Distribution, proposed by Special Master Judah Gribetz and approved by Judge Korman on 22 November 2000, available at www.swiss-bankclaims.com/PDFs_Eng/VolumeIPlan.pdf (visited October 2007).

CRT-II, Rules Governing the Claims Resolution Process (As Amended), available at www.crt-ii.org/governing_rules.phtm (visited October 2007).

'Data Librarian Rules', Appendix A to the CRT-II Rules.

CRT-II, Introduction to the Claims Resolution Process, available at www.crt-ii.org/introduction.phtm (visited October 2007).

CRT-II, *Certified Award in re Account of Helene Rudnicki*, Claim Number 213215/JS, available at www.crt-ii.org/_awards/index.phtm (visited October 2007).

CRPC

CRPC, Book of Regulations on the Conditions and Decision Making Procedure for Claims for Return of Real Property of Refugees and Displaced Persons (Consolidated version), 8 October 2002, available at www.law.kuleuven.ac.be/ipr/eng/CRPC_Bosnia/CRPC/new/en/html/laws/lawsbookofregulations.htm (visited October 2007).

CRPC, Book of Regulations on Confirmation of Occupancy Rights of Displaced Persons and Refugees (Consolidated version), 8 October 2002, available at

www.law.kuleuven.ac.be/ipr/eng/CRPC_Bosnia/CRPC/new/en/html/laws/
lawsbookofregulations.htm (visited October 2007).

ICHEIC

Memorandum of Understanding, 25 August 1998, available at www.icheic.org/
pdf/ICHEIC_MOU.PDF (visited October 2007).
ICHEIC, Appeals Tribunal Rules of Procedure, 15 July 1999, available at www.
icheic.org/pdf/ICHEIC_Appeals.pdf (visited October 2007).
ICHEIC, Holocaust Era Insurance Claims Processing Guide, 22 June 2003, at 9–10,
available at www.icheic.org/pdf/ICHEIC_CPG.pdf (visited October 2007).
ICHEIC, Relaxed Standards of Proof Guide, available at www.icheic.org/docs-
documents.html (visited October 2007).
Principles of the ICHEIC-AWZ Matching Process, Annex F to the AWZ-Settlement
Agreement, 11 July 2003.

IOM programmes

Law on the Creation of the Foundation 'Remembrance, Responsibility and Future', 2
August 2000, as amended on 4 August 2001 (Federal Law Gazette BGBl. 2000 I
1263 and BGBl. 2001 I 2036), commonly know as the 'German Foundation Act'.
IOM Property Claims Commission, Supplemental Principles and Rules of Pro-
cedure, 5 June 2001, available at www.compensation-for-forced-labour.org/
(visited October 2007).
IOM – Press Release 2/2002, 'Many claimants lack sufficient documentation',
Geneva, 7 February 2002.
IOM Appeals Body for Forced Labour Claims, Principles and Rules of Appeals
Procedure, 7 February 2003, available at www.compensation-for-forced-
labour.org/ (visited October 2007).
IOM, 'Slave and Forced Labour: Past Achievements and Challenges Ahead',
Compensation News, Issue 1–2003.

HPD/HPCC

UNMIK Regulation No. 1999/23 on the Establishment of the Housing and
Property Directorate and the Housing and Property Claims Commission, 15
November 1999, available at www.unmikonline.org/regulations/unmikgaz-
ette/index.htm (visited October 2007).
UNMIK Regulation No. 2000/60 on Residential Property Claims and The Rules of
Procedure and Evidence of the Housing and Property Directorate and the
Housing and Property Claims Commission, 31 October 2000, available at www.
unmikonline.org/regulations/unmikgazette/index.htm (visited October 2007).
HPCC, Resolution No 7, 11 April 2003.

Others

Mixed Claims Commission, United States and Germany, Rules of Procedure, *reprinted* in 8 *UN Reports of International Arbitral Awards* 469.

United States and Germany, Administrative Dec. No. 1, 1 November 1923 (7 *UN Reports of International Arbitral Awards* 21).

United States and Germany, Administrative Dec. No. 2, 1 November 1923 (7 *UN Reports of International Arbitral Awards* 23).

United States and Germany, Administrative Dec. No. 3, 11 December 1923 (7 *UN Reports of International Arbitral Awards* 64).

Claims Commissioner (Parker) appointed under Special Agreement of 26 November 1924 between the United States, Austria, Hungary, Administrative Dec. No. 1, 25 May 1927, 6 *UN Reports of International Arbitral Awards* 203.

Claims Commissioner (Parker) appointed under Special Agreement of 26 November 1924 between the United States, Austria, Hungary, Administrative Dec. No. 2, 25 May 1927, 6 *UN Reports of International Arbitral Awards* 212.

American Law Institute/UNIDROIT, Draft Principles and Rules of Transnational Civil Procedure, April 2003, available at www.unidroit.org.

EU Directive 97/80/EC on the burden of proof in cases of discrimination based on sex, 15 December 1997, O.J. 20.0198, L.14/6.

European Commission of Human Rights, Report concerning Applications No. 6780/74 and 6950/75, 10 July 1976, special publication of the Council of Europe.

European Commission of Human Rights, Report on Application No 8007/77, 4 October 1983, in *Decisions and Reports*, Vol. 72 (1992).

ICSID, Rules of Procedure for Arbitration Proceedings, available at www.worldbank.org/icsid/ (visited October 2007).

ICTR Rules of Procedure and Evidence, adopted on 29 June 1995, available at www.un.org/ictr/rules.html (visited October 2007).

ICTY Rules of Procedure and Evidence, 12 July 2007, IT/32/Rev. 40, available at www.un.org/icty/legaldoc-e/index.htm (visited October 2007).

Statute of the International Criminal Tribunal for the Prosecution of Persons Responsible for Genocide and Other Serious Violations of International Humanitarian Law Committed in the Territory of Rwanda and Rwandan Citizens Responsible for Genocide and Other Such Violations Committed in the Territory of Neighbouring States, between 1 January 1994 and 31 December 1994; adopted by Security Council resolution 955 (1994) of 8 November 1994 and amended by Security Council resolutions 1165 (1998) of 30 April 1998 , 1329 (2000) of 30 November 2000, 1411 (2002) of 17 May 2002 and 1431 (2002) of 14 August 2002, available at www.ohchr.org/english/law/itr.htm (visited October 2007).

Statute of the International Tribunal for the Prosecution of Persons Responsible for Serious Violations of International Humanitarian Law Committed in the Territory of the Former Yugoslavia since 1991 (International Tribunal for the Former Yugoslavia); adopted by Security Council resolution 827 (1993) of 25 May 1993 and amended by Security Council resolutions 1166 (1998) of 13 May 1998, 1329 (2000) of 30 November 2000, 1411 (2002) of 17 May 2002 and 1431 (2002) of 14 August 2002, available at www.ohchr.org/english/law/itfy.htm (visited October 2007).

Inter-Allied Declaration against Acts of Dispossession committed in Territories under Enemy Occupation of Control, London, 5 January 1943.

UN documents

UN Security Council Resolutions

UN Security Council Resolution 670, S/RES/670 (1990), 25 September 1990, *International Legal Materials* 29 (1990), 1334.

UN Security Council Resolution 674, S/RES/674 (1990), 29 October 1990, *International Legal Materials* 29 (1991), 1561.

UN Security Council Resolution 686, S/RES/686 (1991), 2 March 1991, *International Legal Materials* 30 (1991), 567.

UN Security Council Resolution 687, S/RES/687 (1991), 3 April 1991, *International Legal Materials* 30 (1991), 847.

UN Security Council Resolution 692, S/RES/692 (1991), 20 May 1991, *International Legal Materials* 30 (1991), 864.

UN Security Council Resolution 1244, S/RES/1244 (1999), 10 June 1999, *International Legal Materials* 34 (1999), 1451.

UNCC Governing Council Decisions
(also available at www2.unog.ch/uncc)

UNCC Governing Council, Decision No. 1: Criteria for Expedited Processing of Urgent Claims, S/AC.26/1991/1, 2 August 1991, *International Legal Materials* 30 (1991), 1712.

UNCC Governing Council, Decision No. 3 on Personal Injury and Mental Pain and Anguish, S/AC.26/1991/3, 23 October 1991, *International Legal Materials* 30 (1992), 1028.

UNCC Governing Council, Decision No. 4: Business Losses of Individuals Eligible for Consideration under the Expedited Procedures, S/AC.26/1991/4, 23 October 1991, *International Legal Materials* 31 (1992), 1030.

UNCC Governing Council, Decision No. 10: Provisional Rules for Claims Procedure, S/AC.26/1992/10, 26 June 1992, *International Legal Materials* 31 (1992), 1053.

UNCC Governing Council, Decision No. 11: Eligibility for Compensation of Members of the Allied Coalition Forces, S/AC.26/1992/11, 26 June 1992, *International Legal Materials* 31 (1992), 1067.

UNCC Governing Council, Decision No. 114: Review of Current UNCC Procedures, 7 December 2000, UN Doc. S/AC.26/Dec.114 (2000).

UNCC, Report and Recommendations Made by Panels of Commissioners (available at www2.unog.ch/uncc/).

UNCC, Report and Recommendations Made by the Panel of Commissioners Concerning Individual Claims for Serious Personal Injury or Death (Category "B" claims), 26 May 1994, UN Doc. S/AC.26/1994/1.

UNCC, Report and Recommendations Made by the Panel of Commissioners Concerning the First Instalment of Claims for Departure from Iraq or Kuwait (Category "A" Claims), 21 October 1994, UN Doc. S/AC.26/1994/2.

UNCC, Report and Recommendations Made by the Panel of Commissioners Concerning the First Instalment of Individual Claims for Damages up to $100,000 (Category "C" Claims), 21 December 1994, UN Doc. S/AC.26/1994/3.

UNCC, Report and Recommendations Made by the Panel of Commissioners Concerning the Second Instalment of Claims for Departure from Iraq or Kuwait (Category "A" Claims), 22 March 1995, UN Doc. S/AC.26/1995/2.

UNCC, Report and Recommendations Made by the Panel of Commissioners Concerning the Fourth Instalment of Claims for Departure from Iraq or Kuwait (Category "A" Claims), 12 October 1995, UN Doc. S/AC.26/1995/4.

UNCC, Report and Recommendations Made by the Panel of Commissioners Concerning the Fifth Instalment of Claims for Departure from Iraq or Kuwait (Category "A" Claims), 13 December 1995, UN Doc. S/AC.26/1995/5.

UNCC, Report and Recommendations Made by the Panel of Commissioners Concerning the Second Instalment of Individual Claims for Damages up to US $100,000 (Category "C" claims), 30 May 1996, UN Doc. S/AC.26/1996/1.

UNCC, Report and Recommendations Made by the Panel of Commissioners Concerning the Sixth Instalment of Claims for Departure From Iraq or Kuwait (Category "A" Claims), 16 October 1996, UN Doc. S/AC.26/1996/3.

UNCC, Report and Recommendations Made by the Panel of Commissioners Concerning the Fifth Instalment of Individual Claims for Damages up to US $100,000 (Category "C" Claims), 25 June 1997, UN Doc. S/AC.26/1997/1.

UNCC, Report and Recommendations Made by the Panel of Commissioners Concerning Part One of the First Instalment of Individual Claims for Damages Above US $100,000 (Category "D" Claims), 3 February 1998, UN Doc. S/AC.26/1998/1.

UNCC, Report and Recommendations Made by the Panel of Commissioners concerning the Sixth Instalment of Individual Claims for Damages up to US $100,000 (Category "C" Claims), 2 July 1998, UN Doc. S/AC.26/1998/6.

UNCC, Report and Recommendations Made by the Panel of Commissioners Concerning the First Instalment of "E3" Claims, 17 December 1998, UN Doc. S/AC.26/1998/13.

Other UNCC documents

Report of the Secretary-General Pursuant to Paragraph 19 of Security Council Resolution 687, S/22559, 2 May 1991, *International Legal Materials* 30 (1991), 1706.

UNCC Secretariat's Memorandum of 18 May 1995, submitted to the Commissioners of Panel "A".

UNCC, Technical Description of Statistical Modelling, Annex I to Report and Recommendations Made by the Panel of Commissioners Concerning the Second Instalment of Individual Claims for Damages up to US $100,000 (Category "C" Claims), 29 April 1996, UN Doc. S/AC.26/1996/R.3/Add.1.

Other UN documents

UNCITRAL Arbitration Rules, G. A. Res. 31/98, 31 U.N.GAOR, Supp. No. 17, UN Doc. A/31/17 (1976), *International Legal Materials* 15 (1976), 701.

Van Boven, Theo, Study Concerning the Right to Restitution, Compensation and Rehabilitation for Victims of Gross Violations of Human Rights and Fundamental Freedoms, UN Doc. E/CN.4/Sub.2/1993/8, 2 July 1993.

Report of the Secretary-General on the United Nations Interim Administration Mission in Kosovo, 12 July 1999, UN Doc. S/1999/779.

INDEX

283